T0330068

European Entrepreneurship in the Globalizing Economy

EUROPEAN RESEARCH IN ENTREPRENEURSHIP

Series Editors: Alain Fayolle, *Professor of Entrepreneurship, EMLYON Business School and CERAG, France and Visiting Professor at Solvay Brussels School of Economics and Management, Belgium and* Paula Kyrö, *Professor of Entrepreneurship Education, Aalto University School of Economics, Finland*

This important series is designed to highlight the unique characteristics and rich variety of European research in entrepreneurship. It provides powerful lenses to help identify and understand the importance of European cultural roots within the international entrepreneurship landscape.

Titles in the series include:

Entrepreneurship Research in Europe
Outcomes and Perspectives
Edited by Alain Fayolle, Paula Kyrö and Jan Ulijn

The Dynamics between Entrepreneurship, Environment and Education
Edited by Alain Fayolle and Paula Kyrö

European Entrepreneurship in the Globalizing Economy
Edited by Alain Fayolle and Kiril Todorov

European Entrepreneurship in the Globalizing Economy

Edited by

Alain Fayolle

Professor of Entrepreneurship, EMLYON Business School, France and Visiting Professor, Solvay Brussels School of Economics and Management, Belgium

Kiril Todorov

Professor of Industrial Management and Entrepreneurship, University of National and World Economy, Sofia, Bulgaria

EUROPEAN RESEARCH IN ENTREPRENEURSHIP

Edward Elgar
Cheltenham, UK • Northampton, MA, USA

Published by
Edward Elgar Publishing Limited
The Lypiatts
15 Lansdown Road
Cheltenham
Glos GL50 2JA
UK

Edward Elgar Publishing, Inc.
William Pratt House
9 Dewey Court
Northampton
Massachusetts 01060
USA

A catalogue record for this book
is available from the British Library

Library of Congress Control Number: 2010930123

ISBN 978 1 84980 821 7

Typeset by Servis Filmsetting Ltd, Stockport, Cheshire
Printed and bound by MPG Books Group, UK

Contents

Contributors

Kaija Arhio is a Principal Lecturer (Wood Technology) in Central Ostrobothnia University of Applied Sciences in Ylivieska, Finland.

Jovo Ateljevic is Professor of Strategic Management at the Faculty of Economics, University of Banja Luka, Bosnia and Herzegovina, and has research interests in local/regional development, institutional frameworks for entrepreneurship and SME development and entrepreneurial behaviour in different socio-political contexts including countries in transition.

Olivier Basso is Research Professor in Corporate Entrepreneurship at the Singleton Institute of Brussels, Belgium.

Véronique Bouchard is Associate Professor in Strategic Management at EMLYON Business School, France.

Alain Fayolle is Professor of Entrepreneurship and Director of the Entrepreneurship Research Centre at EMLYON Business School, France. He is also Visiting Professor at Solvay Brussels School of Economics and Management, Belgium.

Antti Haahti is Professor of Tourism at the Lapland Institute for Tourism Research and Education, University of Lapland, Rovaniemi, Finland. He is the chairperson of the Experience Stratos 2007–2017, an international multidisciplinary research group on entrepreneurship in tourism.

Marja-Liisa Kaakko is Senior Lecturer in Central Ostrobothnia University of Applied Sciences in Ylivieska, Finland specializing in management accounting. She also runs a pre-incubator service for students.

Iliya Kereziev is an Assistant Professor, Chair of Entrepreneurship at the University of National and World Economy (UNWE), Sofia, Bulgaria.

Johan Klaesson is an Associate Professor of Economics at Jönköping International Business School (JIBS), Sweden. He is also the Director of the Research Unit for Rural Entrepreneurship and Growth (RUREG), which aims at being a leading, international centre in research on rural entrepreneurship and innovation.

Massimo Merlino is Professor in Business Administration, Technological Change and Entrepreneurship at Bergamo University, Italy. He has been Associate Professor of Economics and Business Administration at the Managerial Engineering Faculty, Udine and Genoa University since 1987. Professor Merlino is also General Manager of SIA Conseil Italy, a consulting company operating in strategy, change management and logistics in Italian and multinational firms.

Ossi Pesämaa is currently active as a Research Fellow at Queensland University of Technology (Australian Centre for Entrepreneurship Research).

Hanns Pichler is Professor Emeritus of Political Economy and International Development at the Vienna University of Economics and Business and was formerly Senior Schumpeter Fellow and Visiting Scholar at the Center for European Studies, Harvard University, USA.

Raymond Saner is Professor Titulaire in the Economics Department at Basle University, Switzerland and teaches in the Master in Public Affairs programme of Sciences Po in Paris, France. He is co-founder of CSEND, a Geneva-based NGRDO (non-governmental research and development organization), director of its branch DiplomacyDialogue and partner of Organizational Consultants Ltd, Hong Kong.

Stefania Testa is an Assistant Professor at the Department of Communication, Computer and System Sciences at the University of Genoa, Italy. Prior to joining the university as a faculty member she was a consultant in a leading American consulting company.

Kiril Todorov is a Professor of Industrial Management and Entrepreneurship at the University of National and World Economy (UNWE), Sofia, Bulgaria, Director of the Institute for Entrepreneurship Development and Head of the Department of Entrepreneurship at the UNWE. He is also Chairman of the Board of the Bulgarian Association for Management Development and Entrepreneurship and Vice President for Bulgaria of the European Council for Small Business and Entrepreneurship.

Daniel Tolstoy is a researcher at the Department of Marketing and Strategy at the Stockholm School of Economics, Sweden.

David Watkins trained as a natural scientist and science policy analyst. He joined Southampton Solent University as Professor of Management Development after research, teaching and management positions at Bournemouth University and Manchester Business School, UK.

Lichia Yiu was a Professor of Psychology at Chinese Cultural University in Taipei and is currently a Visiting Professor at the Business School of National Chengchi University in Taipei. She is co-founder and President of the Centre for Socio-Eco-Nomic Development (CSEND), a Geneva-based research and development institute.

1. European entrepreneurship in the globalizing economy: an introduction

Alain Fayolle and Kiril Todorov

What role can entrepreneurship play in a European economy that is more and more open to the rest of the world? In this European construction, what is the place of the countries and economies that have only recently converted to a free market economy? It is these questions, among others, that were addressed by the participants at the 'European Entrepreneurship in the Globalizing Economy: Challenges and Opportunities' conference, which took place from 9 to 12 September 2008 in Varna, Bulgaria. Numerous researchers and practitioners from Eastern Europe were brought together during this conference, and we include here a selection of the best papers that were presented on this occasion. Before giving an overview of the various contributions that make up this book, we will briefly outline a few trends in the evolution of entrepreneurship as a field of research.

Entrepreneurship is a phenomenon that depends heavily on the contexts in which it happens and develops. Entrepreneurship, generally defined as 'how, by whom and with what effects opportunities to create new goods and services are discovered, evaluated and exploited',[1] is very much conditioned by the level of economic development and the cultural, political and social contexts in which it appears.[2] It is common knowledge, for example, that entrepreneurship in developing countries, or countries in transition, is quantitatively and qualitatively different from what we observe in developed countries.

Moreover, the nature of entrepreneurship changes by moving from a narrow and simplistic vision (new-venture creation) to a far more complex and sophisticated concept.[3] As the phenomenon gains impetus, we are witnessing a multiplication of its definitions and forms. Some authors evoke the emergence of an entrepreneurial economy in which knowledge in particular would play a key role.[4] Implicitly, they also talk of an entrepreneurial society and institutional or cultural norms, applied nationally or locally, that would contribute to naturally shaping entrepreneurs by influencing individual behaviour.[5] For others, entrepreneurship is a method, a frame of mind, a way of thinking, of raising and solving problems. The systemic view is adopted by many practitioners and researchers.[6] The new firm is seen as an open system that evolves in its environment: it is not surprising therefore to see the importance granted to actor networks, social interactions and exchanges with the institutional environment. Whatever the context under consideration, the development of entrepreneurship seems largely conditioned by the implementation of a specific ecosystem. The entrepreneur is a component of this system, but he or she is far from playing the leading role, or at least his/her expertise and skills have evolved into a situational intelligence, that is to say a capacity to decode contexts (political, economic, legal, social and cultural environments) with which he/she intends to interact.

As a consequence, the environment in its broadest sense, entrepreneurial action support systems and entrepreneurial stakeholders are becoming more and more important. Researchers put forward, for example, the need to create an entrepreneurial ecosystem[7] in order to develop rural entrepreneurship[8] or to enable the environment to specialize and allocate structures and resources that will dynamically encourage the process of new venture creation.[9] Finally, several authors consider that entrepreneurship and its benefits can only develop within a formal institutional framework designed to promote and support entrepreneurial activity. This suggests a rethinking of public policies, which are often founded on illusions and old ideas.[10] The results of public entrepreneurial policies are disappointing and there are myths regarding entrepreneurs' contribution to economic growth and employment. Some believe that public policies target all and sundry whereas many researchers attribute the inefficiency of measures to the huge variety of entrepreneurial situations and contexts in which they are deployed. Finally, we must insist on the necessity, on the one hand, to find the most appropriate frameworks and methods to evaluate public policies and, on the other hand, to simplify and make clearer (more comprehensible to entrepreneurs) public policies, measures and support initiatives.

In view of these trends and fundamental evolutions, and the numerous questions they raise, in what follows we will present the various authors' contributions to this work.

MACRO-ECONOMIC FACTORS IN DEVELOPING ENTREPRENEURSHIP

The entrepreneurial process needs to be conceptualized in order for entrepreneurs' actions and contributions to be better understood. Each of the five chapters that make up the first part of the book sheds a little light on the role of environmental factors in the development of entrepreneurial behaviour.

In Chapter 2 ('Innovative Schumpeterian entrepreneurship: a systemic perspective'), Hanns Pichler helps us rediscover the work and thoughts of Joseph Schumpeter. In trying to depict the background and scientific 'environs' in which Schumpeter's visionary *Theory of Economic Development* (1912) came out, classical and neoclassical thought as well as Marx's 'Capital' had already for some time been exposed to academic scrutiny by the learned community. The entrepreneur explicitly figures in neither classical-neoclassical nor Marxian visions. Schumpeter's truly seminal interpretation of the capitalist process sees the entrepreneur as such taking centre stage as the 'pioneer' and driving force in a dialectic sense as, in fact, a kind of villain, as the 'antithesis' to the market system. The entrepreneur is indeed depicted as an element constantly striving to outmanoeuvre constraining competition, to 'trick' given market conditions and, thereby, forever challenging the 'system' itself; or more pointedly still: when and wherever possible to be, or to become, a monopolist. When relating this to modern entrepreneurship and its pivotal role in a regional and global or, more specifically, in a structural as well as developmental context, Schumpeter's vision may nowadays, more than ever in these times of dynamic change, serve as a guide for any entrepreneurially oriented policy formulation.

Chapter 3, 'Sustainable transborder business cooperation in the European regions: the importance of social entrepreneurship', by Raymond Saner and Lichia Yiu, highlights the importance of social entrepreneurship in making cross-border business cooperation sustainable. Three social roles are put forward that could facilitate transborder integration, namely those of Business Diplomats, Entrepreneurial Politicians and Cultural Ambassadors. These roles are proposed as complementary social competencies for business people, government officials and representatives of social society who play a leading role in transborder cooperation. The tri-national region of the Upper Rhine Valley is used to illustrate the potential usefulness of these new concepts. The area in question encompasses the neighbouring provinces of Switzerland (Basle), France (Alsace) and Germany (Baden and Southern Palatinate).

In Chapter 4, 'Understanding the impact of culture on a firm's entrepreneurial orientation and behaviour: a conceptual framework', Alain Fayolle, Olivier Basso and Véronique Bouchard propose a cultural model of firms' entrepreneurial orientation. The entrepreneurial orientation construct is at the heart of corporate entrepreneurship. Built around dimensions such as innovativeness, risk-taking, pro-activeness, autonomy and competitive aggressiveness, the entrepreneurial orientation construct appears as a useful and powerful tool for assessing entrepreneurial behaviour at firm level. Little empirical research has been devoted to understanding the factors and conditions that produce entrepreneurial orientation. Generic explanatory variables such as environment, organization, strategy and culture have been mentioned in past research, but although a number of hypotheses have been proposed, few have been thoroughly developed and tested. In this chapter, the authors focus on one explanatory variable – culture which they develop on multiple axes. They propose a framework that aims to provide a better understanding of how three interdependent levels of culture – national, industrial and corporate – influence firms' entrepreneurial orientation.

David Watkins, author of Chapter 5, 'Probioprise: engaging entrepreneurs in formulating research and innovation policy at the European level', presents a project commissioned by the EU Directorate General for Research. Its goal is to identify a research programme which will help entrepreneurs address simultaneously two major cornerstones of EU policy: the Lisbon Agenda, which seeks to make Europe globally more competitive by encouraging enterprising behaviour; and the Gothenburg Declaration, which aims to halt and reverse the loss of biodiversity in Europe by 2010. As we can see, this project covers two issues, entrepreneurship and biodiversity, that are extremely important for Europe in that they relate both to its competitiveness in the global economy and to the preservation of its ecological resources.

In Chapter 6, 'The third sector in action: a cross-border partnership in the western Balkans', Jovo Ateljevic explains how an NGO (nongovernmental organization) engages in activities of social and institutional entrepreneurship. A western Balkans region, known as the Drina Valley Tourism Region, encompasses eight municipalities, four from each side of the Drina river which forms the border between Bosnia and Herzegovina and Serbia. The regional economy is heavily dependent upon agriculture and a few tourism activities with good prospects for innovative tourism development. One of the main problems facing all the municipalities is negative population growth and an increasing number of younger people permanently leaving the region. The chapter underlines the role of institutional entrepreneurship in bringing solutions to these problems and in contributing to the regional economic development.

MICRO-ECONOMIC FACTORS IN NURTURING HIGH POTENTIAL SMES

In the second part of the book, the five chapters examine the role of organizational factors in the development of young firms with high growth potential.

Chapter 7, 'Board network characteristics and company performance in Sweden: the case of Gnosjö companies and their board members in southern Sweden', by Ossi Pesämaa, Johan Klaesson and Antti Haahti, focuses on selected characteristics of enterprise boards and their influence on performance in companies located in Gnosjö, one of Sweden's best known industrial districts. The aim and contribution of this chapter is to propose and test a model that reflects the relationship between board characteristics, administration, company age and performance. The results show that the number of commitments among board members, as well as company age, impacts significantly on company performance based on sales and sales per employee. Support for the model is significant, and the authors believe these results have valuable practical as well as theoretical implications.

In Chapter 8, 'Knowledge creation and management in an Italian biotech startup', Massimo Merlino and Stefania Testa explore knowledge management in small technology-based firms. Although knowledge management is important for all industries, it is particularly relevant to the so-called knowledge-intensive sectors, due to a need for high innovativeness. The biotechnology industry features among these and, due to its high growth rate and impact on economic output, it has attracted the attention of the managerial and academic communities. There are essentially two types of companies within this industry: integrated companies or product-oriented firms (pharmaceutical, food and agricultural, chemical, and so on) that utilize biotechnologies for production or research purposes; and specialized biotechnology companies or technology-oriented firms. Specialized companies are usually small young companies and play a very important role in the development of biotechnologies. The survival and growth of such firms depend mainly on their ability to absorb and exploit new technological advancement, and this creates an incentive to enter networks at a faster pace than other less knowledge-intensive companies. Under these conditions, the way in which these new technological firms create and manage advanced knowledge through internal and external sources remains of major strategic importance.

Chapter 9, 'The international product venturing of a biotech SME: knowledge combination in upstream and downstream networks', is centred on similar questions in the same biotechnology industry. Daniel

Tolstoy states that research has highlighted the fact that international product venturing is critical for the competitiveness of SMEs in foreign markets. Despite the academic consensus, researchers still have limited knowledge about the predictors of international product venturing of SMEs. In response to this research gap, this chapter advances the argument that knowledge input from both upstream and downstream networks provides a multitude of options for knowledge combinations and therefore determines the trajectory for international product venturing. The purpose of the study is to examine knowledge combinations in and across upstream/downstream networks in the context of a biotech SME's international product venturing.

Chapter 10, 'Building competitive advantages in the process of business growth: the case of Bulgarian technology-based SMEs', studies the growth of technology-based SMEs, which attract intense attention from political and economic leaders. In this chapter, Kiril Todorov and Iliya Kereziev reveal and highlight the relationship between the creation and development of competitive advantage and growth management of SMEs. On this basis they attempt to identify and analyse the main competitive advantages of Bulgarian technology-based SMEs and their prospects for development. The authors use Wickham's conceptual framework as a theoretical basis for analysing competitive advantage and its relationship with business growth.

Finally, Chapter 11, 'Business pre-incubator as a learning network: a case study in the University of Applied Sciences', written and proposed by Kaija Arhio and Marja-Liisa Kaakko, takes as a starting point the significant role of business incubators in promoting entrepreneurship in higher education institutes. The business incubating process can be seen as an organizational learning process. The concept of the learning network has been used mainly in the context of web-based learning environments, regional development and knowledge and technology transfer between universities and small enterprises. It has also been discussed as an aid to developing strategic capability among SMEs. In this chapter the authors use and discuss the concept in the context of business incubators. The main aim of this chapter is to present a practical example of how to support entrepreneurship as a part of university studies.

NOTES

1. Shane and Venkataraman (2000).
2. Atamer and Torres (2008).
3. Which, of course, does not question its economic and social importance.

4. Audretsch and Thurik (2004).
5. See, for example, Audretsch (2007).
6. See in particular Bruyat (1993).
7. All the interconnected elements including individual risk takers, resource providers, intermediaries, needs and demand for goods and services, should act together in order to create a virtuous circle of wealth creation (Lee and Phan, 2008).
8. Lee and Phan (2008).
9. Venkataraman (2004).
10. See, for example, articles by Philippe Albert and Didier Chabaud in the first issue of *L'Expansion Entrepreneuriat* (January 2009).

REFERENCES

Albert, P. (2009), 'Le high-tech, grande illusion du décideur', *L'Expansion Entrepreneuriat*, (1), January.

Atamer, T. and O. Torres (2008), 'Modèles d'entrepreneuriat et mondialisation', in A. Fayolle (ed.), *L'Art d'entreprendre*, Paris: Editions Village Mondial, pp. 29–37.

Audretsch, D.B. (2007), *The Entrepreneurial Society*, Oxford: Oxford University Press.

Audretsch, D.B. and A.R. Thurik (2004), 'A model of the entrepreneurial economy', *International Journal of Entrepreneurship Education*, 2, 143–66.

Bruyat, C. (1993), 'Création d'entreprise: contributions épistémologiques et modélisation', unpublished doctoral dissertation in Management Science, Université Pierre-Mendès-France, Grenoble.

Chabaud, D. (2009), 'Pour sortir de la naïveté sur la création d'entreprise', *L'Expansion Entrepreneuriat*, (1), January.

Lee, S.H. and P.P. Phan (2008), 'Initial thoughts on a model of rural entrepreneurship in developing countries', Working Paper, World Entrepreneurship Forum, EMLYON Business School.

Shane, S. and V. Venkataraman (2000), 'The promise of entrepreneurship as a field of research', *Academy of Management Review*, 25 (1), 217–26.

Venkataraman, S. (2004), 'Regional transformation through technological entrepreneurship', *Journal of Business Venturing*, 19, 153–60.

PART I

Macro-economic Factors in Developing
Entrepreneurship

2. Innovative Schumpeterian entrepreneurship: a systemic perspective

Hanns Pichler

Schumpeter states in the early German edition of his seminal *Theory of Economic Development* (1912),[1] that underlying hypotheses and observations, were not invented or merely fictitious, but were taken and gleaned from economic reality in contrast to the then prevailing equilibrium-oriented and essentially 'static' views of interpreting the market-based capitalist process as 'conditioned by given circumstances' (as he subtitled the very first chapter). Hence the telling motto right on the title page of the first edition: 'Hypotheses non fingo'. (This never appeared again in any later editions, including the English translation of 1934; see Appendices 2A.1 and 2A.2.)

In retrospect one might be left wondering what, in fact, makes Schumpeter's early conceived vision of the leadership role of the entrepreneur in 'economic life' still so very topical, if not outright indispensable for explaining the dynamics of the 'capitalist' system. In recognizing the role and importance of entrepreneurially driven innovation with the related forces of 'creative destruction' as intrinsically market-based phenomena, Schumpeterian notions indeed seem to have gained new momentum in today's economic debate about the very understanding of entrepreneurially driven systems, including competitive entrepreneurial behaviour with emphasis on related entrepreneurship education.[2] This is against a bibliographical background of his 'Theory' which, from time to time almost forgotten, widely misread or misinterpreted, took a full 14 years until its second, in parts radically revised and modified edition was published in 1926.[3]

In the foreword to the second edition Schumpeter explicitly voices his irritation that readers of the earlier version obviously 'mistook' the book as a kind of 'history' of economic development in line with the – methodologically more descriptive – German 'Historical Schools' to which, nonetheless, the very flow and partly rather verbose style of the original text undoubtedly shows a certain affinity. In restating and emphasizing the theoretical thrust of his argument, the somewhat lengthy subtitle[4] was added from the second edition onwards (and retained in the English translation) to bring home the very essence, together with substantial revisions to the core second chapter on 'The fundamental phenomenon of economic development'.[5]

In the context of such revisions Schumpeter, in our view, perpetrated two 'sins': first, by trying in the second chapter to schematize, thereby narrowing down and rather 'sterilizing', the very role of the entrepreneur to the meanwhile famous, constantly referred to, 'five cases' in 'the carrying out of new combinations'.[6] As such he conveyed a rather bloodless, sort of descriptive 'listing' of implied entrepreneurial traits and 'characteristics', lending itself to a rather limited, yet tempting interpretation as a sort of proxy for defining the 'Schumpeterian entrepreneur', quite in contrast to the full-blooded picture so vividly painted in the original version, which refrained from such schematization. The second transgression was the omission of the entire seventh chapter (from 1926 onward),[7] wherein Schumpeter tried to put his vision and overall conceptualization in a systemic context by way of a 'holistic' topping off in form of a socio-economic synopsis of the expositions in the preceding chapters. It seems a pity that the reader, especially the English reader, remains deprived of a possibly still more comprehensive and deeper understanding of the very thrust of the Schumpeterian message even if, admittedly, this chapter (of nearly 90 pages in the German original) might appear less rigorously argued.

A 'THEORY' AGAINST THE MAINSTREAM

In order to fully appreciate the very boldness of Schumpeter's message, his 'Theory' needs to be viewed in light of the prevailing mainstream of economic thought at the time of its first edition. Classics and neoclassics, notably of the Viennese marginal ('Grenznutzen') tradition with Eugen von Böhm-Bawerk and Friedrich von Wieser as principal advisers to Schumpeter's habilitation at the Vienna University,[8] were clearly dominating the discipline's common body of knowledge. So too was Marx's quite different, non-market based ('socialist') interpretation of the economic process, all of which Schumpeter was very familiar with, while more specifically having been exposed, of course, to neoclassical thinking in the Viennese academic 'style'. His above-mentioned habilitation thesis, submitted in 1908, was indeed devoted to a theoretical treatment and discussion of the 'state of the art' at the time, including a rather shrewd reception and re-interpretation of Walrasian equilibrium as an exposition of 'pure economics' on essentially static grounds.[9]

These scientific environs and ingredients are important to note as points of departure in Schumpeter's own 'Theory', wherein his critical stand against the prevailing 'mainstream' finds ample expression right in the first chapter.[10] Here he points to the intrinsically static, 'circular flow'-type view of 'economic life' and voices his discontent over the obvious deficiency of such theorizing to adequately capture and explain the underlying dynamics of the market-based 'capitalist' process. By contrast, he explicitly commends Marx – with his (dialectic) methodology – as being able to indeed grasp the intrinsically dynamic nature of 'economic development'.[11]

Of specific relevance in this very context is Eugen von Böhm-Bawerk's profoundly neoclassical – and pointedly anti-Marxist – *The Positive Theory of Capital*,[12] for Schumpeter yet another bone of contention and point of critical departure since, despite its erudite theoretical reasoning, it again rests on essentially 'static' grounds and, therefore, is bound to miss the intrinsic nature of 'capitalist' dynamics. (For an ingenious early re-interpretation of *The Positive Theory* with Böhm-Bawerk's subtle theorizing on the 'roundaboutness' of capitalist accumulation by his contemporary Swedish economist Knut Wicksell, see the figure in Appendix 2A.4.)[13]

It is against this background and the dissatisfaction with mainstream 'circular flow' concepts then prevailing, that Schumpeter's own 'Theory' evolved and took shape: as a theoretical – and in its endeavour similar to Böhm-Bawerk's preceding, albeit 'static' – attempt to, for his part, provide a non-Marxist dynamic interpretation of capitalist 'development' driven by its inherent systemic forces 'from within'.[14] We shall try in the following to pinpoint – against such a background – what seems to emerge as a kind of 'hidden agenda' behind Schumpeter's vision, rendering it such a lasting legacy for interpreting capitalist development and its dynamics.

TOWARD ENTREPRENEURIALLY DRIVEN 'CAPITALISM'

In taking a profoundly critical stand against mainstream 'statics', Schumpeter in his 'Theory' endeavours to depict market-based (long-term) 'economic development' as an ever-changing – and as such never-toward-equilibrium-tending – process of 'economic life' generally. This, in fact, constitutes the all-pervading thrust of his argument; and indeed no one – apart from Marx in his systemic theorizing – had done so before in a similarly rigorous fashion which, no doubt, lends such seminal and lasting fascination to his 'Theory'.

The essence of capitalist dynamics, in Schumpeter's view, thus boils down to a continuous pursuit of 'carrying out . . . new combinations'[15] as an entrepreneurially driven process which proves 'that economic life never is static; it lies in the very nature of development.'[16] The question then arises: who is 'carrying out', what stands for the 'new' and how are 'new combinations' being carried through?

Schumpeter's straightforward answer to that is: the entrepreneur, being depicted and singled out in the very 'Schumpeterian' meaning (or 'in our sense' as he repeatedly emphasizes). In any given economic moment or situation, he argues, there exist 'numerous possibilities for new combinations', yet only a small group has the drive and takes 'leadership' to, in fact, carry them through, while 'most do not see them'.[17] Thus, 'the carrying out of new combinations is a special function . . . of people who are much less numerous than all those who have the "objective" possibility of doing it. Therefore, . . . entrepreneurs are a special type, and their behaviour . . . the motive power of a great number of significant phenomena.'[18]

Hence it is, with Schumpeter, the entrepreneur – and only he – who '"leads" the means of production into new channels . . . drawing other producers . . . after him', thereby rendering 'a service, the full appreciation of which . . . is not so easily understood by the public at large'.[19]

From there it follows, 'the most typical incorporation of future value creating potentials is a new enterprise', and the 'specific type' as characteristic of 'a special class of economically active individuals has taken on a name of its own, namely *entrepreneur*'.[20] The entrepreneur is the driving or 'leading' force in economic life, whether as 'business founder'[21] or as 'creative innovator', who through 'anti-hedonist'[22] activity and initiatives creates future values. 'They [these values, J.H.P.] correlate with new combinations, . . . new combinations translated in value terms . . . the shadows of things to come.'[23]

In carrying out new combinations, the entrepreneur, first singles out from a 'multitude of various moments . . . the related right decision . . . which is given to few people only with specific capabilities, and secondly, carries them through. These are the characteristics of our entrepreneur, of our man of action. They are inseparable and of equal importance. And the result is economic development, progress'.[24] This development or progress is being triggered by 'our type' of (Schumpeterian) entrepreneur.

UNCOVERING THE SUBTLETY OF IMPLIED 'DIALECTICS'

The role of the Schumpeterian entrepreneur, as being inseparably geared to the very essence of 'economic development', thus resembles a kind of 'hidden' form of what might be called Schumpeterian 'dialectics' for interpreting the dynamics of capitalist development from a (non-Marxist) systemic perspective.

The market system itself, under 'given circumstances', thereby consti-tutes the *thesis*; the entrepreneur in the Schumpeterian sense as the driving (also the 'creatively destructive') force is the *antithesis* of the system, ever striving to 'out compete' given circumstances by way of new combina-tions and thus – temporarily at least – trying to be or to become a kind of 'monopolist'.[25] Finally, the *synthesis* of such a scenario is to be seen taking the system in such process to an ever higher level of welfare; not, however, as a kind of 'resting place' in equilibrium, since the very dynam-ics of prevailing market forces tends forever to catch up with, to 'compete down', temporarily dominating (monopolistic) entrepreneurial niches and initiatives provoking, by force of such process, entrepreneurial creativity yet anew in trying to tackle or outmanoeuvre the system 'from within' and, as such, is quite distinct from Marxist 'dialectics'. The entrepreneur in such a scenario takes on the role of unsettling 'disequilibrator', as an ever-disturbing element to static or 'circular flow' tendencies toward equilibrium in the very sense of 'creative destruction'; as a *movens* of forever challenging the system 'conditioned by given circumstances',[26] of constantly trying to trick competitive market constraints and forces through innovative 'new combinations', thus providing the intrinsic drive for (Schumpeterian) 'economic development'.

Unlike Marx, also unlike the classical-neoclassical and as such essen-tially 'static' concepts, Schumpeter in his 'Theory' boldly presents an alternative (non-Marxian) interpretation of the 'capitalist' process with the entrepreneur taking centre stage. It is this very boldness too, which in good measure seems to account for the lasting relevance, if not fascination of his 'Theory' up till now (shortly, by the way, to celebrate its 100-year anniversary since the first edition).

LEGACY AND TOPICAL RELEVANCE IN TODAY'S PERSPECTIVE

By provocatively casting the entrepreneur – traditionally being considered the 'epitome' of capitalism itself – as a kind of villain or 'antithesis' to the market system with its 'mainstream' proclaimed tendencies toward (static) equilibrium, amply testifies to the originality of Schumpeter's own theorizing. Thereby depicting the specific role of the entrepreneur under systems-related aspects further implies that the very same ('capitalist') system essentially derives its inherent strength and dynamics from ever self-renewing entrepreneurial drive and initiatives: dynamics and strength, in the end, for sustained reproduction of the system out of its own forces, or 'from within'.

Notwithstanding Schumpeter's later scepticism under changed economic conditions in the face of World War II as to whether entrepreneurially led capitalism indeed may 'survive',[27] we can witness today a sheer global revival of Schumpeter's early vision: be it in the form of a new and growing awareness of the need for entrepreneurial initiatives, values and attitudes as crucial for sustainable development and more broadly based welfare; be it in recognizing the specific relevance of 'entrepreneurship education', or the importance of diversified entrepreneurially based small and medium sized business structures; be it in the context of fostering business startups combined with venture capital financing and concomitant tendencies toward privatization worldwide (including related emphasis on economies 'of scope' rather than just one-sidedly 'of scale').[28] This all relates to the very notion of Schumpeterian 'entrepreneurship' as being reflected in entrepreneurially driven initiatives, creativity and 'leadership', leadership that in any market-based system stands for structural diversification, for sustained viability and capabilities of success and sheer systemic 'survival' under competitive conditions.[29]

From a contemporary perspective, the relevance and importance of Schumpeter's vision nowadays seems to be demonstrated vividly in the ongoing – and partly still painful – restructuring from formerly centrally-planned to market-oriented systems in Central and Eastern Europe. For this transformation, the final verdict over regarding success or failure in large measure hinges on how effectively these economies are able to build and rebuild their entrepreneurially based business structures over which have been ruthlessly weakened, if not outright ruined over decades. This rebuilding is a prerequisite for economic dynamics and sustained development in an increasingly competitive environment with more and more diversified markets.[30]

It seems that more than ever, under today's regional or indeed world-wide challenges, Schumpeter's erstwhile vision can serve as a valuable guide, as a kind of compass with a view to policy formulation for entrepreneurially conducive framework conditions, or more plainly: for creating conditions wherein entrepreneurial initiatives, creativity and leadership in the very Schumpeterian meaning can thrive and be adequately rewarded.

To conclude on that note in Schumpeter's own words: 'Look around – and you will see, things really are like that'.[31] Or in conformity to his early motto again: 'Hypotheses non fingo'.[32]

NOTES

1. Newly edited and reprinted with an 'Introduction' by J. Röpke and O. Stiller (2006). References are here identified as follows: if relating to the earlier German editions (in particular, the first or second) as 'Theorie' followed by year; if relating to the English version as 'Theory' (1934 or reprints). Quotations translated from the German editions, being either omitted or referred to only *passim* in the 1934 English version, are marked 'transl. J.H.P.'

2. Witness the numerous university chairs and programmes on 'entrepreneurship' which have sprung up, and which are still expanding, over recent decades. More recently see also Thomas K. McCraw (2007) with extensive references to Schumpeter's 'Legacy'; or the relevance of innovative elements and factors in the context of the New (endogenous) Growth Theory (cf. Romer, 1990, and others), as well as distinct Schumpeterian traits in the relatively new discipline of 'Evolutionary Economics'.

3. This was essentially the basis for the subsequent English translation, published in 1934 at Harvard after the third and fourth German editions (1931, 1934), which were both largely unchanged.

4. In German: 'Eine Untersuchung über Unternehmergewinn, Kapital, Kredit, Zins und den Konjunkturzyklus'; in English: 'An inquiry into profits, capital, credit, interest and the business cycle' ('profits' to be understood as entrepreneurial or 'private').

5. In German: 'Das Grundphänomen der wirtschaftlichen Entwicklung' (Theorie, 1912, pp. 103–98; 1926, pp. 88–139; Theory, 1934, pp. 57–94).

6. Theorie 1926, p. 100f.; Theory, 1934, p. 66, in contrast to the German version not explicitly 'listed', but less conspicuously integrated in the text (see Appendix 2A.3).

7. In German: 'Das Gesamtbild der Volkswirtschaft' ('Overall view of the economy', transl. J.H.P.) (Theorie, 1912, pp. 463–548).

8. Based on his first book, entitled: 'Das Wesen und der Hauptinhalt der theoretischen Nationalökonomie' (1908) ('The nature and content of theoretical economics'), also referred to repeatedly (as 'Wesen' for short) in Schumpeter's subsequent 'Theorie'.

9. Cf. Walras (1874–7); English translation by W. Jaffe (1954).

10. Entitled 'The circular flow of economic life as conditioned by given circumstances' (Theory, 1934, pp. 3–56); in German: 'Der Kreislauf der Wirtschaft in seiner Bedingtheit durch gegebene Verhältnisse' (Theorie, 1912, pp. 1–102). The 'Physiocrats', Schumpeter argues, in grasping 'the fact of circular flow . . . ipso facto describe a static economy . . . And this remained the objective of pure economics to our days.' Also with A. Smith, 'wherever his arguments rest on firm ground, his view is essentially static . . . Wherever he speaks of progress, he never explains this on the basis of economic processes in themselves. . .' (Theorie, 1912, pp. 92ff., transl. J.H.P.).

11. 'The only major attempt toward the problem of development is the one of Karl Marx . . . He strived to treat the development of economic life itself on basis of economic theory. His accumulation, his immiserization, his crisis theories follow from pure economic reasoning . . . aiming at the evolution of economic life as such . . . not just its circular flow . . .' (Theorie, 1912, p. 98; transl. J.H.P.) And if he 'had not been more than a purveyor of phraseology, he would be dead by now. Mankind is not grateful for that sort of service and forgets quickly the names of the people who write the librettos for its political operas.' (Schumpeter, 1942, p. 5)

12. Translated with a 'Preface' by W. Smart (1891); German original: *Positive Theorie des Kapitales* (1889), as Vol. 2 of *Kapital and Kapitalzins*. A centrepiece until today of

neoclassical capital theory, which propelled its author to international fame. Böhm-Bawerk by the way, as Schumpeter states himself, never really approved of his 'Theory' (see Theorie, 1926, 'Vorwort').

13. See Wicksell (1893/1933).
14. 'By development, therefore, we shall understand only such changes in economic life as . . . arise by its own initiative, from within.' (Theory, 1934, p. 63.) 'Development in our sense is then defined by the carrying out of new combinations.' (Ibid., p. 66; with the 'five points' to follow, see Appendix 2A.3.)
15. Theory (1934, p. 66).
16. Theorie (1912, p. 162) (transl. J.H.P.).
17. Theorie (1912, p. 162) (transl. J.H.P.).
18. Theory (1934, p. 81f).
19. Theory, (1934, p. 89); yet, such 'leadership in particular . . . must be distinguished from "invention". As long as they [inventions, J.H.P.] are not carried into practice, inventions are economically irrelevant.' (Ibid., p. 88). However, 'In as much as the carrying out of new combinations constitutes form and substance of development, so much so is the leader's initiative its driving force.' Alas, not all are 'equally far sighted and energetic . . .' (Theorie, 1912, p. 162, footnote; transl. J.H.P.)
20. Theorie (1912, p. 170f.) (transl. J.H.P.); or somewhat more concisely in the subsequent English version: 'The carrying out of new combinations we call "enterprise"; the individuals whose function it is to carry them out we call "entrepreneurs".' (Theory, 1934, p. 74).
21. In merciless Schumpeterian understanding: If a business founder merely continues to manage his 'enterprise . . . in simply a static way, he ceases to be an entrepreneur!'. His very nature 'is linked to creating [to combining, J.H.P.] something new'. (Theorie 1912, p. 174, footnote; transl. J.H.P.).
22. Theory (1934, p. 94); the entrepreneur as – in a 'non-hedonist' way – ever being absorbed by 'the joy of creating, of getting things done, or of just exercising . . . ingenuity'. (Theory, 1934, p. 93).
23. Theorie (1912, p. 170) (transl. J.H.P.).
24. Theorie (1912, p. 177) (transl. J.H.P.).
25. Since, with Schumpeter, 'perfect competition' temporarily having been 'suspended whenever anything new is being induced . . .' thereby provides 'the fundamental impulse that sets and keeps the capitalist engine in motion.' (Schumpeter, 1942, p. 104f.)
26. Cf. heading of the very first chapter of the 'Theory' (in German: '. . . Bedingtheit durch gegebene Verhältnisse', Theorie, both 1912 and 1926).
27. Cf. his famous *Capitalism, Socialism and Democracy* (1942) and numerous related references; it is in this later work (not in his 'Theory') that Schumpeter explicitly coins the popular and much cited phrase, 'creative destruction' (later on back-translated into German as 'schöpferische Zerstoerung').
28. Cf. Aiginger and Tichy (1984).
29. Cf. Heertje (1981); Heertje and Perlman (1993); Heilbroner (1993); Scherer (1992); Scherer and Perlman (1992).
30. Cf. Becker and Knudsen (2002); Backhaus (2003); Giersch (1984, 1987); Scherer (1999); Shionoya and Perlman (1994).
31. Theorie 1934, 'Vorwort' (Preface) to 4th German edition (transl. J.H.P.).
32. See Appendix 2A.1; as a kind of invitation to scientifically 'creative destruction' Schumpeter, by the way, sums up the preface to the first edition, wishing for himself 'nothing more than that this work as soon as possible be rendered obsolete and forgotten.' (Transl. J.H.P.) – And this invitation, now after almost 100 years, apparently still holds.

BIBLIOGRAPHY

Aiginger, K. and G. Tichy (1984), *Die Größe der Kleinen: Die überraschenden Erfolge kleiner und mittlerer Unternehmungen in den achtziger Jahren*, Vienna: Signum Verlag.

Allen, R.L. (1991), *Opening Doors: The Life & Work of Joseph Schumpeter*, 2 vols, New Brunswick, NJ: Transaction Publishers.

Anderson, B.M. (1915), 'Schumpeter's dynamic economics', *Political Science Quarterly*, **30**, December, 645–60.

Backhaus, J.G. (ed.) (2003), *Joseph Alois Schumpeter. Entrepreneurship, Style and Vision*, Boston, MA: Kluwer Academic Publishers.

Becker, M.C. and T. Knudsen (2002), 'Schumpeter 1911: farsighted visions on economic development, *American Journal of Economics and Sociology*, **61**, April, 387–403.

Böhm, S. (ed.) (1987), *Joseph A. Schumpeter. Beiträge zur Sozialökonomik*, Vienna: Boehlau Verlag.

Böhm-Bawerk, E. von (1889/1921), *Positive Theorie des Kapitales* (Innsbruck 1889), 4th printing, ed. by F. von Wieser, Jena: Fischer Verlag, 1921 (= Vol. 2 of *Kapital und Kapitalzins*)

Bottomore, T. (1992), *Between Marginalism and Marxism: The Economic Sociology of J.A. Schumpeter*, New York: St. Martin's Press.

Chandler, A.D., Jr (1997), *The Visible Hand: The Managerial Revolution in American Business*, Cambridge, MA: The Belknap Press of Harvard University Press.

Chandler, A.D., Jr (1990), *Scale and Scope: The Dynamics of Industrial Capitalism*, Cambridge, MA: The Belknap Press of Harvard University Press.

Clark, J.B. (1912), 'Theorie der wirtschaftlichen Entwicklung', *American Economic Review*, **2** (4), 873–5.

Clemence, R.V. (ed.) (1951), *Joseph A. Schumpeter: Essays on Entrepreneurs, Innovations, Business Cycles and the Evolution of Capitalism*, Cambridge, MA: Kennikat Press.

Dopfer, K. (1994), *The Phenomenon of Economic Change: Neoclassical vs. Schumpeterian Approaches*, in L. Magnusson (ed.), *Evolutionary and Neo-Schumpeterian Approaches to Economics*, Boston-Dordrecht-London: Kluwer Academic Publishers.

Ebner, A. (2003), 'The institutional analysis of entrepreneurship: historist aspects of Schumpeter's development theory', in J.G. Backhaus (ed.), *Joseph Alois Schumpeter. Entrepreneurship, Style and Vision*, Boston, MA: Kluwer Academic Publishers.

Elliott, J.E. (1983), 'Schumpeter and the theory of capitalist economic development', *Journal of Economic Behavior and Organisation*, **4** December, pp. 277–308.

Fagerberg, J. (2003), 'Schumpeter and the revival of evolutionary economics: an appraisal of the literature', *Journal of Evolutionary Economics*, **13** (2), 125–59.

Giersch, H. (1984), 'The age of Schumpeter', *American Economic Review*, **74**, May, 103–9.

Giersch, H. (1987), 'Economic policies in the age of Schumpeter', *European Economic Review*, **31** Feb./March, 35–52.

Haberler, G. (1981), *Schumpeter's Capitalism, Socialism and Democracy After*

Forty Years, ed. by M. Okada, Kyoto; also in A. Heertje (1981), *Schumpeter's vision*: Capitalism, Socialism and Democracy *after 40 Years*, New York: Praeger.

Harris, S.E. (ed.) (1951), *Schumpeter: Social Scientist*, Cambridge, MA: Harvard University Press.

Hedtke, U. and R. Swedberg (eds) (2000), *Joseph Alois Schumpeter. Briefe/Letters*, Tübingen: J.C.B. Mohr.

Heertje, A. (ed.) (1981), *Schumpeter's Vision:* Capitalism, Socialism and Democracy *after 40 Years*, New York: Praeger Publishers Inc.

Heertje, A. and M. Perlman (eds) (1990), *Evolving Technology and Market Structure: Studies in Schumpeterian Economics*, Ann Arbor, MI: University of Michigan Press, 3rd edition 1993.

Heilbroner, R.L. (1981), 'Was Schumpeter right?', *Social Research*, **48** (3), 456–71.

Heilbroner, R.L. (1993), Was Schumpeter right after all?', *Journal of Economic Perspectives*, **7** (3), Summer, 87–96.

Klausinger, H. (1993), 'Schumpeter und die Grosse Depression: Theorie-Diagnose-Politik', discussion paper, Institut für Volkswirtschaftslehre der Universität Hohenheim, No. 78.

Kurz, H.D. (2005), *Joseph A. Schumpeter: Ein Sozialökonom zwischen Marx und Walras*, Marburg: Metropolis Verlag.

Kurz, H.D. (2006), 'Schumpeter on innovations and profits: the classical heritage', paper, presented at Conference 'Neo-Schumpeterian Economics: An Agenda for the 21st Century', 27–29 June, Trest, Czech Republic.

Langlois, R. (1998), 'Schumpeter and personal capitalism', in G. Eliasson and C. Green (eds), *Microfoundations of Economic Growth: A Schumpeterian Perspective*, Ann Abor, MI: University of Michigan Press.

Magnusson, L. (ed.) (1994), *Evolutionary and Neo-Schumpeterian Approaches to Economics*, Boston-Dordrecht-London: Kluwer Academic Publishers.

McCrae, R.C. (1913), 'Schumpeter's economic system', *Quarterly Journal of Economics*, **27** (3), 520–46.

McCraw, T.K. (2007), *Prophet of Innovation: Joseph Schumpeter and Creative Destruction, Cambridge*, MA and London: The Belknap Press of Harvard University Press.

Mokyr, J. (1990), *The Lever of Riches: Technological Creativity and Economic Progress*, New York: Oxford University Press.

Mugler, J. (1990), 'Entrepreneurship and the theory of the firm', in R. Donckels and A. Miettinen (eds), *New Findings and Perspectives in Entrepreneurship*, Aldershot, UK: Avebury.

Mugler, J. (2002), 'Strategic development of SMEs in turbulent environments', in B. Piasecki (ed.), *Entrepreneurship and Small Business Development in the 21ˢᵗ Century*, Lodz: Wydawnictwo Uniwersytetu łódzkiego.

Nelson, R. and S.G. Winter (1982), *An Evolutionary Theory of the Firm*, Cambridge, MA: The Belknap Press of Harvard University Press.

Nicholas, T. (2003), 'Why Schumpeter was right: innovation, market power, and creative destruction in 1920s America', *Journal of Economic History*, **63**, December, 1023–58.

Perelman, M. (1995), 'Retrospectives: Schumpeter, David Wells and Creative Destruction', *Journal of Economic Perspectives*, **9** (3), 189–97.

Röpke, J. (2002), *Der lernende Unternehmer: Zur Konstruktion und Evolution unternehmerischen Bewusstseins*, Marburg: Marburger Förderzentrum für Existenzgründer aus der Universität (Mafex).

Röpke, J. and O. Stiller (eds) (2006), *Joseph Schumpeter: Theorie der wirtschaftlichen Entwicklung: Nachdruck der 1. Auflage von 1912, ergänzt um eine Einführung*, Berlin: Duncker & Humblot.

Romer, P.M. (1990), 'Endogenous technological change', *Journal of Political Economy*, **98** (5), S71–S102.

Scherer, F.M. (1984), *Innovation and Growth: Schumpeterian Perspectives*, Cambridge, MA: MIT Press.

Scherer, F.M. (1992), 'Schumpeter and plausible capitalism', *Journal of Economic Literature*, **XXX**, September, 1416–33.

Scherer, F.M. (1999), *New Perspectives on Economic Growth and Technological Innovation*, Washington DC: Brookings Institution Press.

Scherer, F.M. and M. Perlman (eds) (1992), *Entrepreneurship, Technological Innovation and Economic Growth: Studies in the Schumpeterian Tradition*, Ann Arbor, MI: University of Michigan Press.

Schmidt, K.-H. (1987), '*Vorläufer und Anfänge von Schumpeters Theorien der Wirtschaftlichen Entwicklung*', working paper, Neue Folge No. 8, Universität Paderborn.

Schumpeter, J.A. (1908), *Das Wesen und der Hauptinhalt der Theoretischen Nationalökonomie*, Leipzig: Duncker & Humblot.

Schumpeter, J.A. (1912), *Theorie der Wirtschaftlichen Entwicklung*, Leipzig: Duncker & Humblot.

Schumpeter, J.A. (1934), *The Theory of Economic Development: An Inquiry into Profits, Capital, Credit, Interest and the Business Cycle*, translated by R. Opie, Cambridge, MA: Harvard University Press.

Schumpeter, J.A. (1942/1946), *Capitalism, Socialism and Democracy*, New York: 5th edn, Introduction by T. Bottmore, New York: Harper and Brothers.

Schumpeter, J.A. (1946), 'Capitalism', *Encyclopaedia Britannica*, London: Encyclopaedia Britannica.

Schumpeter, J.A. (1949a), 'Science and Ideology', *American Economic Review*, **39**, March, 345–59 (Presidential Address, December 1948).

Schumpeter, J.A. (1949b), 'The Communist manifesto in sociology and economics', *Journal of Political Economy*, **57**, June, 199–212; reprinted in R.V. Clemence (1951), *Joseph A. Schumpeter: Essays on Entrepreneurs, Innovations, Business Cycles and the Evolution of Capitalism*, Cambridge, MA: Addison-Wesley.

Schumpeter, J.A. (1949), 'Economic theory and entrepreneurial history, in Center for Research in Entrepreneurial History, Harvard University (ed.), *Change and the Entrepreneur. Postulates and Patterns for Entrepreneurial History*, Cambridge, MA: Harvard University Press, pp. 63–84.

Schumpeter, J.A. (1991), 'Comments on a plan for the study of entrepreneurship', reprinted in R. Swedberg (1991), *Joseph A. Schumpeter: His Life and Work*, Oxford: Polity Press.

Seidl, C. (ed.) (1984), *Lectures on Schumpeterian Economics*, Berlin: Springer.

Shionoya, Y. and M. Perlman (eds) (1994), *Innovation in Technology, Industries and Institutions: Studies in Schumpeterian Perspectives*, Ann Arbor, MI: University of Michigan Press.

Stolper, W.F. (1991), 'The theoretical bases of economic policy: the Schumpeterian perspective', *Journal of Evolutionary Economics*, **1** (3), 189–205.

Stolper, W.F. (1994), *Joseph Alois Schumpeter: The Public Life of a Private Man*, Princeton: Princeton University Press.

Stolper, W.F. and C. Seidl (eds) (1985), *Joseph A. Schumpeter: Aufsätze zur Wirtschaftspolitik*, Tübingen: J.C.B. Mohr.

Streissler, E.W. (1992), 'The influence of German and Austrian economics on Joseph A. Schumpeter', paper presented at Conference of the International Joseph A. Schumpeter Society, Kyoto.

Swedberg, R. (1991a), *Joseph A. Schumpeter: his Life and Work*, Oxford: Polity Press.

Swedberg, R. (1991b), *Joseph A. Schumpeter: The Economics and Sociology of Capitalism*, Princeton: Princeton University Press.

Swedberg, R. (1992), 'Schumpeter's early work', *Journal of Evolutionary Economics*, **2** (1), 65–82.

Vecci, N. de (1995), *Entrepreneurs, Institutions and Economic Change. The Economic Thought of J. A. Schumpeter (1905–1925)*, translated by A. Stone, Aldershot, UK: Edward Elgar.

Walras, L. (1874–7), *Elements d' Economie Politique Pure, ou Théorie de la Richesse Sociale*, Lausanne: Rouge; English translation by W. Jaffe, *Elements of Pure Economics*, Homewood, IL and London: Irwin.

Wicksell, K. (1893/1933), *Über Wert, Kapital und Rente nach den neueren nationalökonomischen Theorien*, Jena: Fischer; reprinted in London School of Economics Series No. 15, London: London School of Economics.

Wicksell, K. (1895/1997), 'Zur Lehre von der Steuerinzidenz', doctoral dissertation, Uppsala, 1895; translated as 'Income taxes and duties', in B. Sandelin (ed.), *Knut Wicksell: Selected Essays in Economics*, Vol. I, London and New York: Routledge, 1997, pp. 40–45 (esp. Part II, Appendix to Eugen von Böhm-Bawerk).

Winter, S.G. (1984), 'Schumpeterian competition in alternative technological regimes', *Journal of Economic Behaviour and Organisation*, **5** (3–4), 287–320.

APPENDICES

Appendix 2A.1

Theorie
der wirtschaftlichen
Entwicklung

Von

Dr. Joseph Schumpeter.

Hypotheses non fingo.

Leipzig,
Verlag von Duncker & Humblot.
1912.

Figure 2A.1   Title page of first German edition

Appendix 2A.2

THE THEORY OF ECONOMIC DEVELOPMENT

*An Inquiry into Profits, Capital, Credit, Interest,
and the Business Cycle*

JOSEPH A. SCHUMPETER

TRANSLATED BY
REDVERS OPIE

*COPYRIGHT 1934
BY THE PRESIDENT AND FELLOWS OF HARVARD COLLEGE*

*FIRST PUBLISHED BY THE DEPARTMENT OF ECONOMICS
OF HARVARD UNIVERSITY AS VOLUME XLVI IN THE
HARVARD ECONOMIC STUDIES SERIES, 1934*

Figure 2A.2   Title page of first English edition

Appendix 2A.3

Schumpeter's famous 'five cases' characterising entrepreneurially driven development 'by the carrying out of new combinations':

> (1) The introduction of a new good – that is one with which consumers are not yet familiar – or of a new quality of a good. (2) The introduction of a new method of production, that is one not yet tested by experience in the branch of manufacture concerned, which need by no means be founded upon a discovery scientifically new, and can also exist in a new way of handling a commodity commercially. (3) The opening of a new market, that is a market into which the particular branch of manufacture of the country in question has not previously entered, whether or not this market has existed before. (4) The conquest of a new source of supply of raw materials or half-manufactured goods, again irrespective of whether this source already exists or whether it has first to be created. (5) The carrying out of the new organisation of any industry, like the creation of a monopoly position (for example through trustification) or the breaking up of a monopoly position. ('Theory', 1934, p. 66)

Appendix 2A.4

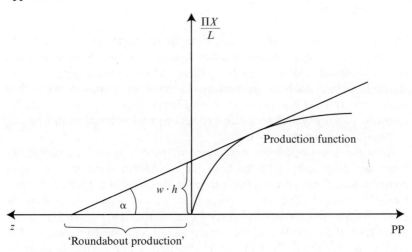

Notes: $\Pi X/L$: output: employment (= labour productivity); PP: ϕ production period; z: 'roundabout production' (= $2/i$); $w \cdot h$: given (real) wage rate times hours worked (to produce output).

Sources: * Böhm-Bawerk (1889/1921); ** Wicksell (1893/1933, Figure, p. 97).

Figure 2A.4   Böhm-Bawerk's 'roundabout production' (in Wicksell re-interpretation)***

3. Sustainable transborder business cooperation in the European regions: the importance of social entrepreneurship

Raymond Saner and Lichia Yiu

1 INTRODUCTION

1.1 Importance of Sustainable Transborder Cooperation for European Integration

Studying regions requires an interdisciplinary approach consisting of, among other things, microeconomics (competitive firm behaviour, local labour markets), spatial economics (rural and urban planning and architecture), policy analysis (regulatory function of government), urban geography (migration patterns), institutional sociology (administrative culture), social psychology (social cohesion) and cultural anthropology (comparative religion and values).[1]

Regional economics, the precursor of today's spatial economics or economic geography, goes back to the nineteenth century with major contributions from continental European theorists like Thünen, Weber, Christaller and Lösch (Arnott, 1996). Some of their studies focused on the causes for variance in regional development in the newly unified Germany at the time of the creation of the German Zollverein (customs union). The main impact of the Zollverein was the creation of new market boundaries offering economies of scale, which previously did not exist in the earlier era of multiple German kingdoms and city-states. Some of the German regions thrived with the creation of a larger internal market; others stagnated or decreased in importance. The cause for growth and decline of these German regions was one of the research interests of the above-cited continental European spatial economists.

In a similar way, a growing number of today's researchers in the field of regional development focus on the impact of enlarged market boundaries;

this time, however, not within a national context but rather at the level of the global economy. Liberalization of trade through continuous tariff reductions has resulted in a broadening of market scope from national to global levels. Within this enlarged context of a liberalizing and globalizing world economy, some countries have been more successful than others in making use of the new opportunities. However, successful competition in globalized markets is not evenly spread across a nation but is rather concentrated in some of its regions that have prospered more, while others stagnated or even declined. The quest for understanding why some regions succeed while others fail to meet the challenges of globalization has led to a renewed interest in regional development theory, spatial economics and economic geography, particularly in North-America and Western Europe.

1.2   National Competitiveness Cluster

Porter (1990) has conducted an extensive comparative research of ten countries and has come up with reasons why some nations succeed in some industries but fail in others. According to Porter, the home base plays a critical role in that firms tend to build up competitive advantage in industries for which the local environment is the most dynamic and challenging. He has conceptualized his findings in his analytical 'diamond' frame, which consists of: a) factor conditions (for example, labour, capital, land); b) demand conditions; c) dynamism of related and supporting industries; and d) firm strategy, structure and rivalry. In addition to the four factors, chance (such as inventions and war, etc.) and government also play an important role in supporting a nation's aim to achieve economic success (see Figure 3.1).

Concretely, a successful region according to Porter's diamond would show the following features:

- several competing companies belonging to the same regional key industry or industries
- a large dynamic and sophisticated internal market (demand conditions)
- suppliers specialized in the activities of the regional key industry/ industries
- qualified and highly qualified manpower specialized in the activities of the regional key industry/industries; educational and research institutes (factor conditions) (Borner, et al., 1991, p. 62).

Role of government
Porter's original concept consisted only of the four diamond conditions. In later publications, Porter added more factors to his diamond model,

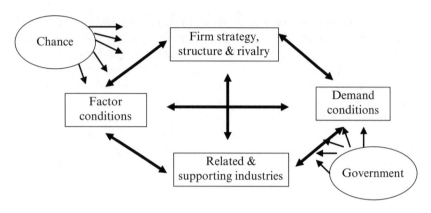

Source: Porter (1990).

Figure 3.1   Successful factors of national competitiveness

namely: 1) chance and 2) government. Concerning the role of government
and chance in Porter's model, Oez (1999) interprets Porter's findings as
follows:

> The proper role of the government should be reinforcing the underlying deter-
> minants of national advantage rather than trying to create the advantage itself.
> It is necessary to note that Porter anticipates a more direct but still partial role
> for the government in the early stage of development of a country since 'the
> tools at its disposal, such as capital, subsidies and temporary protection are
> most powerful at these stages in a nation's competitive development' (p.4).

The role of government, and by extension the mandate and discretion-
ary power of its civil servants, might hence vary according to the level of
economic development of each country. Role adjustments are necessary
to help a country move up the developmental ladder as, for instance, has
been the case in Singapore since independence in 1965. This in return
would imply that a country needs to know how to shift gear, so to speak,
and to change policy and governmental behaviour according to levels of
economic development. The question might hence be asked: what is the
right policy mix for what kind of stage of economic development?

Commenting on the differences between general macroeconomic principles pertaining to, for example, the competent application of inflation or
monetary policy instruments, Frey (1998) points out that:

> Regional Clusters and well functioning Centers are pre-conditions to ensure
> the following: international competitiveness; the protection of the natural
> environment, transport and energy; agriculture and tourism; elimination of

regional disparities between the mountainous areas and the cities and between the periphery and the center, sustainable spatial planning and utilization of land. All these issues are incompatible with economic reasoning of the type: 'wonderland of no dimension' (p. 177).

1.3   Social Dimension of Economic Competitiveness

There is more to regional competitiveness than the assumed rational economic behaviour of firms and the equally assumed efficient allocation of resources through assumed perfect and transparent market mechanisms as postulated by neo-classical and neo-liberal economic theory. These unsubstantiated claims have been refuted by institutional economics whose economic models offer a more interdisciplinary and holistic picture of human behaviour. Regional development consists of different, at times contradictory and conflictual factors of human behaviour which together create a mix which makes regions so uniquely different from each other.

In recent publications, Porter and Sölvell (1998) offer a more holistic explanation of regional competitiveness. Discussing innovation and sustainable competitive advantage of firms, Porter states: 'While some knowledge is embedded in materials, components, products and machinery, other knowledge is embedded in human capital, part of which is tacit' (p. 447).

Expanding on some aspects of his previous work on competitive advantage in the 1980s (Porter, 1985), Porter suggests that:

> clusters are characterised by a specific set of tangible (firms, infrastructure), intangible (knowledge, know-how) and institutional (authorities, legal framework) elements. These elements make up a complex web of *relations* that tie firms, customers, research institutions, schools and local authorities to each other. The interaction between economic, sociocultural, political and institutional actors in a given location triggers learning and enhances the ability of actors to modify their behavior and find new solutions in response to competitive changes (Porter, 1990, p. 443, emphasis added).

With this more complete multifactor and multidisciplinary point of view, Porter joins the existing school of institutional economists and sociologists and political scientists who have been studying the non-economic factors of regional competitiveness for quite some time and who see, for example, the emergence of new industries from the framework of a social system (Van de Ven and Garud, 1988), and from the perspective of social capital theory (Hollingsworth & Boyer, 1997; Putnam, 1993; 2000).

Van de Ven and Garud (1989, 1993) define the industrial social system as a structure which contains three key components, namely institutional, resource endowments and instrumental subsystems. These three subsystems interact in reciprocal relations, depending on an industry's conditions and development.

In particular, when looking at the non-economic contribution of a social system to competitiveness, Van de Ven and Garud (1988) suggest a framework based on the accumulation theory of change applied in the study of the social system. This framework allows the study of the process of industry emergence, as well as the role individual firms may play in this process, from a social system perspective. Putnam (1993, 2000) further elaborated on the theory of social capital by drawing a distinctive line between social and human capital. He argues that human capital relates to inherent properties of the individual, whilst social capital refers to the linkages among these individuals that create social networks. A critical distinction exists between 'bonding' social capital – connections with others 'like us'– and 'bridging' social capital connections with those 'not like us' (Gittel and Vidal, 1998). Far from being mutually exclusive, bonding and bridging ties often interact to support the healthy function of a social system (Putnam, 2000).

If we link these contributions to Porter and Sölvell's (1998) more recent conceptualization, it becomes evident that developing social capital, be it at an individual, firm or industry level, is instrumental to the competitiveness and economic development of a firm, industry, region or nation.

1.4   Regional Competitiveness Cluster

Summarizing the results of a cross-regional survey covering 20 regions in Europe and North America, Koellreuter (1997) identified 50 factors that have an influence on a region's economic advantage. The most decisive factors are listed in Table 3.1.

Many of the factors listed in Koellreuter's chart fall into the sphere of responsibility of the respective regional government (development of highly skilled labour force, efficient tax system and issuing of permits and so on). Creating the right mix of efficient economic factor conditions, effective (consistent and predictable) regulatory framework, transparent and efficient administrative services, and high quality social and cultural institutions and services all combined obviously constitutes the right ingredients for a truly competitive region.

The table is even more significant in light of globalization. Foreign companies investing in other regions of the world make investment decisions based on most of the factors listed in Table 3.1. In other words, the ability of respective governments to design and sustain an appropriate policy environment is crucial. Equally crucial is the ability of the civil servants to apply the rules in a transparent, non-discriminatory manner to local as well as foreign investors. All this results in an increase of challenges to a

Table 3.1   Factors with the most decisive influence on comparative advantages of a region with a future

Ranking	Factors
1	Availability of highly skilled labour
2	Price/performance of highly skilled labour
3	Permits (legislation, processing)
4	Corporate tax system
5	Price/performance of skilled labour
6	Availability of skilled labour
7	Work permits of transnational labour
8	Telecommunication
9	Quality of life
10	Access to EEA (EU) market
10	Working hours
11	Predictability of the politico-legal environment
⋮	⋮
24	Energy supply
25	Price/performance of unskilled labour

region's government and civil servants, who have to honour the increasingly global requirements of good governance, meaning transparency, accessibility, non-discrimination, customer orientation and predictability. Without these requirements, foreign direct investment will go to more promising pastures and local investors might 'vote with their feet' and invest elsewhere.

1.5   Competitive Advantage and Transborder Regional Development

From a European integration perspective, it would be useful to add to the existing literature on competitiveness of national regions a new focus on the specificities of transborder regional competitiveness. Since existing insights on competitiveness of national regions are mostly nation-specific, they are not directly transferable to the complexities of transborder cooperation and integration in the larger EU context. Hence, the discussion on competitiveness needs to be broadened in order to tackle the inter-cultural and inter-institutional aspects of transborder regional integration.

Data covering transborder regional cooperation in Europe are either scarce, incomplete or non-existent. A most useful comparative source of information on regional comparative data covering most of Europe and North America is the International Benchmark Report published annually by the BAK research group in Basle since 1998.

Collecting information concerning transborder regions (for example, the Upper Rhine Valley) has been difficult because cross-border data are not easily comparable and hence cannot easily be aggregated due to different practices of national statistical data processing. Lack of regional aggregate data, such as transborder investment flows, cross-border joint ventures and ownership patterns or comparative cross-border migration flows, makes it impossible to apply Porter's diamond concept as a means to assess competitiveness of a given European transborder region.

A second source of information which provides very illustrative insights on the importance of cross-border initiatives in the context of regional development is the Economic Reconstruction and Development in South East Europe (ERDSEE), a programme under the auspices of two joint institutions (European Commission and World Bank) and several donor institutions (European Investment Bank, European Bank for Reconstruction and Development, and so on). Among the many efforts of the ERDSEE, there are several infrastructural programmes (World Bank, 2001) and environmental projects (European Commission, 2000) destined to support economic growth and regional integration, as well as cross-border projects which focus on the promotion of networks and exchanges among the South Eastern Europe (SEE) countries.

It is important to stress that economic development is not the only focal point of all these efforts. There is also a strong emphasis on the importance of developing social capital as a pre-condition for regional and transborder development. For example, the infrastructure programmes define from the outset that '*Building large infrastructure without* sound policies and institutions for private sector development and *social cohesion and inclusion, means wasting large amounts of resources without achieving* the objective of sustainable *economic growth and prosperity* for the region' (World Bank, 2001, emphasis added)

The current efforts demonstrate the recognition that regional development in a politically and religiously fragmented region cannot solely be achieved through economic conditioning. It needs to be streamlined with the improvement of social cohesion and social capital, if sustainable economic competitiveness at transborder and regional level is sought.

2   CASE STUDY OF A TRANSBORDER REGION: UPPER RHINE VALLEY

Making use of a concrete example of a transborder region, challenges will be described and analysed which local businessmen, government officials and social society representatives have to face when they attempt to create transborder competitiveness. The case in point is the Upper Rhine Valley region consisting of adjacent sub-regions from Switzerland (Province of Basle), France (Province of Alsace) and Germany (Province of Baden and Southern Palatine).

Transborder cooperation in the Upper Rhine Valley has been in existence for centuries, and movement of goods and people across the three borders were very common practice dating back to the late Middle Ages. In addition, parts of this transborder region have been politically connected in the past, and economic exchanges have only been restricted during the last two World Wars when the German and French provinces were drawn into war which opposed France and Germany and left Switzerland in an isolated position of neutrality. Today, the transborder cooperation has been formalized within the framework of a tri-national convention and organization called Conférence du Rhin Supérieur (CRS)

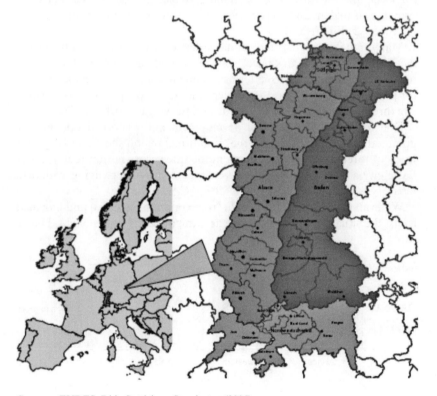

Source: EURES–Rhin Supérieur, Strasbourg (2005).

Figure 3.2   Tri-national Upper Rhine region

which was established in 1975 by the respective three country governments (France, Germany, and Switzerland) as depicted in Figure 3.2.

The territorial dimension of the CRS is 21 500 km² of which 38.5 per cent is French (Alsace), 44.8 per cent German (Baden and Southern Palatine), and 16.7 per cent Swiss (Basle and Northwest Switzerland). The total population in 2003 amounted to 5.813 million people who live and work in one of Europe's most densely populated territorial regions. The CRS transborder region has four main universities (Basle, Freiburg, Strasbourg and Karlsruhe), several world-renowned multinational companies (such as Novartis, Hofmann-LaRoche, UBS, Schlumberger SA) and houses the seat of the Council of Europe, the EU Parliament, European Court of Human Rights and Eurocorps (Strasbourg). The estimated per capita GNP for 2005 as compared to 1998 showed the following progression: namely, 25 800 (22 500) euros for Alsace province, 36 600 (30 900) euros for Basle and Northwest Switzerland province, 29 300 (26 300) euros for province of Baden, and 23 100 (19 100) euros for the Province of Southern Palatine (see Figure 3.3).

Many inhabitants of the transborder region speak or understand Allemanisch, a German dialect spoken around the Upper Rhine Valley region. The common roots in terms of language and history make it easier for people to move across the border, and 94 000 people cross the respective three borders both ways every day on the way to work (see Figure 3.4).

Due to a mix of economic development and historical openness to immigration, all three parts of the tri-national region show relatively high levels of foreign populations living in the three cross-border regions, with Basle city showing the highest percentage of foreigners living within its territory (see Figure 3.5).

While all three subregions benefit from common historical and linguistic roots, the situation is not as simple as it might sound at first sight. Due to

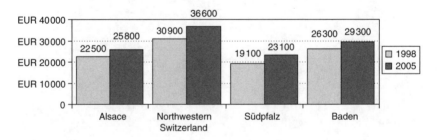

Source: *Rhin Supérieur: Faits et chiffres*, No. 8, Strasbourg (2008).

Figure 3.3   GDP per capita in 1998 and 2005

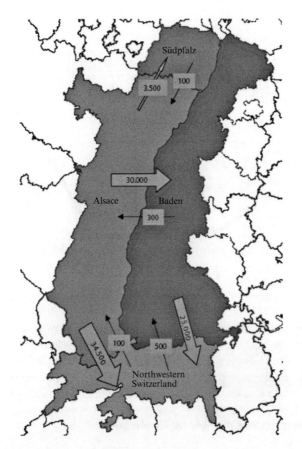

Source: EURES – Rhin Supérieur, Strasbourg (2005).

Figure 3.4 Daily cross-border movement of workforce

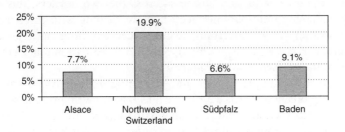

Source: Rhin Supérieur: Faits et chiffres, No. 8, Strasbourg (2008).

Figure 3.5 Foreigners living in region

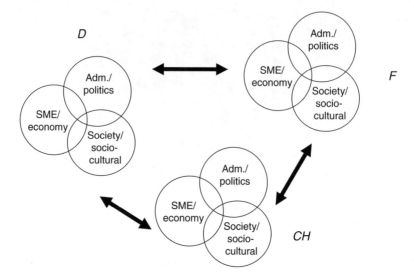

Figure 3.6   Reality of transborder cooperation for local enterprises

mandatory and exclusive use of French in the Alsatian province, French has become the preferred language of many Alsatians living in larger urban agglomerations like Strasbourg, Mulhouse or Colmar. Also, with regard to the official language to be used for legal, political and contractual trans-actions, French and German are the two official and mandatory languages.

2.1   Complexity of Cross-border Cooperation

Cross-border regional cooperation between companies, governments and social society requires the management of more interfaces than is the case within national regions. To take the example of small enterprises of one country conducting business across the two borders, this would imply managing multiple interfaces: namely, dealing with three national administrations (e.g. concerning business licences), three national labour markets (e.g. recruitment of employees) and three national markets (e.g. potential buyers–sellers) (see Figure 3.6).

Taking this example further and imagining a Basle-based enterprise conducting business in Alsace/France and Baden/Germany, the complex-ity of interfaces would include dealing with German and French national and provincial administrations (e.g. in order to obtain business licences), German and French national and provincial labour organizations (e.g. in order to employ people), French and German local and sometimes national associations (e.g. in order to become a member of a professional

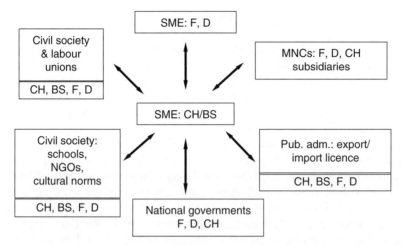

Figure 3.7 *Reality of transborder socio-economic cooperation: managing business and non-business stakeholders*

organization, religious group or neighbourhood organization). This complexity of multiple interfaces would further increase with a change of personal residence or the opening of companies on the other side of the national borders. Figure 3.7 visualizes some of these interfaces mentioned above.

In addition, the hypothetical Swiss entrepreneur domiciled in Basle would also have to interface with Swiss administration officials (e.g. concerning customs declarations for goods exported or imported into Swiss territory), provincial and national authorities (e.g. federal, cantonal and municipal tax declarations and payments). The interfaces are multiple and to each cross-border interface one has to add the inevitable difficulties that would arise due to difference in national laws, administrative practices, local values and customs, including the mandatory use of the French language if business or administrative transactions involve official exchanges between Alsace and Basle.

The difficulties encountered by this hypothetical Basle entrepreneur illustrate the current limitations to the creation of competitiveness within the CRS transborder region. Transaction costs remain high, administrative obstacles substantial and the influence of the respective three national governments cannot be ignored despite all the official pronouncements of pan-European integration. All these could make it prohibitive for small to medium-sized companies to benefit from growth potential of such transborder cooperation.

2.2   Need for Additional Boundary Spanners

Realizing the limits of existing cooperation mechanisms, different think-tanks have come up with suggestions regarding how the CRS transborder region could deepen cooperation mechanisms by creating common physical and social infrastructures and by further increasing the existing, albeit still lightweight, cooperation in areas such as education, joint marketing, joint venturing and so on.

Taking into account the existing competitiveness in all three sub-regions with regard to financial resources, highly educated and skilled workforces, world-class research institutes and large companies, successful SMEs and established cultural affinities, such efforts at transborder cooperation should succeed, provided the people involved in these cross-border development actions are cultural and professional boundary spanners who can be at home in different professional and cultural milieux, thus being instrumental in fostering bonding and bridging social capital for transborder cooperation.

The need for boundary spanners becomes clear when one considers the actions which have been proposed to create a CRS Technology Valley. Detailed proposals have been tabled to strengthen economic integration across the three national borders. However, as long as the three borders with their separate legal and administrative realities exist, it will be difficult to see either full economic integration or leveraging of the potential synergy from combined resources and competitive advantages.

What follows is a selected list of the economic initiatives that have been proposed by CRS planners. Specifically, six of the 22 proposals are identified here to illustrate the competencies needed to meet these challenges.

Unbundling the existing proposals from a social capital perspective

The six initiatives have been grouped into three categories according to the presumed role competencies required of the experts who might be selected to implement some of them in the near future (Table 3.2). The three boundary-spanning roles are: a) Business Diplomat (Saner et al., 2000); b) Entrepreneurial Politician (Saner, 2001); and c) Cultural Ambassador (Bassand and Hainard, 1985).

The three roles suggested above should be seen as competencies which would complement or expand the expertise of traditional actors. They are entrepreneurs, government officials and politicians and representatives of civil society and cultural institutions. Together, they form the team to accumulate the social capital in support of the CRS regional development strategy.

Figure 3.8 highlights the complementary social roles as discussed above,

Table 3.2   Transborder initiatives and role competencies requirements

Proposed transborder initiatives	Suggested competencies required of experts
A.	Business Diplomats
Promote regional economic market structures and networks. Develop inter-municipal energy grids and telecommunication services (groupings of municipalities as 'market partners').	Ability to develop and discuss business plans with business partners and non-business stakeholders (e.g. communes, schools, associations), understanding different national laws and practices governing employment, creation of companies and foundations, being familiar with different national management and leadership styles dominant in French, German and Swiss businesses.
B.	Entrepreneurial Politicians
Put in place legal and financial inter-municipal structures in order to better respond to entrepreneurial needs. Establish the coordination mechanism and/or define specializations once the location of sites on the Upper Rhine Valley has been attributed. Establish collaboration among the training and research centres and between them and the enterprises of the region.	Ability to initiate projects spanning German, Swiss and French legal and administrative laws, creating efficient cross-border administrative procedures, involving private and public sector actors to create new ventures, knowing how to mobilize financing for cross-border physical and social infrastructure projects.
C.	Cultural Ambassadors
Develop the project titled 'Cultural roadmap of the region'. Create a joint offer for the regional tourism sector. Develop an administration which can manage the transborder region in a competent and effective manner.	Ability to appreciate German, French and Swiss contemporary and classical art and culture, creating cultural events offering participation and benefits to existing cultural institutions of all three sub-regions, understanding processes of budgeting and approval of new initiatives in the domain of culture and tourism in all three sub-regions and respective national governments.

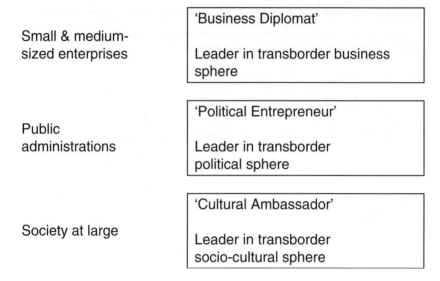

Small & medium-
sized enterprises

'Business Diplomat'

Leader in transborder business
sphere

Public
administrations

'Political Entrepreneur'

Leader in transborder
political sphere

Society at large

'Cultural Ambassador'

Leader in transborder
socio-cultural sphere

Figure 3.8   The transborder social roles and corresponding linkages to
main domain of activities and constituencies

namely the Business Diplomat, the Entrepreneurial Politician and the
Cultural Ambassador.

3   CONCLUSION

The goal of this chapter was to describe the importance of social entrepreneurship for sustainable cross-border business cooperation in the
European Region. Successful transborder cooperation requires an expanding social role repertoire of the entrepreneurs, politicians and community
leaders who play a leading role in the respective transborder regions.

Creating competitiveness for transborder regions requires different
inputs and personal competencies than in the case for regional development at national level. This is partially due to the fact that the number of
cross-border interfaces is greater and partially because specific competencies are needed to manage these inter-cultural (administrative, entrepreneurial, individual) interfaces (Gmür and Rakotobarison, 1997). Specific
competencies would include for instance:

1.   foreign language proficiency (for example, French and German for
     the CRS region)

2. 'global-regional' mindset and a natural curiosity which enables the transborder actor to remain open for continuous learning
3. basic knowledge regarding administrative law and regulations of all three member countries
4. basic knowledge regarding policy-making procedures and framework in all three member countries
5. cross-culturally effective negotiation and communication skills
6. skills in leading and working with temporary and project task teams from one, two or all three member countries
7. networking skills suitable for different cultural contexts.

Transborder regional development requires political will, business acumen and, most importantly, the bridging roles of the Business Diplomat, Political Entrepreneur and Cultural Ambassador. These social, economic and political actors could span the social and institutional boundaries and generate social capitals to support new business development and regional dynamism.

Future research will help identify differences in achieving competitiveness in different transborder regions of Europe. It will also help deepen the understanding of the formation of bridging and bonding social capitals required for different transborder regions of Europe. It is further hypothesized that knowing more about how to create transborder competitiveness will further strengthen European competitiveness and strengthen the process of European integration. Insights gained through further research in the European region concerning the integrative dynamics and social capital formation might also be useful for sustainable transborder cooperation in other parts of the world.

NOTE

1. This chapter builds on a previously published article by both authors (Saner and Yiu, 2000). This chapter also appears in Alain Fayolle and Harry Matlay (eds) (2010), *Handbook of Research on Social Entrepreneurship*, Cheltenham, UK and Northampton, MA, USA: Edward Elgar, pp. 125–41.

REFERENCES

Agence de Développement et d'urbanisme de l'agglomération Strasbourgeoise (ADEUS) (1999), *Lire et construire l'espace du Rhin Supérieur. Atlas transfrontalier pour aménager un territoire commun*, 99/48 PLA, Strasbourg: ADEUS.

Arnott, R. (1996). *Regional and Urban Economics*, Amsterdam: Harwood Academic Publishers.
BAK Kulturforschung (1998), *International Benchmark Report*, No. 1/1998, Basel: BAK Basel Economics.
Bassand, M. and F. Hainard (1985), *Dynamique socio-culturelle régionale*, Lausanne: Presses Polytechniques Romandes.
Borner, S., M. Porter, B. Weder and M. Enright (1991), *Internationale Wettbewerbsvorteile: ein strategisches Konzept fuer die Schweiz*, Frankfurt, Zuerich: Campus Verlag.
Conférence du Rhin Supérieur (CRS) (2002), *Donnés statistiques 2002*, Conférence de Rhin Supérieur, Strasbourg: Conférence Franco-Germano-Suisse du Rhin Supérieur.
European Commission (2000), 'Regional environmental reconstruction program. Cross border projects: promotion of networks and exchanges in the countries of South Eastern Europe', Regional Funding Conference, 29–30 March, Brussels: European Commission.
Frey, R.L. (1998), 'Räumliche Ökonomie', in A. Brunetti, P. Kugler and S. Schaltegger (eds), *Economics Today: Konsens und Kontroverse in der modernen Ökonomie*, Zurich: Verlag Neue Zürcher Zeitung (NZZ), pp. 177–92.
Gittell, R. and A. Vidal (1998), *Community Organizing: Building Social Capital as a Development Strategy*, Thousand Oaks, CA: Sage.
Gmür, M., and A. Rakotobarison (1997), 'Organisationslehre in Deutschland und Frankreich. *Organisations Wissen*, **5**, Glattbrugg: Gesellschaft für Organisation.
Grootaert, C. and T. van Bastelaer (eds.) (2002a), *Understanding and Measuring Social Capital: A Multidisciplinary Tool for Practitioners*, Washington, DC: The World Bank.
Grootaert, C. and T. van Bastelaer (eds) (2002b), *The Role of Social Capital in Development: An Empirical Assessment*, Cambridge, UK: Cambridge University Press.
Hollingsworth, R. and R. Boyer (1997), *Contemporary Capitalism: The Embeddedness of Institutions*, New York: Cambridge University Press.
Koellreuter, C. (1997), 'Increasing globalisation: challenge for the European regions', *Basler Schriften zur Europäischen Integration*, no. 26, pp. 6–27. Basle: Europa Institut, Universität Basel.
Oez, O. (1999), *The Competitive Advantage of Nations: The Case of Turkey*, Aldershot: Ashgate.
Porter, M.E. (1985), *Competitive Advantage: Creating and Sustaining Superior Performance*, New York: The Free Press.
Porter, M.E. (1990), *The Competitive Advantage of Nations*, New York: The Free Press.
Porter, M.E. and O. Sölvell (1998), 'The role of geography in the process of innovation and the sustainable competitive advantage of firms', in A. Chandler, P. Hagström and O. Sölvell (eds), *The Dynamic Firm: The Role of Technology, Strategy, Organization and Regions*, Oxford: Oxford University Press, pp. 440–57.
Putnam, R.D. (1993), *Making Democracy Work. Civic Traditions in Modern Times*, Princeton: Princeton University Press.
Putnam, R.D. (2000), *Bowling Alone. The Collapse and Revival of American Community*, New York: Simon and Schuster.
Saner, R. (2001), 'Globalisation and its impact on leadership qualifications in

public administration', *International Review of Administrative Sciences*, **5**(4), 650–61.

Saner, R. and L. Yiu (2000), 'The need for business diplomats, entrepreneurial politicians and cultural ambassadors', in W. Kraus and P. Trappe (eds), *Social Strategies*, Berne: Peter Lang Publishers, pp. 411–28.

Saner, R., L. Yiu and M. Sondegaard (2000), 'Business diplomacy management: a core competency for global companies', *Academy of Management Executive*, **14**(1), 80–92.

Van de Ven, A. and R. Garud (1989), 'A framework for understanding the emergence of new industries', in R. S. Rosenbloom and R. Burgelman (eds), *Research on Technological Innovation, Management and Policy*, Vol. 4, Greenwich, CT: JAI Press, pp. 195–225.

Van de Ven, A. and R. Garud (1993), 'Innovation and industry development: the case of cochlear implants', in R. S. Rosenbloom and R. Burgelman (eds), *Research on Technological Innovation, Management and Policy*, Vol. 5, Greenwich, CT: JAI Press, pp. 1–46.

Weder, B. (1998), *Economics Today*, Zürich: Verlag Neue Zürcher Zeitung.

World Bank (2001), 'The road to stability and prosperity in South Eastern Europe', a regional Strategy Paper, Washington, DC: The World Bank.

4. Understanding the impact of culture on a firm's entrepreneurial orientation and behaviour: a conceptual framework[1]

Alain Fayolle, Olivier Basso and Véronique Bouchard

INTRODUCTION

For almost four decades now, both practitioners and scholars have shown a marked interest in corporate entrepreneurship. In a changing world, large and small companies have to innovate and react quickly just to maintain their competitiveness (Ireland et al., 2001). They have to continually identify new opportunities and turn these opportunities into revenue streams: they have to behave entrepreneurially (Stevenson and Jarillo, 1990; Shane and Venkataraman, 2000).

In the entrepreneurship literature, corporate entrepreneurship is defined in a variety of ways and there is an abundance of empirical research linking corporate entrepreneurship to performance. In all these studies, the entrepreneurial orientation construct holds a particularly important place (see, for example, Lumpkin and Dess, 1996; Wiklund, 1999; Wiklund and Shepherd, 2003). Measured through dimensions such as innovativeness, risk-taking, proactiveness, autonomy and competitive aggressiveness (Miller, 1983; Covin and Slevin, 1989; Lumpkin and Dess, 1996), the entrepreneurial orientation construct appears as a useful (and powerful) tool for assessing entrepreneurial behaviour at firm level and its effect on firm performance. According to Lumpkin and Dess (1996, p. 136), 'firms that want to engage in successful corporate entrepreneurship need to have an entrepreneurial orientation'.

Entrepreneurial orientation is often described in entrepreneurship literature as the mindset of firms engaged in the pursuit of new opportunities. Research on entrepreneurial orientation focuses on its definition, its measure and its relationship with the performance of firms. More precisely, the discussion of the impact of entrepreneurial orientation on performance, in different contexts and for different types of firms, remains an important research topic (Wiklund and Shepherd, 2005; Hughes and Morgan, 2007) whereas little research has been dedicated to the factors and/or the conditions which produce this specific mindset.

For a long time now, researchers have recognized the impact of cultural factors on entrepreneurial behaviour, but even though national culture has sometimes been included as an independent variable in some models, generally speaking, cultural variables have been rather neglected (see, for example, Hayton et al. 2002). Even more neglected has been the study of the impact of different levels of culture (for example national or regional, industry and corporate) and, more importantly, their interaction and their impact on corporate entrepreneurship and specifically on entrepreneurial orientation, though cultural variables can probably help account for the huge variability in the entrepreneurial behaviour of firms.

Based on an in-depth review of literature, we propose a conceptual framework that aims to provide a better understanding of how interdependent levels of culture (national, industry and corporate) influence the entrepreneurial orientation of firms and their associated behaviour. We postulate that corporate and industrial culture can reinforce or weaken the effects of national culture on a firm's entrepreneurial orientation. In our view, national culture is mainly influenced by the history, traditions, norms, values and collective beliefs of a given country; by contrast, an industry culture is a specific sub-culture reflecting the competitive environment, the skills, resources and organization that are characteristic of a given industry, while the corporate culture remains strongly influenced by the history of the company and the main values of its founders and initial stakeholders.

In the first section of this chapter, we describe the entrepreneurial orientation concept, underlining its history, content and use in the field of entrepreneurship. In a second section, we develop the relationship between national culture and entrepreneurship. We then study, in a third section, the relation between industry culture and entrepreneurship, and finally the fourth section allows us to highlight the role and influence of corporate culture on entrepreneurial behaviours.

1   ENTREPRENEURIAL ORIENTATION: A RELEVANT CONSTRUCT TO CHARACTERIZE ENTREPRENEURIAL FIRM-LEVEL BEHAVIOURS

There is a strong consensus within the research community that entrepreneurship as an academic field suffers from a lack of clear-cut definitions and concepts. Personality trait approaches, process-related studies and environmental factor analyses provide the reader with various distinct, overlapping and sometime conflicting characterizations of entrepreneurship, be they at individual or firm level (see, for example, Lumpkin and Dess, 1996).

One concept, however, appears to be quite robust and has been adopted by various scholars throughout the last two decades (see for recent years Wiklund and Shepherd, 2003; 2005; Covin and Green, 2006; Keh et al., 2007). The entrepreneurial orientation, in fact, 'represents one of the few areas of entrepreneurship where we are beginning to see a cumulative body of knowledge developing' (Rauch et al., 2004).

1.1   Entrepreneurial Orientation Definitions

Entrepreneurial orientation, also labelled 'entrepreneurial posture' (Covin and Slevin, 1989), refers to 'the processes, practices and decision-making activities' that lead to corporate entrepreneurship. There are various salient 'behaviours' that entrepreneurial firms may exhibit (Lumpkin and Dess, 1996). The identification of these dimensions results from a cumulative process and the ongoing conversation between a group of scholars. The starting point of this 'conversation' is a seminal paper by Miller (1983) which characterizes the entrepreneurial firm as 'one that engages in product-market innovation, undertakes somewhat risky venture and is first to come up with proactive innovations, beating competitors to the punch'.

A similar definition is proposed by Covin and Slevin (1991). These authors associate 'entrepreneurial posture' with three salient firm characteristics: (1) top management risk-taking with regard to investment decisions, and strategic actions in the face of uncertainty; (2) the extensiveness and frequency of product innovation and the related tendency toward technological leadership; and (3) the pioneering nature of the firm as evident in the firm's propensity to compete aggressively and proactively with industrial rivals. This approach has been praised, criticized and enriched with diverse improvement suggestions (for example Zahra, 1993).

In the literature, entrepreneurial orientation is always described as a multidimensional concept which alternatively includes two dimensions: innovation and risk-taking (Miller and Friesen, 1982); three dimensions: innovation, proactiveness and risk-taking (Miller, 1983; Covin and Slevin, 1991; Zahra and Covin, 1995) or five dimensions: autonomy, innovativeness, risk-taking, proactiveness and competitive aggressiveness (Lumpkin and Dess, 1996; Dess et al., 1997).

1.2 A Dominant Topic: Entrepreneurial Orientation–Performance Relationship

Most of the articles we have mentioned are interested in the relationships between entrepreneurial orientation and performance. They propose various contingency or configurational models that include external (environment) and internal (structure, strategy, organizational culture) variables. Contingency approaches (Dess et al., 1997) concentrate on one variable and explore how the entrepreneurial orientation-performance relationships are dependent on a given factor such as a firm's competitive environment (Covin and Slevin, 1989), its structure (Covin and Slevin, 1988), or its strategy. Configuration models study firm performance as the combined effects of several variables, for instance entrepreneurial orientation, strategy and environment (for example Dess et al., 1997). Results have been contrasted: some studies show a positive correlation between entrepreneurial orientation and performance (for example Wiklund, 1999; Zahra, 1991; Zahra and Covin, 1995), while others conclude there is no significant relationship between the two (for example Auger et al., 2003; Smart and Conant, 1994; Dess et al., 1997). Some studies even argue that, in some cases, entrepreneurial-type strategies are associated with poor performance (Hart, 1992).

A common conclusion of these studies is that the extent to which entrepreneurial orientation is useful for predicting firms' performance is contingent on external factors, such as industry globalization, product/market life cycle stage and government regulations, or internal factors, such as the organization structure or the leader's personality. Most of the proposed models are therefore moderating-effects models in which entrepreneurial orientation–performance relationships vary as a function of one specific variable, such as 'organicness' (quoted by Lumpkin and Dess, 1996; Covin and Slevin, 1988; 1991) or other variables (see Figure 4.1).

1.3 Scope of our Research

Our goal is different, and to some extent more modest: we take a step back and explore the conditions of emergence of an entrepreneurial orientation.

More precisely, we investigate whether cultural variables can significantly modify or condition the three entrepreneurial orientation dimensions mostly commonly mentioned (innovativeness, risk-taking and proactiveness) and how these cultural variables interact. This chapter is an attempt at delineating a theoretical framework that will allow us to explore the relationships between entrepreneurial orientation and various dimensions of culture (see Figure 4.2).

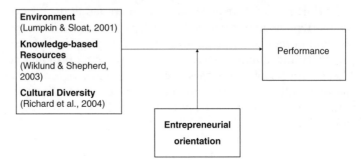

Source: Gregory G. Dess, IACMR Research Methods Workshop Xian, PRC (2005).

Figure 4.1   Moderating role of entrepreneurial orientation

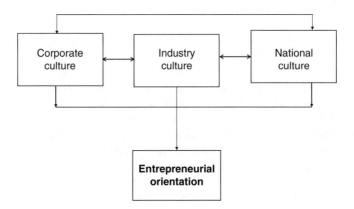

Figure 4.2   Cultural variables and entrepreneurial orientation

2   THE INFLUENCE OF NATIONAL CULTURE ON ENTREPRENEURIAL BEHAVIOUR

2.1   Entrepreneurship and National Culture[2]

The first works focusing on demonstrating the influence of culture on national entrepreneurial activity are anything but recent[3] (see for instance Landes, 1953). Some researchers even give this factor a central role, for instance Berger (1993, p. 16), who specifies that 'culture is the conductor and the entrepreneur is the catalyst' of entrepreneurial activity. Of course, one cannot deny the influence of other institutional factors (legal, financial, political and technological), as highlighted by North and Thomas (1973). In this regard, North distinguishes formal institutions (which correspond roughly to the factors mentioned previously) from informal institutions, which he defines as follows: 'They [the informal institutions] come from socially transmitted information and are part of the heritage that we call culture'. In short, as far as entrepreneurial activity is concerned, formal institutions (political, financial and regulating structures) contribute to creating opportunities, whereas informal institutions (values and cultural norms) shape society's and individuals' perceptions of these opportunities (Welter, 2007).

Countries and societies therefore have collective perceptions and images that lead them to admire entrepreneurial activities more or less (Busenitz et al., 2000). As Hayton et al. (2002) stated, 'Cultural values indicate the degree to which a society considers entrepreneurial behaviors, such as risk taking and independent thinking, to be desirable' (p. 33). Moreover, Casson (1991, 1995) suggests that countries differ in their entrepreneurial culture and shows that variations in the level of confidence within cultures can affect transaction costs, and as a result global economic performance. In an empirical comparative study on European Jews who emigrated to New York or London, Godley (2001) shows that Jewish immigrants in New York chose entrepreneurial careers more often than those who had immigrated to London. From this observation, he deduced that US and British cultures value entrepreneurship differently. Morris et al. (1994), relying on studies by numerous authors, have underlined the link, in the United States, between a high level of entrepreneurial activity and cultural values such as freedom, independence, individualism and achievement. The study by McGrath et al. (1992) in 10 countries, reaches the conclusion that cultural values influence entrepreneurial behaviour. Despite regular criticism of this factor (Gerschenkron, 1962, 1966), national culture remains a solid reference whenever one tries to explain variations in terms of entrepreneurial activity: 'Among the many factors that contribute to entrepreneurship, perhaps the most critical is a set of social and cultural values along with the appropriate social, economic and political institutions that legitimize and encourage the pursuit of entrepreneurial opportunity' (Reynolds et al., 1999). This shows how important it is to develop research aimed at better understanding how much different attitudes and behaviours towards entrepreneurship may depend on national and cultural factors (Venkataraman, 2004; Todorovic and McNaughton, 2007). However, surprisingly, empirical and conceptual studies in the field of entrepreneurship that have included cultural factors are rare, and rarer still are those concerned with corporate entrepreneurship.

2.2   The Effects of National Culture on Entrepreneurial Behaviours[4]

In disciplines such as sociology, economic history, or even anthropology, researchers have tried to explain differences in terms of national economic performance.[5] Landes (1949), for example, links France's weak economic performance in the nineteenth century to the lack of boldness and the conservatism of its entrepreneurs, who based their activities on a patrimonial logic. For half a century, Landes has extended his research to many different countries, trying to explain the development of entrepreneurial activity, and thus, national economic performance, through national culture, social values and attitudes. As a result, he published what is probably regarded as his reference work: *The Wealth and Poverty of Nations* (Landes, 1998).

In Landes' work, the 'measure' of national culture is the nationality (national belonging) itself, and it is not really easy to always identify precisely to what extent a given level of economic performance depends on specific cultural factors. Empirical works that focus on measuring differences between countries in terms of individual or collective entrepreneurial behaviours follow the same logic (see Antoncic and Hisrich, 2000). The research works that rely on existing conceptualizations of national cultures such as Hofstede's (1980) seem more interesting. In their study, Morris et al. (1994) only consider one of Hosftede's four characteristic dimensions of national culture: individualism vs. collectivism. They show that this dimension is important not only at the national level, but also at the level of the firms' corporate culture in the three countries they studied. Mueller and Thomas (2000) tested two of Hofstede's (1980) cultural dimensions, individualism and uncertainty avoidance, on the entrepreneurial potential of a sample of 1800 individuals from nine different countries. They define entrepreneurial potential through two main personality traits, the locus of control and innovativeness. The results of the study give empirical evidence that on the one hand, individualistic cultures have a more internal locus of control than collectivist cultures, and on the other hand, an internal locus of control combined with innovativeness is more often found in individualistic cultures with a low uncertainty avoidance than in collectivist cultures with a high level of uncertainty avoidance. Lee and Peterson (2000) use all Hofstede's dimensions, individualism, uncertainty avoidance, power distance and masculinity, to which they add two extra dimensions borrowed from Trompenaars (1994): achievement and universalism. The cultural model proposed by these authors suggests that only countries with a culture that is favourable to entrepreneurship are able to generate a strong entrepreneurial orientation in the sense of Lumpkin and Dess (1996), leading to the development of entrepreneurial activity and the increase of global competitiveness. One last study (O'Brien and Nordtvedt, 2006) uses Hofstede's four original dimensions as well as a fifth dimension that was later developed by the same author (Hofstede, 1991): long-term orientation. This work deals with the effects of national culture on entrepreneurial intention, drawing on the theory of planned behaviour (Ajzen, 1991) and Shapero's model (Shapero and Sokol, 1982).

The research works we have briefly presented here constitute a representative sample of what can be done to study, conceptually or empirically, the influence of national culture on entrepreneurial behaviour. They all refer, to a greater or lesser extent, to Hofstede's cultural dimensions, to tried and tested constructs such as entrepreneurial intention, entrepreneurial potential, and entrepreneurial orientation, and they all address the three levels of analysis: individual, organizational and national.

2.3   National Culture Dimensions and Research Propositions

Drawing from Hofstede (1985) we define in our research model four national cultural dimensions which could influence and shape entrepreneurial orientation of firms. For each of them we derive a possible research proposal.

1. *Power distance.* This indicates the degree of tolerance for hierarchical or unequal relationships, 'that is the extent to which the members of a society accept that power in institutions and organizations is distributed unequally' (Hofstede, 1985, p. 347). A low degree of tolerance for unequal relationships leads to a more conducive entrepreneurial culture (Lee and Peterson, 2000) and consequently influences in a positive sense the entrepreneurial orientation of firms (P1).
2. *Uncertainty Avoidance.* This dimension clearly underlines the degree of acceptance for uncertainty or the willingness to take risk, 'that is the degree to which the members of a society feel uncomfortable with uncertainty and ambiguity, which leads them to support beliefs promising certainty and to maintain institutions protecting conformity' (Hofstede, 1985, pp. 347–8). A weak degree of uncertainty avoidance leads to a more conducive entrepreneurial culture (Lee and Peterson, 2000) and consequently influences in a positive sense the entrepreneurial orientation of firms (P2).
3. *Individualism.* This dimension is opposed to collectivism and indicates the degree of emphasis placed by a country on individual

accomplishment, 'which stands for a preference for a loosely knit social framework in society in which individuals are supposed to take care of themselves and their immediate families only; as opposed to *Collectivism*, which stands for a preference for a tightly knit social framework in which individuals can expect their relatives, clan, or other in-group to look after them, in exchange for unquestioning loyalty' (Hofstede, 1985, p. 348). A high level of individualism in a given country leads to a more conducive entrepreneurial culture (Lee and Peterson, 2000) and consequently influences in a positive sense the entrepreneurial orientation of firms (P3).

4. *Masculinity.* This dimension gives the degree of stress placed on materialism and wealth, which stands for a preference for achievement, heroism, assertiveness, and material success; as opposed to *Femininity*, which stands for a preference for relationships, modesty, caring for the weak, and the quality of life. In a masculine society even the women prefer assertiveness (at least in men); in a feminine society, even the men prefer modesty. A high level of masculinity in a country leads to a more conducive entrepreneurial culture (Lee and Peterson, 2000) and consequently influences in a positive sense the entrepreneurial orientation of firms (P4).

3   THE INFLUENCE OF INDUSTRY CULTURE ON ENTREPRENEURIAL ORIENTATION

The influence of national culture on individual entrepreneurial behaviour has been well ascertained. Because a firm's behaviour is to some extent the product of its individual members' behaviour and orientations, we can legitimately assume that national culture will also have an impact on the entrepreneurial orientations of firms. However, such a line of reasoning can easily turn into a massive oversimplification. If we push it to its natural conclusion, American companies should all be characterized by a strong entrepreneurial orientation, while French or Scandinavian firms should be characterized by a weak entrepreneurial orientation, since American culture values entrepreneurship more than French or Scandinavian culture, and since Americans create proportionally more new businesses than Europeans. We know that this is not the case: high-tech companies in Europe are more entrepreneurially oriented than utilities and insurance companies in the United States and, in fact, probably as entrepreneurially oriented as their American counterparts. Industry, therefore, appears to be as significant a variable as nationality when it comes to identifying the cultural factors at the origin of entrepreneurial orientation.

3.1 Industry Culture as a Substitute for the Environment

Most entrepreneurial orientation models (Miller, 1983; Covin and Slevin, 1991; Zahra, 1993; Lumpkin and Dess, 1996; Dess et al., 1997) attribute a significant role to the firm's external environment, together with internal variables such as the firm's strategy, its organization and culture. The external dimensions most commonly cited are the *dynamism, hostility* and *heterogeneity* of the firm's environment. Also proposed are the environment's *munificence* (the existence of development opportunities), its level of *technological sophistication*, the *life cycle stage of the industry* and finally its overall *level of uncertainty*.

No student of the organization would deny the impact of the external environment on organizational structure, culture and behaviour. Environment–organization relationships are complex, however, and have been described as loosely coupled (Pfeffer and Salancik, 1978; Weick, 1978). The impact of the external environment on an organization, and more specifically on its entrepreneurial orientation, is mediated by the prevailing basic assumptions and values, cultural norms and rules (Gordon, 1991). On the other hand, the culture of the organization is not wholly idiosyncratic but reflects its adaptation to environmental and technological conditions. In our model, therefore, the entrepreneurial orientation of a firm greatly depend on the attitude and the beliefs of its employees, which depend on the organizational culture which, in turn, is influenced by environmental and technological conditions.

3.2 Industry Culture

An industry is a set of firms that use similar technologies, have similar clients and suppliers (Porter, 1985). As a result, the firms that belong to the same industry tend to compete in similar environments, that is, environments characterized by similar levels of dynamism, hostility, technological sophistication, and so on. One will observe some differences across countries and industry segments but, overall, one can expect significant resemblance.

To the extent that the culture of an organization reflects not only its founders' values but also its history, which is largely a process of adaptation to environment and technology changes, the firms that belong to the same industry share organizational and cultural traits (Huff, 1982; Spender, 1989; Gordon, 1991; Abrahamson and Fombrun, 1994; Chatman and Jehn, 1994). The resemblance that results from similar external and internal conditions is further reinforced by the exchanges and interactions that take place among members of these firms via trade fairs, trade magazines, shared suppliers, managers' transfers, further consolidating what can be rightly called an 'industry culture' (Hambrick, 1982; Abrahamson and Fombrun, 1994). By integrating the industry culture dimension in our model, we are able to take into account the external environment's impact on the entrepreneurial orientation of a firm, while acknowledging the mediated nature of this impact.

For Huff (1982), an industry 'is defined by shared or interlocking metaphors or world views'. Hambrick (1982) observes that 'a common body of knowledge appears to exist within an industry. . . which is disseminated through media equally available to and used by executives within the industry'. Spender (1989), who has studied different British industries, finds 'an altogether surprising degree of homogeneity amongst the constructs being applied by managers. . . in each industry'. Gordon (1991) sustains that 'although culture is unique to each organization, industries exert influences that cause this unique culture to develop within defined parameters'. Thus, 'within industries, certain cultural characteristics will be widespread among organizations, and these most likely will be quite different from the characteristics found in other industries'.

Abrahamson and Fombrun (1994) defend the existence of 'macrocultures' shared by all participants of a given industry. Macrocultures result from the exposure of value-added network members (suppliers, producers and clients of an industry) to similar conditions, and are reinforced by the socialization that takes place in the network. A process of closure can often be observed: by fixing the network members' attention on certain aspects of their environment, the shared 'macroculture' can hinder the questioning of basic assumptions and lead to collective inertia.

In an empirical study that includes 15 firms belonging to four different industries, Chatman and Jehn (1994) demonstrated the existence of stable organizational culture dimensions which varied more across industries than within them. A later empirical study by Christensen and Gordon (1999) reached similar conclusions.

3.3   Culture and Industry Descriptors

Chatman and Jehn (1994) qualify industry culture by measuring the degree of identification of employees belonging to different industries to seven basic orientations (Innovative, Stable, Respecting of people, Outcome oriented, Detail oriented, Team oriented and Aggressive). The dimensions used by Christensen and Gordon (1999) to qualify industry culture are very similar (Aggressiveness, Innovation, Confrontation, Planning orientation, Results orientation, People orientation, Team orientation, Communication).

According to Gordon (1991), dynamic environments – as opposed to stable ones – elicit specific organizational responses and give rise to specific values and patterns of behaviour. One can expect firms competing in dynamic environments to value innovation, risk-taking and flexibility, while firms competing in stable environments tend to value institutionalization and specialization. The same logic applies to firms competing in high growth vs. low growth markets (Chatman and Jehn, 1994). Customer requirements are also important (Gordon, 1991). When customers demand reliability above all, as in the banking, insurance and utilities industry, stability and detail orientation, become central values, while innovation and risk-taking tend to be rejected. On the other hand, when customers demand novelty, as in the fashion industry, risk-taking, innovation and flexibility constitute central corporate values.

One of the most salient similarities among firms belonging to the same industry is technology. Technology, in its turn, determines how things are done and can have a strong impact on organizational culture (Chatman and Jehn, 1994). Industries relying on standardized and automated production processes value precision, discipline and predictability. Industries relying on customized production processes value innovation, team spirit and personal responsibility.

Selecting relevant industry descriptors will be an important and challenging task. At this stage, we plan to take into consideration the most often cited and, in our opinion, most significant ones:

- industry dynamism (technology, competition and demand changes);
- industry heterogeneity (customer, products, channels, business models, variety);
- importance of reliability as a customer requirement.

3.4 Implications

By integrating the industry culture dimension in our model, we are able to take into account the external environment's impact on entrepreneurial orientation while acknowledging the mediated nature of this impact. Two options are possible from thereon: (1) we can either emphasize this dimension by studying firms belonging to two or three different industries, or (2) we can neutralize it by studying firms all belonging to the same industry. In the second case, the industry selected should not belong to 'extremes' (very favourable or very unfavourable to entrepreneurial orientation) but have intermediate characteristics so as to maximize the salience of organizational and national culture variables.

3.5   Propositions Concerning the Industry Culture Variable

The most often cited and, in our opinion, most significant industry descriptors are:

- industry dynamism (of technology, competition, demand);
- industry heterogeneity (customer, products, channels, business models, variety);
- importance of reliability as a customer requirement.

If our model is correct, these descriptors of the industry should have a significant impact on the major dimensions of the entrepreneurial orientation.

1. *Industry dynamism.* Industry dynamism puts pressure on firms, forcing them to innovate, to continuously adapt and thus to take risk. It is also a source of new opportunities which can be turned into first mover advantages by proactive firms. Industry dynamism (measured by the rate of change observable at the level of technology, demand and competition) should be positively correlated with the entrepreneurial orientation of firms (P5).
2. *Industry heterogeneity.* Industry heterogeneity implies that there are many niches, several sources of competitive differentiation and consequently many ways to succeed. As a result, proactive firms, able to preempt a niche, and innovative ones, able to conceive new client and product segmentations, to create new distribution channels and business models, should thrive in such industries. Industry heterogeneity (measured by the variety of customer profiles, products, channels and business model) should be positively correlated with the entrepreneurial orientation of firms (P6).
3. *Customers' requirements.* Gordon (1991) underlines the impact of customers' requirements on a firm's culture and in particular the impact of their demand for reliability. In industries where this requirement is high (banking, insurance, utilities, but also aeronautics) we would expect risk-taking to be shunned, and slow, well-tested decisions and operational processes to prevail. Innovation would not be absent but it would be a highly controlled activity. As a result, customers' requirement for reliability should be negatively correlated with the entrepreneurial orientation of firms (P7).
4. *Geographical vs. multi-domestic industry.* High-tech industries are, for the most part, global industries. In global industries, operations are integrated on a global scale, and management practices and product

and/or service offers are very homogeneous, whatever the countries and regions (Porter, 1986). On the other hand, in multi-domestic industries (for example retail, packaged goods, commercial banking), local needs are taken into account, decisions are made locally and national cultures play an important role. In global industries we could therefore expect industry determinants of corporate culture to have a greater impact than national determinants, and the reverse to be true in multi-domestic industries. In global industries, industry culture plays a dominant role and has a major impact on firms' entrepreneurial orientation (P8), while in multi-domestic industries, national culture plays a dominant role and has a major impact on firms' entrepreneurial orientation (P9).

4 THE INFLUENCE OF CORPORATE CULTURE ON ENTREPRENEURIAL ORIENTATION

National and industry cultures are doubtlessly significant explaining factors when it comes to understanding entrepreneurial behaviour at firm level. These macro variables are driving forces that contribute to shape the firm's environment and, as a result, its strategy-making process. Interestingly enough, culture appears in some entrepreneurial orientation models as one of the internal variables susceptible to impact entrepreneurial behaviours (for example Zahra, 1991). Like any social community, firms exhibit tangible and intangible traits that contribute to form their unique organizational identity; it has been contended that an effective corporate culture as a hard-to-imitate asset can lead to superior performance (Barney, 1986). Because corporate culture is an important determinant of a firm's strategic behaviour, we believe that it has to be taken into account in our model, together with national and industry culture.

4.1 Definitional Elements

As mentioned before, research devoted to entrepreneurial orientation does not focus on corporate culture. Moreover, there is some conceptual overlapping between corporate culture (sometimes labelled 'organizational values') and other internal variables like management philosophy, managerial structure or even strategy (Lumpkin and Dess, 1996, p. 139). We therefore believe the concept calls for some clarification.

Corporate culture can be characterized through several dimensions and according to different lenses (Smircich, 1983).

First, corporate culture acts as a pervasive context for everything individuals do and think in an organization. As such, it can be expressed through different media, both tangible and intangible (Schein, 1984; 1996). A company's culture is manifested in the values, business princi-ples and ethical standards preached and practised by management, in the approaches to personnel management and problem-solving adopted, in official policies and procedures, in the spirit and character permeating the work environment, in the interactions and relationships that exist among managers and employees, in the peer pressure that reveals core values, in revered traditions and oft-repeated stories, in relationships with external stakeholders and so on.

Secondly, corporate culture defines what is expected by others, what behaviours are rewarded by the community, how and what things are valued, be they a dress code, the office space, work habits, or anything else. The majority of definitions emphasize the constraining effect of culture on *individual* behaviours: organizational norms, guidelines or expecta-tions prescribe appropriate kinds of employee behaviour in particular situations and regulate the behaviour of organizational members towards one another. Culture acts as a coordinating principle and plays an active role in the way organizations are governed (Meek, 1986). Researchers abundantly use the metaphor of social or normative 'glue' that holds the organization together and guides and shapes the attitudes and behaviours of employees. Its benefits are clear: it facilitates delegation, reduces moni-toring, and improves communication.

Thirdly, the genesis of such normative dimensions has been related to collective history, past successes and lessons drawn from experience. Schein's (1984) often referred-to definition of corporate culture stresses this aspect and explicitly connects it with organizational knowledge. Corporate culture consists of 'the pattern of basic assumptions that a given group has invented, discovered, or developed in learning to cope with its problems of external adaptation and internal integration, and that have worked well enough to be considered valid, and, therefore, to be taught to new members as the correct way to perceive, think, and feel in relation to those problems'. With regard to this historical process, the founder's role in establishing norms and culture has been studied and characterized as the embedding of cultural elements into the organiza-tion. It occurs when the founder/leader gets the group to try out certain responses (Schein, 1983). As the founders and their successors manage by their principles, their experiences lead them to modify the system through the process of incremental change. A newcomer 'may be chosen, and may choose to join the company, because his personality is compatible with the beliefs of those doing the hiring'.

This last feature refers to the equivocal relations between culture and performance: as previously stated, corporate culture enhances social system stability and serves as a 'sense-making' and control mechanism. First, it differentiates the organization from others and provides a sense of identity for its members. Second, it can be seen as a mechanism enabling the community to deal in a specific way with unforeseen contingencies. Shared beliefs and values lead to homogenized perspectives and behaviours. However, homogeneity of belief can have different effects on the firm performance: shared beliefs imply less variety or diversity amongst different individuals' visions and actions; less creativity and less responsiveness to change will ensue (Sorensen, 2002).

The homogenizing effect becomes a key issue when it comes to envisioning how a corporate culture could be an *entrepreneurial* culture, which by definition is supposed to foster entrepreneurial behaviours.

4.2 Paradoxical Nature of an Entrepreneurial Culture: Its Status and Function in Entrepreneurial Orientation Models

If culture works as a kind of normative frame, it is difficult to figure out how it could promote behaviours that, by definition, escape from homogeneity and standardized conducts. If deviation is considered a serious threat to any social organization and is accordingly sanctioned, then innovativeness and the taking of bold initiatives will be discouraged. In other words, if corporate entrepreneurship has to do with taking risk, innovating and acting proactively (Miller, 1983), how could challenging the status quo be part of culture itself? Is this not self-contradictory?

There are at least four potential ways of solving this apparent paradox. First of all, one can contend that innovation, even as a diverging process, can be managed with *specific* policies and rules (Drucker, 1985). A second option is to refer to the anthropological root of the notion of culture (Smircich, 1983) and argue that an entrepreneurial culture can be viewed as one that from time to time allows a hero or a champion to emerge and take charge of an entrepreneurial or innovative project (Dougherty and Heller, 1994): the intrapreneur appears as a transgressor of taboos and a founder of a new reality. A third option is to consider the existence of sub-cultures and, more specifically, of 'nonconforming enclaves' (Martin and Siehl, 1983). 'If the enclave functions innovatively within the institution's latitude of tolerance, the institution benefits. If not, the institution has isolated the deviance'. Finally, one can also argue that 'weak cultures', as opposed to strong ones, will allow autonomous behaviours: the existence of many sub-cultures, few strong traditions, few values and beliefs widely shared by all employees and no strong sense of company identity should favour the emergence of divergent and creative behaviours.

Strangely enough, there are no papers appearing in first-rank, peer-reviewed publications specifically devoted to entrepreneurial culture even though corporate culture is repeatedly identified as a component of intrapreneurial phenomena and integrated as such in numerous frameworks. For instance, in the opportunity-based approach (Stevenson and Jarillo-Mossi, 1986; Stevenson and Jarillo 1990; Brown et al., Davidsson and Wiklund, 2001), entrepreneurial culture is defined as a climate that encourages idea generation, experimentation and creativity. These are also key ingredients in opportunity recognition dynamics (Drucker, 1985).

Entrepreneurial culture is also identified by researchers as an internal variable of entrepreneurial firm behaviour under different denominations: for instance under the label of 'core values/beliefs' (Guth and Ginsberg, 1990) or 'organizational culture' (Covin and Slevin, 1991). In the latter, organizational culture is considered as an internal variable, together with top management values and philosophies, organizational resources and competencies and organizational structure. It can be more implicitly defined throughout different factors (management support, work discretion, reward/reinforcements) that can be considered as parts or results of corporate culture (Hornsby et al., 1993; 2002; Sathe, 1989). This boils down to characterizing innovative environments as specific cultural settings (Detert et al., 2000) where an institutionalized belief prevails that there is room for constant, continuous improvement.

Several researchers (Kanter, 1985; Sykes and Block, 1989) have pinpointed various components specific to entrepreneurial cultures: organizational tolerance for experimentation and risk-taking, employees' involvement in the firm's development, rejection of turf defence behaviour, ability to form autonomous project teams, official recognition of successes, and so on. Entrepreneurial leaders are often identified as sources and shapers of corporate culture (Schein, 1983), but middle managers in large organizations (Noble and Birkinshaw, 1998) have also been identified as potential generators of an entrepreneurial climate: informally encouraging employees to innovate and take risks, promoting autonomous or informal corporate entrepreneurship activities, championing strategic alternatives, and so on.

4.3   Corporate Culture Descriptors

Given its intangible quality, it proves to be difficult to describe, assess and possibly measure a firm's culture. Scholars have tried to measure a firm's cultural strength in assessing the consistency of responses to survey items across managers in a firm (for example Gordon and DiTomaso, 1992) or across the rival firms' managers in the same industry (Kotter and Heskett,

1992). A very interesting contribution (Hofstede et al., 1990), based on extensive research performed in the 1980s, measures organizational cultures in 20 organizational units in Denmark and the Netherlands. Quantitative measures of the cultures of the 20 units, aggregated at the unit level, showed that a large part of the differences among these 20 units could be explained by six factors, related to established concepts from organizational sociology, which measured the organizational cultures on six independent dimensions. Hofstede's transferable and operationalized definitions are defined as such:

1.   'Process-Oriented vs. Results-Oriented' opposes a concern for means (process-oriented) to a concern for goals (results-oriented).
2.   'Employee-Oriented vs. Job-Oriented' opposes a concern for people (employee-oriented) to a concern for getting the job done (job-oriented).
3.   'Parochial vs. Professional': opposes units whose employees derive their identity largely from the organization, which we have called 'parochial', to units in which people identify with their type of job, which we have called 'professional'.
4.   'Open System vs. Closed System' opposes open systems to closed systems. This dimension describes the communication climate, a focus of attention for both human resources and public relations experts.
5.   'Loose Control vs. Tight Control' refers to the amount of internal structuring in the organization.
6.   'Normative vs. Pragmatic' deals with the popular notion of 'customer orientation'. Pragmatic units are market-driven; normative units perceive their task regarding the outside world as the implementation of inviolable rules.

These descriptors can be used as relevant descriptors of the corporate culture in our planned research.

4.4   Implications

By fully integrating the corporate culture dimension in our model, we are able to take into account its impact on entrepreneurial orientation in a more precise way than previous studies have done. In so doing we aim to bring a more detailed analysis of what has so far been considered as a minor variable (often reduced to a vague labelling), whereas corporate culture, whatever its definition, has always been considered in the managerial and research literature as a key driver of entrepreneurial behaviours within the corporate setting.

Several options are then possible: (1) we can emphasize this dimension by studying firms belonging to the same industries and countries (or at least very close in Hofstede's terms such as north-west European countries); (2) we can partially (because of possible sub-cultures) neutralize it by studying MNC units all belonging to the same industry.

4.5   Propositions Concerning the Corporate Culture Variable

If our model is correct, descriptors of corporate culture should have a significant impact on the major dimensions of entrepreneurial orientation.

- *Focus.* Being result-oriented is recognized as being part of entrepreneurial behaviours, at an individual level and firm level. It distinguishes between entrepreneurs and dreamers; in order not to be stuck at the idea phase, entrepreneurs must be doers too, and transform opportunities into reality. Thus result orientation should be positively correlated with the entrepreneurial orientation of firms (P10). However, this orientation does not lead to the neglect of team-spirited approaches: emphasizing an 'employee-oriented' approach seems to be consonant with the collective spirit often associated with intrapreneurial initiatives; people as sources of resources, talents, competencies and so on are commonly recognized as key assets in the success of any venture (internal or external). Hence employee orientation should be positively correlated with the entrepreneurial orientation of firms (P11).
- *Identification.* Whether employees derive their identity largely from the organization, or identify with their type of job should be neutral as regards entrepreneurial orientation. Entrepreneurial initiatives can stem from different contexts, and individuals can rely upon their organizational identity or the meaning of their job. Consequently one can assume that parochialism vs. professionalism should be neutral as to the entrepreneurial orientation of firms (P12).
- *Control.* Regarding organizational systems and procedures, loose control oriented environments or organically structured organizations are more likely to foster entrepreneurial behaviours (for example Miller, 1983; Covin and Slevin, 1990). For this reason the tight control dimension should be negatively correlated with the entrepreneurial orientation of firms (P13).
- *Permeability.* Finally, permeable and porous organizations are more likely to be open to innovation and welcome novelties from the outside. In the same perspective, market-driven companies are expected to be more entrepreneurial than others, the customers

being a strong driver for innovation. From this, normativeness should be negatively correlated with the entrepreneurial orientation of firms (P14), while open system features should be positively correlated with the entrepreneurial orientation of firms (P15).

CONCLUSION

Although we still find ourselves at an early stage of our enquiry process, we believe that the multi-level cultural model of entrepreneurial orientation we propose can give rise to interesting research questions and results. In effect, our model relies on well-tested concepts which it combines in new, original ways. The strong emphasis given to culture versus other variables – such as external environment or internal structure – in explaining entrepreneurial orientation is partly compensated by the multiple levels of culture the model takes into consideration and is compatible with the general consensus concerning the importance of soft, internal variables when it comes to fostering corporate entrepreneurship.

We are aware that the three cultural levels we have identified interact with each other in complex ways that we still don't fully understand. In certain settings, the national culture variable could be of major significance while it could have only a marginal impact in other settings, and the same holds true for industry and corporate culture.

While all of the 15 industry and culture descriptors we have included in our model have been previously described and used, these descriptors will need to be adapted to our particular research context and design. An effort to harmonize and to avoid overlaps among descriptors will also be required. The descriptors of the entrepreneurial orientation (innovativeness, risk-taking and proactiveness) will have to be turned into operational variables, easy to measure and meaningful, whatever the characteristics of the firms we decide to study. Finally, the scope and focus of our enquiry will have to be properly circumscribed. We will need to select more precise research questions, on the basis of their significance for professional managers, as well as pragmatic research considerations.

At this early stage of our enquiry, it is still difficult to foresee all the implications of our model or to identify its shortcomings. Because our model is quite original, we lack points of comparison and sources of inspiration when it comes to imagining all the directions our enquiry could take and selecting an appropriate research design and methodology. This will be our next step.

NOTES

1. This research paper was presented at the international conference RENT XXI – Research in Entrepreneurship and Small Business, Cardiff, 22–3 November, 2007.
2. There are many definitions of culture or national culture. Drawing mainly from Herbig (1994) and Hofstede (1980), Hayton et al. (2002) propose the following general definition: 'Culture is defined as a set of shared values, beliefs and expected behaviors' (p. 33). They add: 'Deeply embedded, unconscious, and even irrational shared values shape political institutions as well as social and technical systems, all of which simultaneously reflect and reinforce values and beliefs' (p. 33).
3. We could also mention the pioneering works of Weber (1930) on the link between religious values and entrepreneurship, which paved the way for much research work and debate.
4. We do not present in this section all the research that associates national culture and entrepreneurship. For a recent review, see Hayton et al. (2002). In their article, the authors present studies of national culture and corporate entrepreneurship (nine have been identified in an extensive survey).
5. See the works of Jones and Wadhwani (2006), which offer a wide range of examples of research in these disciplines. These authors introduce their research as follows: 'In recent decades, historians have increasingly sought to ground the study of how culture and nationality affect entrepreneurship by examining how specific social structures and relationships shape the influence of entrepreneurial culture. They have examined how social group affiliation – whether ethnicity, race, gender, family or class – mediates entrepreneurial culture by constraining or providing specialized access to opportunities and resources' (p. 14).

BIBLIOGRAPHY

Abrahamson, E. and C.J. Fombrun (1994) 'Macrocultures: determinants and consequences', *Academy of Management Review*, **19**(4), 728–55.

Ajzen, I. (1991), 'The theory of planned behavior', *Organizational Behavior and Human Decision Processes*, **50**, 179–211.

Antoncic, B. and R.D. Hisrich (2000), 'Intrapreneurship modeling in transition economies: a comparison of Slovenia and the United States', *Journal of Developmental Entrepreneurship*, **5**(1), 21–40.

Auger, P., A. Barnir and J.M. Gallaugher (2003), 'Strategic orientation, competition, and Internet-based electronic commerce', *Information Technology & Management*, **4**(2–3), 139–64.

Barney, J.B. (1986), 'Organizational culture: can it be a source of sustained competitive advantage?', *Academy of Management Review*, (11), 656–65.

Berger, B. (1993), *Esprit d'entreprise, Cultures et Sociétés*, Paris: Maxima.

Brown, T.E., P. Davidsson and J. Wiklund (2001), 'An operationalization of Stevenson's conceptualization of entrepreneurship as opportunity-based firm behavior', *Strategic Management Journal*, **22**(10), 953–68.

Busenitz, L.W., C. Gomez and J.W. Spencer (2000), 'Country institutional profiles: unlocking entrepreneurial phenomena', *Academy of Management Journal*, **43**(5), 994–1003.

Casson, M. (1991), *The Economics of Business Culture*, Oxford: Clarendon Press.

Casson, M. (1995), *Entrepreneurship and Business Culture: Studies in the Economics of Trust*, vol.1, Aldershot, UK and Brookfield, VT, USA: Edward Elgar.

Chatman, J.A. and K.A. Jehn (1994), 'Assessing the relationship between industry characteristics and organizational culture: how different can you be?', *Academy of Management Journal*, **37**(3), 522–53.

Christensen, E.W. and G.G. Gordon (1999), 'An exploration of industry, culture and revenue growth', *Organization Studies*, **20**(3), 397–423.

Covin, J.G. and K.M. Green (2006), 'Strategic process effects on the entrepreneurial orientation–sales growth rate relationship', *Entrepreneurship Theory and Practice*, January, **30**(1), 57–82.

Covin, J.G. and D.P. Slevin (1988), 'The influence of organization structure on the utility of an entrepreneurial top management style', *Journal of Management Studies*, **25**, 217–34.

Covin, J.G. and D.P. Slevin (1989), 'Strategic management of small firms in hostile and benign environments', *Strategic Management Journal*, **10**(1), 75–87.

Covin, J.G. and D.P. Slevin (1990), 'New venture strategic posture, structure, and performance: an industry life cycle analysis', *Journal of Business Venturing*, **5**, 123–35.

Covin, J.G. and, D.P. Slevin (1991), 'A conceptual model of entrepreneurship as firm behavior', *Entrepreneurship Theory and Practice*, **16**(1), Fall, 7–25.

Dess, G.G., G.T. Lumpkin and J.G. Covin (1997), 'Entrepreneurial strategy making and firm performance: tests of contingency and configurational models', *Strategic Management Journal*, **18**(9), 677–95.

Detert, James R., Roger G. Schroeder and John J. Mauriel (2000), 'A framework for linking culture and improvement initiatives in organizations', *The Academy of Management Review*, **25**(4), 850–63.

Dougherty, D. and T. Heller (1994), 'The illegitimacy of successful product innovation in established firms', *Organization Science*, May, **5**(2), 200–218.

Drucker, P.F. (1985), 'The discipline of innovation', *Harvard Business Review*, May–June, 67–72.

Gerschenkron, A. (1962), *Economic Backwardness in Historical Perspective*, Cambridge, MA: Belknap Press.

Gerschenkron, A. (1966), 'The modernization of entrepreneurship', in M. Weiner (ed.), *Modernization: The Dynamics of Growth*, New York: Basic Books.

Godley, A. (2001), *Jewish Immigrant Entrepreneurship in New York and London*, Basingstoke: Palgrave.

Gordon, G.G. (1991), 'Industry determinants of organizational culture', *Academy of Management Review*, **16**(2), 396–415.

Gordon, G.G. and N. DiTomaso (1992), 'Predicting corporate performance from organizational culture', *Journal of Management Studies*, **29**(6), 783–98.

Guth, W. and A. Ginsberg (1990), 'Guest editors' introduction: corporate entrepreneurship', *Strategic Management Journal*, **11** (summer special issue), 5–15.

Hambrick, D. (1982), 'Environmental scanning and organizational strategy', *Strategic Management Journal*, **3**, 159–74.

Hart, S.L. (1992), 'An integrative framework for strategy-making processes', *Academy of Management Review*, **17**, 327–51.

Hayton, J.C., G. George and S.A. Zahra (2002), 'National culture and entrepreneurship: a review of behavioral research', *Entrepreneurship Theory and Practice*, Summer, pp. 33–52.

Herbig, P. (1994), *The Innovation Matrix: Culture and Structure Prerequisites to Innovation*, Westport, CT: Quorum.

Hofstede, G. (1980), *Culture's Consequences: International Differences in Work-related Values*, Beverly Hills, CA: Sage.
Hofstede, G. (1985), 'The interaction between national and organizational value systems', *Journal of Management Studies*, **22**(4), 347–57.
Hofstede, G. (1991), *Cultures and Organizations: Software of the Mind*, London, UK: McGraw Hill.
Hofstede, G., B. Neuijen D. Daval Ohayv and G. Sanders (1990), 'Measuring organizational cultures: a qualitative and quantitative study across twenty cases', *Administrative Science Quarterly*, June, **35**, 286–316.
Hornsby, J.S., D.W. Naffziger, D.F. Kuratko and R.V. Montagno (1993), 'An interactive model of the corporate entrepreneurship process', *Entrepreneurship Theory and Practice*, Winter, pp. 29–37.
Hornsby, J.S., D.F. Kuratko and S.A. Zahra (2002), 'Middle managers' perception of the internal environment for corporate entrepreneurship: assessing a measurement scale', *Journal of Business Venturing*, **17**, 253–73.
Huff, A. (1982), 'Industry influences on strategy reformulation', *Strategic Management Journal*, **3**, 119–31.
Hughes, M. and R.E. Morgan (2007), 'Deconstructing the relationship between entrepreneurial orientation and business performance at the embryonic stage of firm growth', *Industrial Marketing Management*, **36**(5), 651–61.
Ireland, R.D., M.A. Hitt, S.M. Camp and D.L. Sexton (2001), 'Integrating entrepreneurship and strategic actions to create firm wealth', *Academy of Management Executive*, **15**(1), 49–63.
Jones, G. and R.D. Wadhwani (2006), 'Entrepreneurship and business history: renewing the research agenda', working paper 07-007, Harvard Business School.
Kanter, R.M. (1985), 'Supporting innovation and venture development in established companies', *Journal of Business Venturing*, Winter, pp. 47–60.
Keh, Hean Tat, Thi Tuyet Mai Nguyen and Hwei Ping Ng (2007), 'The effects of entrepreneurial orientation and marketing information on the performance of SMEs', *Journal of Business Venturing*, **22**(4), 592–611.
Kotter, J.P. and J.L. Heskett (1992), *Culture & Performance*, New York: Free Press.
Landes, D. (1949), 'French entrepreneurship and industrial growth in the nineteenth century', *Journal of Economic History*, **9**, 45–61.
Landes, D. (1953), 'Social attitudes, entrepreneurship and economic development: a comment', *Explorations in Entrepreneurial History*, **6**, 245–72.
Landes, D. (1998), *The Wealth and Poverty of Nations*, New York: W.W. Norton.
Lee, S.M. and S.J. Peterson (2000), 'Culture, entrepreneurial orientation, and global competitiveness', *Journal of World Business*, **35**(4), 401–16.
Lumpkin, G.T. and G.G. Dess (1996), 'Clarifying the entrepreneurial orientation construct and linking it to performance', *Academy of Management Review*, **21**, 135–72.
Lumpkin, G.T. and G.G. Dess (1997), 'Proactiveness versus competitive aggressiveness: teasing apart key dimensions of an entrepreneurial orientation', in P.D. Reynolds et al. (eds), *Frontiers of Entrepreneurship Research*, Wellesley, MA: Babson College, pp. 47–58.
Lumpkin, G.T. and C.B. Sloat (2001), 'Do family firms have an entrepreneurial orientation?', paper presented at the Babson-Kauffman Entrepreneurship Research Conference, June, Jönköping, Sweden.
Martin, J. and C. Siehl (1983), 'Organizational culture and counterculture: an uneasy symbiosis', *Organizational Dynamics*, **12**, 52–64.

McGrath, R.G., I.C. MacMillan and S. Scheinberg (1992), 'Elitists, risk-takers, and rugged individualists? An exploratory analysis of cultural differences between entrepreneurs and non-entrepreneurs', *Journal of Business Venturing*, **7**, 115–35.

Meek, L.V. (1986), 'Organizational culture: origins and weaknesses', *Organization Studies*, **9**(4), 453–73.

Miller, D. (1983), 'The correlates of entrepreneurship in three types of firms', *Management Science*, **29**(7), 770–91.

Miller, D. and P. Friesen (1982), 'Innovation in conservative and entrepreneurial firms: two models of strategic momentum', *Strategic Management Journal*, **3**, 1–25.

Morris, M.H., D.L. Davis and J.W. Allen (1994), 'Fostering corporate entrepreneurship: cross-cultural comparisons of the importance of individualism versus collectivism', *Journal of International Business Studies*, **25**(1), 65–89.

Mueller, S.L. and A.S. Thomas (2000), 'Culture and entrepreneurial potential: a nine country study of locus of control and innovativeness', *Journal of Business Venturing*, **16**, 51–75.

Noble, R. and J. Birkinshaw (1998), 'Innovation in multinational corporations: control and communication patterns', *Strategic Management Journal*, **19**(5), 479–96.

North, D. (1990), *Institutions, Institutional Change and Economic Performance*, Cambridge: Cambridge University Press.

North, D. and R. Thomas (1973), *The Rise of the Western World: A New Economic History*, Cambridge: Cambridge University Press.

O'Brien, R. and L.P. Nordtvedt (2006), 'The conundrum of subjective norms: the moderating effect of national culture on entrepreneurial intentions', paper presented at the Academy of Management Conference, August, Atlanta, GA.

Pfeffer, J. and G.R. Salancik (1978), *The External Control of Organizations: A Resource Dependence Perspective*, New York: Harper and Row.

Porter, M. (1985), *Competitive Advantage*, New York: Free Press.

Porter, M. (1986), *Competition in Global Industries: A Conceptual Framework*, Boston, MA: Harvard Business School Press.

Rauch, A., J. Wiklund, G.T. Lumpkin and M. Frese (2004), 'Entrepreneurial orientation and business performance: a meta analysis', submitted to *Strategic Management Journal*, October.

Reynolds, P.D., M. Hay and S.M. Camp (1999), *Global Entrepreneurship Monitor: 1999 Executive Report*, Kansas City: Kauffman Center.

Richard, O.C., T. Barnett, S. Dwyer and K. Chadwick (2004), 'Cultural diversity in management, firm performance and the moderating role of entrepreneurial orientation dimensions', *Academy of Management Journal*, **47**(2), 255–66.

Sathe, V. (1989), 'Fostering entrepreneurship in large diversified firm', *Organizational Dynamics*, **18**(1), 20–32.

Schein, E. (1983), 'The role of the founder in creating organizational culture', *Organizational Dynamics*, Summer, **12**(1), 13–29.

Schein, E. (1984), 'Coming to a new awareness of organizational culture', *Sloan Management Review*, **25**(2), 3–16.

Schein, E. (1996). 'Culture: the missing concept in organization studies', *Administrative Science Quarterly*, **41**(2), 229–40.

Shane, S. and S. Venkataraman (2000), 'The promise of entrepreneurship as a field of research', *Academy of Management Review*, **25**(1), 217–26.

Shapero, A. and L. Sokol (1982), 'The social dimensions of entrepreneurship', in

C. Kent, D. Sexton and K. Vesper (eds), *The Encyclopedia of Entrepreneurship*, Englewood Cliffs, NJ: Prentice Hall, pp. 72–90.

Smart, D.T. and J.S. Conant (1994), 'Entrepreneurial orientation, distinctive marketing competencies and organizational performance', *Journal of Applied Business Research*, **10**, 28–38.

Smircich, L. (1983), 'Concepts of culture and organizational analysis', *Administrative Science Quarterly*, **28**(3), 339–58.

Sorensen, J.B. (2002), 'The strength of corporate culture and reliability of firm performance', *Administrative Science Quarterly*, **47**(1), 70–91.

Spender, J.C. (1989), *Industry Recipes: The Nature and Source of Managerial Judgment*, Cambridge, MA: Blackwell.

Stevenson, H.H. and J.C. Jarillo-Mossi (1986), 'Preserving entrepreneurship as companies grow', *Journal of Business Strategy*, **7**(1), 10–23.

Stevenson, H.H. and J.C. Jarillo (1990), 'A paradigm of entrepreneurship: entrepreneurship management', *Strategic Management Journal*, Summer special issue, (11), 17–27.

Sykes, H.B. and Z. Block (1989), 'Corporate venturing obstacles: sources and solutions', *Journal of Business Venturing*, **4**, 159–67.

Thornberry, N. (2001), 'Corporate entrepreneurship: antidote or oxymoron?', *European Management Journal*, October, **19**(5), 526–33.

Todorovic, W.Z. and R.B. McNaughton (2007), 'The effect of culture, resources and quality of entrepreneurship on economic development: a conceptual framework', *International Journal of Entrepreneurship and Small Business*, **4**(4), 383–96.

Trompenaars, F. (1994), *Riding the Waves of Culture*, London: Nicholas Brealey.

Venkataraman, S. (2004), 'Regional transformation through technological entrepreneurship', *Journal of Business Venturing*, **19**(1), 153–67.

Weber, M. (1930), *The Protestant Ethic and the Spirit of Capitalism*, New York: Scribner.

Weick, K.E. (1978), *The Social Psychology of Organizing*, 2nd edn, Reading, MA: Addison-Wesley.

Welter, F. (2007), 'Entrepreneurship in West and East Germany', *International Journal of Entrepreneurship and Small Business*, **4**(2), 97–109.

Wiklund, J. (1999), 'The sustainability of the entrepreneurial orientation–performance relationship', *Entrepreneurship Theory and Practice*, **24**(1), 37–48.

Wiklund, J. and D. Shepherd (2003), 'Knowledge-based resources, entrepreneurial orientation and the performance of small and medium-sized businesses', *Strategic Management Journal*, **24**, 1307–14.

Wiklund, J. and D. Sheperd (2005), 'Entrepreneurial orientation and small business performance: a configurational approach', *Journal of Business Venturing*, **20**(1), 71–91.

Zahra, S.A. (1991), 'Predictors and financial outcomes of corporate entrepreneurship: an exploratory study', *Journal of Business Venturing*, **6**, 259–86.

Zahra, S.A. (1993), 'A conceptual model of entrepreneurship as firm behavior: a critique and extension', *Entrepreneurship Theory and Practice*, **17**(4), 5–21.

Zahra, S.A. and J.G. Covin (1993), 'Business strategy, technology policy and firm performance', *Strategic Management Journal*, **14**, 451–78.

Zahra, S.A. and J.G. Covin (1995), 'Contextual influences on the corporate entrepreneurship–performance relationship: a longitudinal analysis', *Journal of Business Venturing*, **10**, 43–58.

5.   Probioprise: engaging entrepreneurs in formulating research and innovation policy at the European level

David Watkins

INTRODUCTION

Probioprise[1] is a project commissioned by the EU Directorate General for Research. Its goal is to identify a research programme which will assist entrepreneurs in simultaneously meeting two major planks of EU policy: the Lisbon Agenda, which seeks to make Europe globally more competitive by encouraging enterprising behaviour; and the Gothenburg Declaration, which aims to halt and reverse the loss of biodiversity in Europe by 2010. Normally, such objectives would appear to be in potential conflict, since enterprise and environmental concerns are not seen as natural bed-fellows. In a counter-intuitive leap of faith, the focus of the project is to identify and work with smaller enterprises, and potential enterprises, which benefit from the sustainable exploitation of biodiversity as a key resource (*pro-bio*diversity enter*prises*, hence Probioprise). The focus is on such firms in protected areas (such as National Parks, Natura2000 locations and Ramsar sites). These sites tend to be located in some of the most rural areas of Europe and are often extremely peripheral in economic and social terms, as well as geographically. The research programme proposed will form one input to the development of EU's Framework 7 and subsequent Framework programmes; it is itself supported under Framework 6 as part of the work programme of EU DG Research. The Commission makes special efforts to involve SMEs in the Framework.

Probioprise is being undertaken by a consortium of European NGOs. Both Fauna and Flora International (FFI) and the European Bureau for Conservation and Development (EBCD) are environmental groups. The third partner is EFMD, formerly known as the European Foundation for Management Development. This evolved as an association of Europe's leading business schools and management development specialists from major international corporations, but has an increasingly global reach. EFMD has a number of initiatives in place to stimulate entrepreneurship research and education in Europe. The author became involved in the project described as a representative of the EFMD's 'Entrepreneurship, Innovation and Small Business Network', and has been particularly involved in writing case studies of SMEs to inform the project's conclusions. The chapter is therefore written from the perspective of a participant-observer; the contribution reports and reflects upon work done by a large international team engaged in organizing and delivering a variety of related outputs, but the opinions expressed are those of the author alone.

The mode of operation of the project is to undertake literature research, hold workshops of entrepreneurs operating in four different ecologically sensitive zones (forests, wetlands, grasslands and maritime/coastal zones), and to follow up the experiences of several of the participants through writing detailed case histories. The focus of this project is to identify management and other socio-economic research that could potentially make entrepreneurs more effective agents for delivering the dual policy aims – while themselves running economically effective businesses.

At the time of writing, the four planned workshops have been held, and more than 100 individual enterprises have been involved in the data collection, with 15 organizations being the subject of detailed case histories. Cases have been written jointly by business experts nominated by EFMD, and biodiversity experts nominated by FFI.

ENTERPRISE AND THE ENVIRONMENTAL AGENDA

A literature review of the intersection of scholarship regarding the smaller enterprise with that on environmental issues identified two major strands, which can be broadly characterized as the *constraints* perspective and the *opportunities* perspective, although the further one investigates, the less clear this distinction seems to become.

Constraints Perspective

The first strand essentially concerns legislation as a constraint on environmentally insensitive behaviour or, in its more sophisticated form, as an incentive for environmental sensitivity. At its simplest, 'environmentalism' is seen as having the same effects as regulation in general; as such it may also lead to innovation as firms try to adapt or circumvent legislation (cf. Clark, 1987). However, it is clear that the responses of firms to environmental regulation – as with regulation and 'red tape' generally – are revealed to be more complex the further one investigates.

Sharfman et al. (2000) observed that a growing number of firms have begun working towards the development of innovative systems that consume fewer resources, reduce waste and enhance productivity, while creating new market opportunities, but argue that since this environmentally friendly innovation occurs under varying types/levels of regulation, the role of such laws is still debatable. On the basis of four case studies undertaken for a US Environmental Protection Agency (EPA)-funded study that describes environmentally conscious product and process innovations in high and low regulation environments, Sharfman et al. modelled the antecedents of environmentally conscious technological innovation under high and low amounts of regulation. More quantitative work was conducted by Hitchens et al. (2003), who sought to measure the relationship between firm competitiveness, management environmental culture, the importance of external advice on the use of cleaner production, and the firm's environmental performance among European manufacturing SMEs in the United Kingdom, Republic of Ireland, Germany and Italy, in furniture and two other sectors. Cost and market drivers appeared to be almost as important as regulation, and the environmental initiatives adopted by firms did have an impact on both cost and market performance. Nevertheless, a statistically significant relationship between overall environmental and economic performance could not be shown. There was no evidence of a relationship between environmental performance and management's environmental attitudes. Moreover, SMEs failed to take up available advice, which often appeared to be of good quality. Further work by the same research group (Hitchens et al., 2005) concluded that more competitive SMEs do not necessarily have any greater capacity to adopt environmental initiatives. In a study which tried to link small firm environmental performance to factors such as profitability, growth, skills and R&D, they examined three interrelated propositions concerned with the impact of environmental initiatives on firm competitiveness: the relevance of management's awareness of environmental issues; the availability of external information and expertise to aid management; and the competitiveness of the firm. There was only scattered evidence to suggest any of these was significantly associated with the firm's environmental performance. The study showed that firms with an average economic performance were just as likely to adopt environmental initiatives as their high-performing competitors. Moreover, regardless of managers voicing personal concerns about the environment, most small firms do relatively little about the environment in practice and are reluctant to seek advice about it.

Blackburn et al. (2005) investigated the effects of state regulation on small firms in three situations, including the response of business owner-managers to increased environmental regulation, in order to provide a holistic analysis of the effects of regulation on business strategy, the behaviour of owner-managers and business performance. They argued for consideration of the 'world views' and experiences of business owners in order to understand their responses to interventions designed to meet wider government objectives, as well as structural factors, including labour force characteristics, supply chain influences and the nature and extent of competition. They concluded that the effects of regulation on smaller enterprises are always potentially more complex than they might appear at first sight and that what is required are sociological analyses, seeking to understand the motivations and meanings of small business owners, as well as economic perspectives. They argued that although business owners operate within certain structural constraints – including their business sector and resource and information limitations – within these parameters they respond according to a set of motivations and world meanings where the logics of intervention and the responses of business owners may not coincide.

Opportunities Perspective

In the second strand, environmental consciousness and concerns are the specific focus of business opportunities. This strand is somewhat piece-meal and at present lacks even a common vocabulary, but is evolving rapidly and may have much promise. Thus studies here may describe the 'green entrepreneur' (Berle, 1991; Fischetti, 1992), 'ecopreneurship' (Bennett, 1991; Isaak, 1998; Pastakia, 1998; Isaak, 2002; Schaper, 2002), 'bioneers' (Schaltegger, 2002), 'environmental entrepreneurship' (Keogh and Polonsky, 1998; Linnanen, 2002) or 'sustainable entrepreneurship' (Anderson, 1998; Cohen and Winn, 2007). Despite this, the focus of the studies is very similar. There is even a small body of literature focusing on the support networks available to such firms, such as specialist sources of risk capital (Randjelovic et al., 2003) and a growing case literature (for example Volery, 2002; Seidl et al., 2003) which might be adapted for peda-gogical use.

Recently, attempts to systematize and theorize the situation have been attempted. These usually start from economic perspectives such as discussion of market failure (for example Pastakia, 2002). Cohen and Winn (2007) suggest that four types of market imperfection (inefficient firms, externalities, flawed pricing mechanisms and information asymmetries) both contribute to environmental degradation but may also provide significant opportunities for the creation of radical technologies and innovative business models. Thus it is possible for 'founders to obtain entrepreneurial rents while simultaneously improving local and global social and environmental conditions'. Similarly, Dean and McMullen (2007) argue that since 'environmental degradation results from the failure of markets . . . environmentally relevant market failures represent opportunities for achieving profitability while simultaneously reducing environmentally degrading economic behaviours'. The key task therefore is to determine how entrepreneurs identify and seize the opportunities that are inherent in environmentally related market failures.

Market failure is one of the few widely accepted reasons for providing assistance to SMEs generally, be it in the form of finance, information services, training or consultancy (cf. Storey, 1994; Bovaird et al., 1995; Bergstrom, 2000; Hinloopen, 2004, among many others. Thus it is unsurprising that there have already been calls to establish 'business biodiversity facilities' to mitigate market failure where the market currently underprices valuable biodiversity goods and services (Bishop et al., 2006).

INVOLVING ENTREPRENEURS IN FRAMING POLICY

It is something of a paradox that as the entrepreneurship/small business field has become an acceptable academic endeavour, it has become more and more detached from the stated interests of the subjects of its research. It is easy to see why this should be so. Verstraete (2002 and 2003) has explained the process of academic institutionalization in France, which has a particularly rigid and statist academic system, although Aldrich (2000) has argued that in Europe more generally[2] entrepreneurship/small business academics are more practically and policy oriented than their colleagues in the USA. Evidence is scant, but Brockhaus (1988) specifically compared the concerns expressed by entrepreneurs to the US President in the 1986 White House Conference on Small Business to research undertaken in the key entrepreneurship niche journals and key conferences (cf. Watkins and Reader, 2003). He found little overlap. Banks and Taylor (1991) and Aldrich and Baker (1997) later reached similar conclusions. Indeed, since that time the situation has probably worsened, as attempts to evaluate academic research around the world have increasingly focused on peer review and bibliometric measures rather than applicability in the outside world. Busenitz et al. (2003) exemplify those who seem to welcome this trend, seeking to locate and confine entrepreneurship research to just one narrow academic subfield, sacrificing all to academic respectability and career progression. This has happened to such an extent that even academics are beginning to worry, but it will be instructive to observe whether the response to the general Academy of Management Conference call for papers by Walsh (2007/8), seeking the development of phronesis, is higher or lower in 'emergent' domains such as entrepreneurship.

MODE 2 RESEARCH IN THEORY

Be that as it may, in the respect described above, entrepreneurship research is just following in the footsteps of much of previous social science, and before that, natural science. In a book which has greatly influenced policy makers, Gibbons et al. (1994) characterize the process by which academics set their own research agenda through peer review and discount the interests and needs of the wider community as 'Mode One'. They contrast this with a form of research that was evolving at the time they were writing and which they characterize as 'Mode Two'. Mode Two research takes into account the interests of other societal stakeholders from the outset and goes beyond traditional disciplines. Specifically, it is construed as research that is undertaken as: part of a socially accountable, reflexive process; is subject to a wider range of quality processes than simple peer review; is transdisciplinary; is performed by heterogeneous research teams; and perhaps crucially, is performed in the context of application (see Figure 5.1 for a schematic of this). Although these characterizations are ideal types, there is no question that the concept of Mode Two research has been extremely and increasingly influential (Nowotny et al., 2001). In particular, it is possible to see elements of all five Mode Two characteristics in the design of the EU Framework programmes. However, even when an effort is made to embrace potential users in the formulation of research policies and projects in order to meet the criterion 'not only of research performed in the context of application', but also those of 'social accountability' and a broader construct of 'quality' (in terms of fitness for *their* purposes), it is much easier to find representatives of large firm interests than of small ones.

MODE 2 RESEARCH IN PRACTICE: PROBIOPRISE PROJECT

As noted earlier, the focus of Probioprise is to identify and work with smaller enterprises, and potential enterprises that benefit from the sustainable exploitation of biodiversity as a key resource, in order to take note of

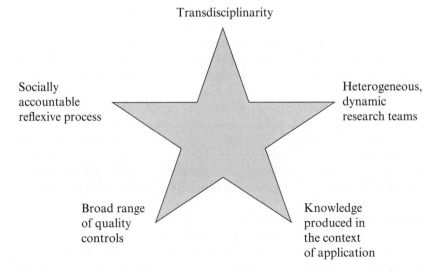

Transdisciplinarity

Socially
accountable
reflexive process

Heterogeneous,
dynamic
research teams

Broad range
of quality
controls

Knowledge
produced in
the context
of application

Source: Adapted from *British Academy of Management* (2002).

Figure 5.1 Schema of mode 2 research

their concerns and interests in the formulation of future Framework initiatives. We can now examine the extent to which this projects falls within the parameters of Mode Two research.

Probioprise is itself a Framework Programme under the EU's 6th Framework; however, it is a special project by virtue of the fact that its aim is to inform the research agenda for Framework 7 and subsequently: in EU parlance, it is what is known as a Specific Support Action, or SSA.

So it is *doubly* important, given that the set of Framework Programmes is intended to support research that is near to application, that Probioprise meets the conditions of Mode Two research. These conditions therefore perfuse the design of the Probioprise project, as can be seen when we address each of the Mode Two characteristics individually.

Heterogeneous, Dynamic Research Teams

We have noted above that Probioprise is being undertaken by a consortium of European NGOs, bringing together expertise in environmental issues, business development and the management and influence of core European institutions. Fauna and Flora International (FFI) is a long-established environmental NGO which focuses on the preservation and re-establishment of biodiversity on a worldwide scale. The European Bureau for Conservation and Development (EBCD) is an organization which was established to undertake environmentally-related tasks for European institutions such as the European Parliament. The third partner is the EFMD, the association of Europe's leading business schools and the management development specialists of major international corporations, which has a number of initiatives in place to stimulate entrepreneurship research and education in Europe. All of these organizations can be described as network organizations, since they can quickly access and animate a wide range of contacts and expertise through their members and sponsors. They therefore pass the tests of heterogeneity and dynamism.

Transdisciplinarity

The core expertise set which FFI brings to the project is in ecological and biological sciences, together with experience of a political nature which comes from dealing with local and national administrations, together with other NGOs, on a worldwide basis. The expertise set that EFMD brings to the project comprises the disciplines that are traditionally taught in European business schools, which range from business history through organizational design and strategy to economics and applied mathematics. A subgroup of its members also has particular expertise in the emerging discipline of entrepreneurship and small business management. EBCD brings expertise in environmental management and law, together with political skills including lobbying. The criterion of transdisciplinarity thus seems well met.

Socially Accountable Reflexive Process

A core element of a socially accountable reflexive process is to involve the key stakeholders in a meaningful way, while not neglecting the legitimate interests of wider civic society. The design of the Probioprise project has addressed this issue in the following way. Following a literature search for publications of all kinds that address issues of SMEs engaging with biodiversity, each of the organizations activated its own networks to establish levels of knowledge and interest in the topic. On the basis of this, academics, consultants, and – above all – SME owner-managers were identified who had both an interest and expertise to share. These groups were divided into four on the basis of the kind of ecological setting in which they mainly operate: forestry, grasslands, wetlands, or the marine and coastal environment. A workshop was then held for each of these groups.

Representative SMEs which had a priori interesting experiences to share were invited to discuss their experiences of creating and developing their businesses, and to indicate the kinds of problems, issues and opportunities they expected to face in future. Discussions were wide-ranging, with both other entrepreneurs and the invited experts commenting on each presentation. Following each workshop, a report was circulated to all participants to invite their comments. In addition, a small number of SMEs from each workshop were chosen to be the basis of an extended case study which documented in more detail the firms' experiences and issues faced. Each case study has been written jointly by authors having respectively business expertise and expertise related to the nature of the biodiversity that was the basis of the business opportunity. Each case study is next sent to the SME for comment and as each becomes finalized it is placed on the project website. All participants in every workshop are encouraged to use the website to check on and contribute to progress and as the basis for contacting firms with which they may wish to do business. The site is also being opened up to other relevant parties. The project has thus established a platform to enable the interaction of firms working with biodiversity, which may continue beyond the life of the project itself.

The penultimate stage will be to write two documents based on the information collected from the workshops, case histories and literature review. The first of these comprises an analysis of the experiences of SMEs seeking to engage in a positive manner with biodiversity, including the issues faced and still to be overcome. The second output is a proposed research agenda to determine how SMEs may more effectively work with biodiversity to meet the joint aspirations of the Lisbon Agenda and the Gothenburg Declaration, and to assist them to do so. These papers will then again be circulated to all participants in the project, as well as being placed on an open website, for wide consultation before being presented to the European Commission and the European Parliament. In this way the criterion of the research being a socially accountable, reflexive process is being met.

Knowledge Produced in the Context of Application

From the discussion above it should be clear that the relevant actors – the entrepreneurs – are being involved throughout the process of determining the kind of research which *they* believe to be most relevant in assisting them to meet their business objectives while maintaining or enhancing the biodiversity on which their continued business success depends. In particular, by beginning the process with a wide-ranging and relatively unstructured set of workshops, rather than with a fully developed, researcher-determined set of topics or formal questionnaire, it is the entrepreneurs who are throughout being encouraged to take the lead in the design of the ultimate research agenda. For the first workshop the organizers/*animateurs* deliberately did no more than set out a list of likely 'issue areas', which might for the most part be of the sort faced by any SME (see below), as a framework within which to capture these. This rather inductive approach is a rarity in the establishment of policy towards SMEs in any field: the aim was to ensure that the research that is ultimately undertaken within the Framework programmes, and which seeks to assist these SMEs by working on issues which they face (or believe they face), is that which the entrepreneurs themselves genuinely feel to be the most salient. As an example of the detailed way in which the project is being implemented, note that the workshops are being held in locations specific to the ecosystem with which the relevant entrepreneurs engage, and – wherever possible – that this is within a protected area and/or co-hosted by a scientific research institute prominent in research on that ecosystem.[3] In this way the team is seeking to ensure both that the research agenda itself is produced in the context of application, and *more importantly* that the research conducted in future on the basis of the research agenda is itself highly contextualized to the needs of the SMEs.

Broad Range of Quality Controls

Without wishing to labour the point, it should be clear that by feeding the results of the research back to a variety of interested parties in 'real time' throughout the project – including the sponsoring group within the European commission, and not least the entrepreneurs themselves – the generalized quality criterion of 'fitness for purpose' is taking priority over the narrowly constructed quality criteria of academic peer review.

PROGRESS TO DATE

Engagement

The project has managed to engage with owner-managers and business experts from nearly all the 27 member states and some other countries in the EEA[4] and beyond. This has been difficult, and it is a tribute to the power of the networks which the project partners have been able to animate.

Criteria for inclusion in the project have actually been the subject of considerable debate within the team throughout. With a limit of 15 case studies and around 100 workshop participants it is difficult simultaneously to ensure good coverage of different firm sizes (EU itself recognizes three within the general rubric of 'SME'[5]), types of enterprise (since the EU rubric again does not insist on the common characterization of the profit-seeking independent enterprise which the term 'SME' immediately suggests to Anglo-Saxon ears) and four (as a minimum) kinds of ecosystem. This is before one even examines the kinds of goods and services offered by the firm, or its position in the supply chain. The team has, however, as discussed below, tried to use such constraints as a springboard for generating aspects of the research agenda.

The Emerging Research Agenda: Stimulated by Issues in the Case Studies

Table 5.1 mainly sets out the characteristics of the case firms from the first round of case writing, comprising eight organizations. The final row of Table 5.1 lists for each organization two important issues arising as a result of the case analysis. Some of these relate to general business issues as faced by any SME (for example seasonality; managing growth), whereas others relate to issues specific to those firms located in or near protected areas and/or otherwise sustainably engaging with biodiversity for profit (boundary effect issues, lack of specialist services (including finance), 'unfair' competition from less ecologically sensitive firms). There are – although not apparent from this table directly – some issues which, although common to all SMEs, are severely compounded by these firms engaging with biodiversity. For example, lack of continuity in EU policies as experienced by the Portuguese firm Imobiente is compounded by the industry in which it works – forestry – which has one of the longest product cycles found in *any* industry (Watkins, 2006).

However, although the case studies constitute the most intensive interaction between those on the project team and the SMEs, and are therefore likely to be the source of the deepest and most complex insights into the potential research agenda, they are by no means the only source. Team members have been compiling potential items from a variety of sources since the project began.

Emerging Research Agenda: Stimulated by Literature Review and Follow-through

Given that the ultimate objective of the Probioprise project is the establishment of a research agenda appropriate to the needs of the firms characterized in this chapter, it has been vital to record contributions towards this agenda as and when they are signalled at each stage of the project;

Table 5.1 Sample cases and issues identified

Firm	Heylen bvba	Koli National Park	Aranyponty Rt. Rétimajor Fish Farm & Eco-tourism	Field Fair	De Boerinn Farm	Taxus and Kolbon Sawmills	Imobiente
Location	Herentals, Belgium	Koli, North Karelia, Finland[1]	Sáregres-Rétimajor, Hungary[2]	Lower Danube Basin – Ukraine, Bulgaria, etc	Kamerik, The Netherlands	Malopolska, Poland	Albufeira, Portugal
Principal ecosystem	Forest + wetlands	Forest	Wetlands	Wetlands	Wetlands	Forest	Forest
Nature of business	Eco-sensitive contracting	National Park + economic development	Freshwater fish-farming, processing + angling and eco-tourism including accommodation, restaurant, health spa	Diversified, including investment funds + technical assistance to firms, NGOs etc.	Traditional wetlands farm + associated eco-tourism including farm sports	Timber processing + some downstream activities	Forest consultancy/management, including land reclamation and water management
Status/ownership	Private company set up for purpose	Infrastructure owned by Finnish state. Partners licensed to operate facilities. Spins-off	Private family business. Post-communist era successor to collective farm.	Private firm with overtly stated ecological role. Registered in UK but activities are	Family farm (held as two separate limited (b.v) companies)	Private firms with unlimited liability (spółka jawna – sp.j)	Private micro-firm

Size and scope	9 employees. Right at micro-firm/small firm transition point	independent SMEs as policy. Small core staff. Hotel staff + about 25 people in SMEs within park, plus many more in area surrounding	30 on main site; 70–80 FTE overall. Beginning to structure by activity.	in Eastern Europe Micro-firm. Creates employment in other firms	7 FT plus around 50 PT staff. Management structures in place	Taxus≈6 Kolbon≈40	2.5 FTE employees including owner. Many PT operatives on project basis, often in disadvantaged rural areas
Typical issues of concern	Managing growth Cheap competition from less eco-aware firms.	Institutionally anomalous Boundary effects on periphery of protected areas	Extra costs of operating in protected area. Low market premium for quality products	Credibility issues outside home country Lack of finance aimed at biodiversity firms	Over-regulation Seasonality	Access to finance for SMEs problematic. Quality advisory services lacking	Continuity of EU policies HRM issues

Notes:
1. For an extended discussion of this case see Watkins (2007).
2. For an extended discussion of this case see Watkins (2011).

they are then followed through to other phases. Thus the ongoing literature review (of which some of the introductory material in this chapter forms a part) suggests some areas where new knowledge is likely to be both appropriately generated through academic research *and* of value to the target firms. One example suggested in part by works cited above such as Pastakia (2002), Cohen and Winn (2007) and Dean and McMullen (2007), is the issue of the extent to which there is market failure in respect of the biodiversity services provided by SMEs. This is something which is being inducted into the case studies: thus the firm Imobiente has customers who provide positive externalities in the form of water management where they are nevertheless unable to capture (or completely capture) the economic benefits. However, another firm (which is the subject of a case not otherwise reported here: Nordic Shell, a seafood producer) has been able to construct and implement a business model where the improvement of water quality for its community also generates real economic value for the firm.[6] It is in this way that parts of the research agenda have been identified and developed.

Emerging Research Agenda: Stimulated by Definitions and Methodological Issues

Internal discussions relating to definitions, categorizations of firms and methodological issues have also directly generated useful research questions. Thus the issue of what constitutes an 'SME' in EU parlance – as noted above – leads directly to important questions regarding the extent to which business and ecological motivations can be co-resolved, and what constitutes an appropriate context for doing this (cf. Watkins, 2007). Consideration of these issues has led the team to engage more strongly with the social/community enterprise literature, which in turn has generated further appropriate research questions regarding the applicability and development of these strands of management research.

Emerging Research Agenda: Stimulated by Issues from the Workshops

The other main input into the research agenda has been to capture and analyse the issues emerging from discussion in the workshops. Although it was noted earlier that the approach to the whole study has been largely inductive, it would have been inappropriate for the team to have organized workshops which were totally unstructured. Thus, *inter alia*, a short checklist of headings within which more specific issues might be identified was developed (mainly on the basis of the business research expertise within the group, deriving from the business school participants), as a means of helping to capture research issues manifesting themselves in the first workshop. This list was as follows:

- typological/definitional (including eligibility criteria for EU and other support);
- motivational issues among environmental entrepreneurs specifically;
- organizational issues;
- customer/market threats/opportunities;
- supplier and logistical issues;
- position in supply chain;
- staffing beyond the entrepreneurial core;
- financial strength and sourcing finance;
- knowledge management (including absorptive capacity for new business expertise);
- scalability (and awareness of this);
- existence of networks/clusters of similar or interacting firms;
- use/need for common services (marketing, KM, etc.);
- role of public sector (at local, member state and EU level);
- economic factors;

Brief scrutiny of Table 5.2, which displays the outcomes from the first (and typical) workshop, shows that many of the issues which concern pro-diversity enterprises are similar or identical to SMEs in general. However, some of these are complicated by the multidimensional objectives which many of these firms seek to achieve. Consider just two of these.

It is not uncommon for an entrepreneur to establish a pro-diversity enterprise with environmental considerations predominating and the business being seen as a simple tool.[7] If the environmental objectives could be met more simply through other means (establishing an NGO, working in the public sector, and so on) then the business-as-tool might well be sacrificed. Even if it continues indefinitely, a motivation based on extreme satisficing behaviour may have implications for the extent to which public programmes should support such firms, whatever the apparent benefits. However, if others depend on the continued existence of the firm *qua* business entity, this could cause a range of problems in future with which public agencies might have to engage. Clearly the *milieu* in which some of these pro-diversity enterprises exist could create difficult problems for public support.

However, it would be very wrong to leave an impression that all proprietors of pro-diversity firms lack the motivation and expertise to be successful in business; many of the firms whose experiences informed Table 5.2 are innovative, profit-oriented businesses such as those which might be found in *any* sector. Their profitability may be constrained at present by a

*Table 5.2   Research issues emerging directly from a typical workshop
(forestry)*

A.	Typology etc	1. What is best level of aggregation in considering BD-based business since some firms work across ecologies?
		2. Are issues of ecological restitution different in kind at a business level from those of maintenance?
		3. BD-based business is a confusing concept for consumers. (BD-based businesses both cut trees/plant trees, etc). What are implications of this for mobilizing public opinion?
B.	Motivation	4. How do we balance eco motivation against business motivation?
		5. How big a problem is growth (since it *can* create greater role strain here than when eco motivation is absent)?
C.	Organization	6. Given that most – if not all – investment in maintenance of BD and all in the recreation of BD is derived from public funding in some way, what is the appropriate organizational form of 'SMEs'?
		7. Given that BD-based businesses exist in quasi-markets, what are implications for legal status and how do these vary across EU?
		8. How does this vary with historical background of member states? What are opportunities for inter-state learning on bilateral or EU basis?
		9. Given that most BD issues are long-term, is the SME, with known short-term time horizons, an appropriate policy instrument? If it is, how can issues of long vs. short-termism be identified and resolved?
D.	Customers/ markets	10. To what extent are opportunities for sustainable exploitation of BD compromised by *non*-sustainable exploitation by others?
		11. Certification/labelling seems important, but *how* do customers value labelling? E.g. Is mental map to pay premium for ecologically sound products or to pay less for products that are not? (Needs detailed level consumer behaviour research)
		12. What would be the technical and legal bases of any BD labelling scheme?
E.	Suppliers	13. No issues identified at this point.
F.	Staffing	14. What are specific training needs/how should these be delivered? How can they be best financed? Do we need to pay people to train if time is spent away from firm?
		15. Is there evidence that the capital/labour trade-off is different in BD-friendly firms, intrinsically and/or by choice? What are implications for this? Does this vary between member states?
G.	Financial strength and sourcing	16. If loans are at a commercial rate, *why* is a special fund required?
		17. Is the timing of investment/cash flow affected in a BD-based business compared with a 'normal' one? If so, how? How can this be managed?
		18. What are implications of having to use much more specialized equipment (e.g. low-impact machinery) in terms of amount and term of finance?

Table 5.2   (continued)

	19.	In general, not just regarding SMEs and/or BD, should there be greater consideration of EU forestry policy since the time frames are so long? (Importance *re* carbon fixing; future energy resources, etc)
H. Knowledge management including absorptive capacity of new business expertise	20.	How do we communicate necessary information/impart knowledge to BD active/potentially active SMEs (who are severely time/resource constrained)?
I. Scalability and awareness of this	21.	Are typical BD-based businesses scalable or, by their very nature, apparently constrained to remain small?
	22.	Do existing business models and processes exist to overcome this?
J. Position in supply chain	23.	Is certification system common throughout chain? Should it be?
	24.	Does this vary by ecosystem?
K. Existence of networks/ clusters	25.	In forestry long time scales and geographical isolation may contribute to weak networking. If true, how can this be redressed?
L. Use/need for common services (marketing, KM, etc.)	26.	To what extent are SMEs aware of *general* issues facing them? (not just *re* BD-based business issues, but SME problems generally)
	27.	How can common services best be developed and marketed to SMEs? (BD a lower priority than directly profit-related issues, so these need to be fixed first).
M. Role of public sector in member states and EU	28.	What should role(s) of public sector be?
	29.	How should this be split between different levels of government (subsidiarity issue)?
	30.	Levers include taxation, subsidy, regulation and certification. What else is possible? What should the balance be?
N. Economic factors	31.	Can a market in BD be established (cf. carbon emission trading)?
	32.	What are the circumstances under which BD may be 'marketized'?
	33.	How big is the 'market' for BD likely to be? Can we extrapolate from existing local pilot studies?

failure to capture the full benefits of the ecological services they provide, but they are keenly aware of this and often surprisingly anxious to seek out market mechanisms to do this rather than relying on soft loans or other state support. There are clearly emerging opportunities, for example in cooperative action for direct marketing, sustainability certification and elsewhere, that could be business-rather than public sector-led, at least in the medium term.

For the Probioprise team at present the most important thing is that the emerging research agenda can be speedily completed and made available to pro-diversity enterprises for comment. Hopefully, in the light of their feedback, there will exist a research agenda that a large number of BD-based businesses feel they can 'own'. If so, this will have been a relatively rare example of successfully engaging SMEs in Mode Two research. . .but could well become a useful model for the future both in environmental entrepreneurship and elsewhere in the Framework Programme.

NOTES

1. 'Probioprise: creating a European platform for SMEs and other stakeholders to develop a research programme for pro-biodiversity business', *Framework 6* Priority 1.1.6.3 Global Change and Ecosystems, SSA #018356.
2. Probably most true of the UK and Nordic countries.
3. For example, the forestry workshop was co-hosted by METLA, the Finnish Forest Research Institute; the grasslands workshop was held in Croatia in association with Žumberak-Samborsko Gorje Nature Park.
4. European Economic Area. Broadly, these countries are economically integrated with the EU without subscribing to the aspect of political integration that membership would entail. Switzerland and Norway are important members of this group.
5. This is based on numbers employed. Less than 10 are called micro-firms; up to 50 are small firms, and above that are medium-sized firms. The main rationale for this is that the different sizes will have different organizational characteristics.
6. In essence there is an 'off-set' for the fixation of nitrogen run-off analogous in some ways to a carbon sequestration off-set.
7. It has long been recognized that entrepreneurship may be an instrumental strategy for the continued pursuit of non-economic motivations or specific technical activities rather than a rational economic choice. (*e.g.* Watkins, 1973).

REFERENCES

Aldrich, H. (2000), 'Learning together: national differences in entrepreneurship research', in D.L. Sexton and H. Landström (eds), *The Blackwell Handbook of Entrepreneurship*, Oxford: Blackwell: pp. 5–25.

Aldrich, H.E. and T. Baker (1997), 'Blinded by the cites? Has there been progress in entrepreneurship research?', in D.L. Sexton and R.W. Smilor (eds), *Entrepreneurship 2000*, Chicago: Upstart Publishing Company: pp. 377–400.

Anderson, A.R. (1998), 'Cultivating the garden of Eden: environmental entrepreneuring', *Journal of Organisational Change Management*, **11**(2), 135–43.

Banks, M.C. and S. Taylor (1991), 'Developing an entrepreneur- and small business owner-defined research agenda', *Journal of Small Business Management*, **29**(2), 10–18.

Bennett, S.J. (1991), *Ecopreneuring: The Complete Guide to Small Business Opportunities from the Environmental Revolution*, New York: John Wiley.

Bergstrom, F. (2000), 'Capital subsidies and the performance of firms', *Small Business Economics*, **14** (3), 183–193.

Berle, G. (1991), *The Green Entrepreneur: Business Opportunities that can Save the Earth and Make You Money*, Blue Ridge Summit, PA: Liberty Hall Press.

Bishop, J., S. Kapila, F. Hicks and P. Mitchell (2006), 'Building biodiversity business: report of a scoping study', International Union for Conservation of Nature, IUCN/Shell.

Blackburn, R., M. Hart and D. Smallbone (2005), 'Regulation, regulation, regulation: Understanding the effects on entrepreneurship and small business performance', paper presented at the RENT XIX Conference: 'Entrepreneurship, Competitiveness and Local Development', Naples: Edizioni Scientifiche Italiane for University of Naples Federico II, with EIASM and ECSB.

Bovaird, T., L. Hems and M. Tricker (1995), 'Market failures in the provision of finance and in business services for small and medium sized enterprises', in R. Buckland and E.W. Davis (eds), *Finance for Growing Enterprises*, London: Routledge: pp. 13–39.

British Academy of Management (2002), Special Research Forum on Mode 2 Knowledge Production: 'Exploring practice-oriented research approaches', Summary Materials, Glasgow, March.

Brockhaus, R.H. (1988), 'Entrepreneurial research: are we playing the correct game?', *American Journal of Small Business*, **11**(3), 55–61.

Busenitz, L.W., G. Page West, D. Shepherd, T. Nelson, G.N. Chandler, and A. Zacharakis (2003), 'Entrepreneurship in emergence: past trends and future directions', Special Issue on Entrepreneurship of *Journal of Management*, **29**(3), 285–308.

Clark, S.H. (1987), *Farmers as Entrepreneurs: Regulation and Innovation*, Connecticut: Brown University.

Cohen, B. and M.I. Winn (2007), 'Market imperfections, opportunity and sustainable entrepreneurship', *Journal of Business Venturing*, **22**(1), 29–49.

Dean, T.J. and J.S. McMullen (2007), 'Toward a theory of sustainable entrepreneurship: reducing environmental degradation through entrepreneurial action', *Journal of Business Venturing*, **22**(1), 50–76.

Fischetti, M. (1992), 'Green entrepreneurs', *Technology Review*, **5**(3), 38–45.

Gibbons, M., C. Limoges, H. Nowotny, S. Schwartzman, P. Scott and M. Trow (1994), *The New Production of Knowledge: The Dynamics of Science and Research in Contemporary Societies*, London: Sage.

Hinloopen, J. (2004), 'The market for knowledge brokers', *Small Business Economics*, **22**(5), 407–415.

Hitchens, D., J. Clausen, M. Trainor, M. Keil and S. Thankappan (2003), 'Competitiveness, environmental performance and management of SMEs', *Greener Management International*, **44** (Winter), 45–57.

Hitchens, D., S. Thankappan, M. Trainor, J. Clausen and B. de Marchi (2005), 'Environmental performance, competitiveness and management of small businesses in Europe', *Tijdschrift voor Economische en Sociale Geografie*, **96**(5), 541–57.

Isaak, R. (1998), *Green Logic: Ecopreneurship, Theory and Ethics*, Sheffield: Greenleaf Publishing.

Isaak, R. (2002). 'The making of the ecopreneur', *Greener Management International*, **38** (Summer), 81–91.

Keogh, P.D. and M.J. Polonsky (1998), 'Environmental commitment: a basis for environmental entrepreneurship?', *Journal of Organisational Change Management*, **11**(1), 38–48.

Kollberg, S. (2000), *The Swedish Mussel Industry*, Gothenburg: Swedish Aquaculture Association.

Lindahl, O., R. Hart et al. (2005), 'Improving marine water quality by mussel farming: a profitable solution', *Ambio*, **34**(2), 131–138.

Linnanen, L. (2002), 'An insider's experiences with environmental entrepreneurship', *Greener Management International*, **38** (Summer), 71–80.

Nowotny, H., P. Scott and M. Gibbons (2001), *Re-Thinking Science: Knowledge and the Public in an Age of Uncertainty*, Cambridge: Polity Press.

Pastakia, A. (1998), 'Grass-roots ecopreneurs: change agents for a sustainable society', *Journal of Organisational Change Management*, **11**(2), 157–70.

Pastakia, A. (2002), 'Assessing ecopreneurship in the context of a developing country: the case of India', *Greener Management International*, **38** (Summer), 93–108.

Randjelovic, J., A.R. O'Rourke, and R.J. Orsato (2003), 'The emergence of green venture capital', *Business Strategy and the Environment*, **12**(4), 240–53.

Schaltegger, S. (2002), 'A framework for ecopreneurship: leading bioneers and environmental managers to ecopreneurship', *Greener Management International*, **38** (Summer), 45–58.

Schaper, M. (2002), 'The essence of ecopreneurship: introduction to special issue on environmental entrepreneurship', *Greener Management International*, **38** (Summer), 26–30.

Seidl, I., O. Schelske, J. Joshi and M. Jenny (2003), 'Entrepreneurship in biodiversity conservation and regional development', *Entrepreneurship and Regional Development*, **15**(4), 333–50.

Sharfman, M.P., M. Meo and R.T. Ellington (2000), 'Regulation, business, and sustainable development: the antecedents of environmentally conscious technological innovation', *American Behavioral Scientist*, **44**(2), 277–02.

Storey, D.J. (1994), *Understanding the Small Business Sector*, London: Routledge.

Verstraete, T. (2002), 'Essai sur la singularité de l'entreprenariat comme domaine de recherche', Association pour la Diffusion de la Recherche sur l'Entrepreneuriat et la Gestion, les éditions de l'ADREG, available at: http://asso.nordnet.fr/adreg/ADREG1.htm.

Verstraete, T. (2003), 'On the singularity of entrepreneurship as a research domain', in D.S. Watkins (ed.), *Annual Review of Progress in Entrepreneurship Research, 2000/2001*, Brussels: European Foundation for Management Development: pp. 10–65.

Volery, T. (2002), 'An entrepreneur commercialises conservation: the case of Earth Sanctuaries Ltd', *Greener Management International*, **38** (Summer), 109–16.

Walsh, J.P. (2007/8), 'Program chair's remarks: the questions we ask', AoM 2008 Annual Conference Invitation, available at Academy of Management website, http://meeting.aomonline.org/2008/index.php?option=com_content&task=view&id=1&ltemid=63, accessed November 2010.

Watkins, D. (1973), 'Technical entrepreneurship: a cisatlantic view', *R&D Management*, **3**(2), 65–70.

Watkins, D. (2006), 'Involving entrepreneurs in designing and developing the EU research agenda: ecopreneurs in the EU's framework programme', in U. Fueglistaller, T. Volery and W. Weber (eds), *Rencontres de St-Gall 2006: Understanding the Regulatory Climate for Entrepreneurship and SMEs*, Wildhaus,

Switzerland: Swiss Research Institute of Small Business and Entrepreneurship, University of St. Gallen (KMU-HSG).

Watkins, D. (2007), 'Koli National Park: incubation for regional economic development and environmental protection through multi-level Entrepreneurship', paper presented at Annual Babson College Entrepreneurship Research Conference, Madrid, June.

Watkins, D. (2011), 'From obsolescent fish farm to developing ecotourism destination: the Aranyponty ('Golden Corp') fishponds complex in rural Hungary', in D.V.L. Macleod and S.A. Gillespie (eds), *Sustainable Tourism in Rural Europe: Approaches to Development*, Abingdon, UK: Routledge, pp. 181–95.

Watkins, D. and D. Reader (2003), 'Quantitative research on entrepreneurship as a field of study: what do we know? What should we know?', paper presented at 17th Annual RENT Conference, Lodz, Poland: European Institute for Advanced Studies in Management/European Council for Small Business, November.

APPENDIX: A CONTEXTUALIZING CASE –
NORDIC SHELL AS (PRODUCING
MUSSELS WHILE DELIVERING
ENVIRONMENTAL SERVICES)[1]

There is a traditional saying in Yorkshire, England: 'Where there's muck there's brass'. 'Brass' is the local word for money, and although what we think of as money has evolved over the years, people still share a common understanding of the term. 'Muck', however, is a different matter. As societies have evolved, as different material inputs have changed in rela-tive value, and as the by-products from different production processes altered, what we think of as 'muck' has been dramatically transformed. We may no longer collect household urine for tanning, nor do we often scrape horse manure off our streets for fertilizer, but we are now familiar with markets for carbon emitted by industrial processes, and demand that new cars be disassembled at the end of their working lives for their components to be recycled. Clearly, those Yorkshire men knew a thing or two.

Philosophizing about the changing nature of pollution may seem a strange place to start discussion of a firm which produces a pure foodstuff in some of the cleanest waters in Europe; but as we shall see, there is a vital business link – without which this interesting start-up firm may not have come into existence anywhere near as easily.

Nordic Shell's Business

Nordic Shell's business model is to produce high quality shellfish while simultaneously delivering environmental services. Although the latter contribute only a small amount to turnover and profitability, they are absolutely essential to the company's plans, since they enable it to operate in locations which might otherwise be precluded.

Nordic Shell Holding AS was established in 2003. This is the holding company for two other firms which produce, or will produce, shellfish. Nordic Shell Production AB is located at Lysekil in Sweden, and Nordic Shell Production AS is located at Fredrikstad in Norway, where the holding company is also incorporated. The Lysekil company was incor-porated in 2006, but the group has been producing shellfish at this site on an experimental basis since 2005. At present, and for the foreseeable future, the only shellfish in production at Lysekil are blue mussels (*Mytilus edulis*). The major part of this case therefore focuses on that part of the group's activities.

Bivalves and the Suppression of Eutrophication

Mussels are bivalves. As such, they feed by sucking in large quantities of water, filtering out the micro-organisms which sustain them, and excreting mainly the residual water. Typically, mussels grow by filtering out the algae from the water in which they live. Although the blue mussel may not appear to be a large creature, each one typically 'processes' around five litres of seawater per hour. Within reason, the more algae the water contains, the faster the mussels grow.

The term 'processes' here is used deliberately since it characterizes the way that Nordic Shell thinks about its mussels. For this company, mussels are not just a nutritious and delicious foodstuff but also a way of removing algae from seawater – and hence reducing the levels of the nitrogen and phosphorus nutrients on which the algae themselves depend. The significance of this is that an oversupply of such nutrients can cause real problems for oxygen-dependent aquatic life forms such as fish, through a process known as eutrophication (excessive plant growth followed by oxygen depletion). However, as the mussels grow they reduce the likelihood of eutrophication by controlling the algae on which they feed.

In the absence of mussels – or some other organism which feeds on algae – increasing fertilizer run-off from farming, managed lawns and sewage often means that bodies of water such as lakes and estuaries receive excess nutrients that stimulate excessive plant growth (algae, periphyton attached algae, and so on). This is often called an algal bloom. When the dead plant material from the bloom sinks and decomposes, this reduces dissolved oxygen in the water. Water with a low concentration of dissolved oxygen is known as hypoxic, and when it reaches this state fish and other organisms which rely on dissolved oxygen can thus die of suffocation.

Eutrophication of inland and inshore waters is an increasing problem in Europe as populations have grown and farming has become more intensive. This has led to extensive research on the issue and, as we shall see, action at the EU and national level to counteract the problem. The particular insight which Nordic Shell had was – to use that old business strategy cliché – to turn this problem into an opportunity.

The Origins of the Business

The roots of the business lie in an EU Interreg project on blue mussels and nitrogen quotas which ran from 2002–2004. This was a relatively large-scale project ($\approx$€1m) and had partners from both Norway and Sweden. These included Østfold Bærekrafitge Utvikling AS (N) which was the 'promoter' of the project, the Kristineberg Marine Research Institute of the Royal Swedish Scientific Academy and Universities of Stockholm and Gothenburg (S), the Tjærnø Marine Biological Laboratory Institute of the University of Gothenburg (S) and the Lysekil Municipality (S). The focus was to examine the concentration of nitrogen in the Skagerrak,[2] the body of water which divides Norway, Sweden and Denmark, and its relation to algal, and hence bivalve, growth. The stimulant for this was a series of EU Urban Waste Water Treatment Directives.[3] These mandated the reduction of urban nitrogen and phosphorus effluents by 70 per cent in communes of more than 10 000 people – but implementation had been slow and patchy. Sweden takes pride in being a leader in environmental matters and was concerned to be in the forefront of implementing this directive, using novel approaches that could become models elsewhere if possible. It had determined to implement the directive by 1998, but little was done in practice. It was already known that nitrogen levels were increasing rapidly in the waters off this part of Sweden because the University of Gothenburg had long maintained a research station in the area and had noted that plant growth had doubled over the past 50 years. On a more practical level, local mussel farmers already knew that certain locations were much more productive than others, but had no scientific explanation of why this should be so, and thus no means to determine rationally where new beds should be established. There appeared to be a possibility of reducing the nitrogen levels in the water by expanding shell fish production in carefully identified sites rather than using land-based chemical treatments to reduce the nitrogen levels in discharged water. Given that the market for mussels in Europe is strong, the more environmentally sensitive nitrogen reduction regime could in addition produce high quality foodstuffs and generate employment locally: a win–win situation.[4]

The Nordic Shell Team

The Norwegian foundation Østfold Bærekrafitge Utvikling AS, the promoter of the Interreg project, and Nordic Shell Holding AS are linked through the person of Ulf Syversen, who established them both. Ulf Syversen's background is in chemistry and the commercialization of natural resources on a sustainable basis. He has worked for several Norwegian research institutes and companies, including Norsk Hydro, where his task was to find new business development projects. Here he began to specialize in obtaining the permissions and licences needed for exploiting natural resources, including water, and this led naturally to an interest in water quality issues. Ulf used his wide range of industrial and technical contacts to put together the Interreg project in the hope that this might confirm his suspicion that a commercial opportunity existed through the combination of water treatment and mussel production in and around the Gullmar Fjord and elsewhere in the Skagerrak. Nordic Shell was established to take advantage of the opportunity.

The other key person in Nordic Shell is Bernt Asbjørnsen. Bernt is Marketing Director of Nordic Shell. His background complements Ulf's well, since he has a marketing background in seafood and experience as a lobbyist in Brussels. Much of his market knowledge relates to salmon farming and aquaculture generally. Like Ulf he is innovative and entre-preneurial, and currently has interests in another business which trades in derivatives linked to markets for fish such as salmon. Between them the two directors have very detailed knowledge of their industry and strong networks covering the technical, legal and marketing aspects of the business they have entered.

In addition to the directors there are currently 10 employees, a produc-tion manager responsible for six people involved in direct production, a salesperson and two drivers. Most of the work is relatively unskilled and relates mainly to taking care not to crush the products. Training is left to the production manager. Three of the current employees are women. As production expands in the summer of 2007 another ten employees will be taken on to tie in the ropes that the mussels grow on. Probably most of these will be female.

The Start-up Phase

Two of the most difficult aspects of starting any new business are raising finance and securing the first income-generating order. In the case of aquaculture there is the added problem of securing a suitable site against objections from other potential users of the preferred site.

Mussel farming in Norway has a history of failure, so any pitch for finance was likely to be difficult. Also, in moving from the Interreg project, which can be seen as the R&D phase of the development of Nordic Shell, the business itself was unproven, as indeed was the upside potential. In such a situation it would have been easy to give away too great a propor-tion of the firm to early investors and to lose control. Ulf was keen to avoid this, and so employed an advisor to identify a large number of small investors. About 30 per cent of the shares were sold in this way to about 50 investors.[5] About €1.5m was raised in this way. Additional funding of €0.5m came from the Norwegian government.[6] The EU also contributed 20 per cent of the total project funding.

Gullmar Fjord has ideal locations for mussel production, with a growing cycle of 12–15 months. Prior to the waste directive it would have been very unlikely that licences to site the beds so close to shore would have been granted. The difficulty of obtaining licences under normal circumstances is reflected in the rate at which they are rising in price. In Sweden, licenses for inshore fish farming typically cost €700 000 in 2002; today it costs €3–4 million for a similar production site, assuming it is possible to identify one and overcome objections. There are nature reserves and marine reserves in and around the area, although the site itself is outside these. Nevertheless, this is a well-known and popular area of outstanding natural beauty where the competing interests of leisure sailors and environmental objections to perceived 'eyesores' would previously have been too great.[7] The EU directive, however, together with the detailed evidence from the Interreg project, changed all this. The Lysekil local authority was given a clear choice: invest in onshore facilities to remove nitrogen contamination, or – for about one third of the price – let the water run off into the fjord and contract with Nordic Shell to remove the nitrogen as mussels. The initial contract is to remove 39 000 kilos (39MT) of Nitrogen as 3 300MT of mussels. Lysekil has agreed to pay 50 per cent of the cost each year up front, with the balance becoming due when 50 per cent of the total has been harvested.[8]

From the point of view of Nordic Shell this will be a small element in its total income when the Gullmar Fjord mussel beds are at full capacity,[9] but in the start-up phase this income stream goes some way to reducing the cash-flow needs of the emergent firm. Moreover, because of the environmental benefits of the scheme, Nordic Shell has been able to place the beds close to the shore where the conditions for mussel production are optimum, without creating substantial local objections.

Lysekil for its part has solved its problem of nitrogen-rich waste water at a lower cost and without unsightly onshore processing facilities. Moreover, by adopting a natural solution to the nitrogen removal rather than a chemical one, some phosphorus is also removed.[10] Above all, the municipality is able to display its green credentials by entering into a contract with Nordic Shell which is believed to be the first 'Nitrogen Quota' agreement in the world. This is likely to be not only a reputational benefit to Lysekil but a practical one in terms of increased visitor numbers. Extra employment has also been generated, and more jobs will be created as Nordic Shell expands.

The Market for Mussels

Much of the above would be purely academic if no market for mussels existed, or if it were in decline. In practice, mussel production worldwide is declining slightly even as demand continues to increase. European production is also down: from 90 000MT at its peak to 35 000MT in Holland, 90 000MT to 40 000MT in Denmark, with static or declining production in Ireland and France. One reason for this is that mussels are a cool water organism and their seeds begin to die at around 23°C. The tasty bivalve *Mytilus edulis* is becoming an early casualty of global warming.

The total EU market for mussels is about 800 000 tonnes per year. At the European level competition is intense, but determined principally on taste. This is particularly true of the Benelux market, which accounts for around 100 000MT a year. The French market is bigger, at 130 000MT, but less discerning. At tastings in Antwerp and elsewhere with leading industry buyers the reaction to the Swedish mussels has been very positive.

Small farmers predominate in Denmark and Ireland particularly, and there have been few attempts at branding. Formerly it was not even possible to state unambiguously where a mussel came from, since seeds were transported from one country to another to be fattened up. However, tighten regulations have meant that it is now difficult to move mussels even within the same country. Given Nordic Shell's potential to deliver many thousands of tonnes of high quality mussels from closely related sites, there is an obvious opportunity for branding.

With the exception of a small market for mussels in ready meals, the shellfish are usually sold alive to the end consumer. Different markets are used to buying in different quantities: for example, they are bought in small bags in Oslo but in large ones in Holland. The expectation is that not all the shellfish will survive and that dead ones must be discarded. In Holland the final yield averages 70 per cent. Alive to these constraints, Berndt has been experimenting with different kinds of packaging and promotional materials. He has come up with a superior bag containing 2 kilos of mussels, which is delivering a higher yield of 85+ per cent. This is branded 'Moules de Scandanavie' and has pictures of the fjord where the mussels are currently sourced. This cleverly combines the fact that French is the language of gastronomy while emphasizing the wholesome image of Scandinavian waters. Saying 'Scandanavie' leaves open the possibility that mussels will also be produced on the Norwegian side of the border – Nordic shell aims eventually for a 50:50 production split. The packaging furthermore emphasizes that these are *moules de cordes*, since rope-grown mussels are considered the best.

The brand values are thus about a high-quality gastronomic experience of wholesome foods. Deliberately excluded is any specifically 'green' sales pitch. Consumers are not made aware that the mussels they consume are the result of a pioneering nitrogen quota agreement and that 'their' mussels have played a key part in recycling Swedish sewage and fertilizer run-off!

Seafood Toxins and their Control

Omitting the water cleaning aspects of the mussels in the Nordic Shell 'story' is perhaps not surprising given the bad press that shellfish have had over the years for causing stomach upsets and worse. Today there is, in principle, a very strict regime to control the presence of toxins in seafood, with the food safety of mussels regulated in the EU by Directive 91/492EEC.

The main problem facing commercial mussel farming in Sweden is the occurrence of algal toxins, especially diarrhoeic shellfish poisoning (DSP), caused by diarrhoeic shellfish toxins, DST. The major toxins are okadaic acid (OA) and a number of structurally related acids (DTX-1, DTX-2, DTX-3). Herein the problems for mussels farmers begin. Although 91/492EEC is intended to harmonize the toxicity legislation, the interpretation varies from country to country, partly as a result of new scientific knowledge which has emerged since the directive was promulgated. Thus the Swedish legislation allows a maximum of 160 microgrammes of OA equivalents per kilo of mussel meat. It counts OA and DTX-1 towards this total, but discounts DTX-2 and DTX-3. In some countries DTX-2 is included. Germany already does so and Norway is evaluating this. Nordic Shell argues that the limits are anyway extremely cautious and if DTX-2 is to be included, the limit should be raised to 250 microgrammes of OA equivalents per kilo.

Three tests for OA and related compounds are used. Feeding to mice is the only direct test of toxicity; but there are two additional chemical tests. If mussels are found to be over the limit it does not mean they need to be disposed of, since bivalves can clean themselves of toxins, given time. One way is to lower the ropes to greater depths at the same site. Another is to move to another location at sea. A third, and most expensive option is to bring the mussels onshore into detoxification tanks. However, it has been argued that there is insufficient knowledge about the factors that influence the rate of elimination or the best ways in which to achieve this in practice.[11]

These are factors which influence all shellfish producers since regular testing is mandatory and toxins will at some point become a problem for even the best-managed farms because of the uncontrolled nature of the oceans. Nordic Shell is better placed than most to deal with this issue, although it resents the amount of paperwork involved in certifying the quality of its products! Because of Ulf's background and the close links with scientific institutes developed through Interreg and in other ways, Ulf says that the firm is: 'Not at the top of the knowledge curve, but better placed than any other commercial producer to respond appropriately.'

It would be wrong to make too much of the problems faced by shellfish producers. Bivalves are not only tasty and nutritious, they are also very robust. In most cases it is possible to negate the potential effects of a toxic algal bloom by simply lowering the ropes by a further metre or so. And of course, the potential for a bloom is anyway much reduced by the presence of substantial mussel beds straining out the algae at a rate of five litres per hour before a problem develops. Indeed, the mussels are also resistant to that other great fear of inshore fisheries – oil spillage. Tests have shown that the oil only affects the top metre of so of the sea. Lowering the beds by a metre or so avoids any problems, and this is built into the production process as a means of avoiding toxic blooms.

Biodiversity Impacts

This business has clear implications for conservation, but they are indirect. By preventing eutrophication, much sea life is preserved which would otherwise have been killed off unnecessarily by human actions. However, the species involved are not threatened, and the effects on biodiversity are therefore not particularly important.

Indirectly, by improving water quality, other sea life is attracted to the area around and underneath the beds, seeking a source of food. This includes lobsters, langoustines, crabs, flatfish, birds, ducks and cod. In future it may be possible to harvest some of these other creatures. Nordic Shell performs monitoring and research on the environment, including biodiversity, around their production site throughout the entire year, over and above the minimum required by law. They also monitor what is happening on the sea bed below the beds, using cameras.

The other major indirect effect is the existence of an operating nitrogen quota agreement. This could provide a model for many other sites, including those where biodiversity conservation is a much more pressing issue.

Future Plans and Developments

Although Nordic Shell looks poised to become one of the largest mussel producers in Europe, it will still account for only a small proportion of the market. There are additional markets which are as yet barely touched to the east. Here it might be possible to piggy-back export sales on existing distribution systems for Swedish salmon, and Berndt's networks would be invaluable here.

There is also a possibility of harvesting some of the other species which live below the beds and feed on the mussels' detritus. These include crab and lobster. However, there is ample scope for expanding the core business of mussel production in association with environmental services over the next few years, and this remains the main concern of Nordic Shell.

Issues Raised

The successful negotiation of a ground-breaking nitrogen quota agreement is by far the most important issue to emerge from this case. It is a very clear example of the way in which an innovative SME can be formed which helps meet the Lisbon and Gothenburg objectives simultaneously. We have here a win–win situation for the SME and its local community as well as a win–win project in terms of helping to deliver key EU objectives.

The fact that the firm arose from knowledge gained during an Interreg project also shows how skilful exploitation of EU funds can be used to drive this process.

In terms of future research, the case may give hints about how other eco-benefits might be marketized beyond nitrogen removal. Possibly phosphorus removal is the next eco-service that will become amenable to negotiated quotas in the way that nitrogen now has. These models may prove useful in the much more demanding search for 'valuing' biodiversity itself. Detailed studies of the way in which carbon quotas/trading have evolved, and nitrogen quotas are developing, may assist this process.

On the negative side, the slow and uneven adoption of the Urban Waste Water Treatment Directive (91/271/EEC, amended 98/15/EC) demonstrates that even carefully targeted EU policies and laws are not enough to stimulate innovation unless they are systematically adopted and enforced by national governments.

At a more detailed level there is also ambiguity in the way that national governments interpret rules such as those that affect shellfish safety. This is much more likely to be a case of unclear and rapidly developing scientific knowledge than of governments using technical regulations to attempt back-door protectionism. However, for the operating SME the effects are the same. What should be a Single European Market (SEM) is, at the margin, fragmented by technical obstacles which are expensive and time-consuming for an individual SME to contest. More research is needed on the practical problems which prevent the real world completion of the SEM as it affects the pro-biodiversity SME.

Finally, the case hints at the problems facing firms that might want to present a truly green marketing face to the world rather than engage in simply 'greenwashing'. Nordic Shell has a very interesting environmental story to tell, but feels this would be counterproductive in marketing terms. A thoroughgoing study of green marketing by SMEs, carefully separating the rhetoric from the reality, is urgently needed, or there may be a backlash against ecologically sound production.

Notes

1. This case was prepared by Professor David Watkins of Southampton Business School, SSU, UK and Suzanne Tom of Fauna and Flora International, UK on the basis of an extended visit to the business concerned and other materials provided by the firm. Additional input has been provided by other members of the Probioprise Project Team. Opinions expressed are those of the authors and do not necessarily represent the views of the firm or any other parties.
2. And in particular on the Gullmar Fjord.
3. 91/271/EEC, amended 98/15/EC.
4. A review of some of the scientific and economic considerations is given in Odd Lindahl et al. (2005).
5. Minority investors in unquoted SMEs are in a weak position to influence a business. In practice, Nordic Shell's controlling director is now seeking to buy out these small shareholders.
6. Note that this was from Norway rather than Sweden, despite the fact that the first production site of Nordic Shell is in Sweden. Since the operating company is on the Swedish side of the border, it was possible to get export subsidies for Norwegian-produced equipment. This factor, and a somewhat more permissive licensing regime, determined the initial preferred location as being in Sweden rather than Norway, although expansion into Norwegian waters is planned in future. A Norwegian registered production company, Nordic Shell Production AS, exists but is currently dormant.
7. In practice, three kinds of licence are required for aquaculture in Sweden. One relates to the volume of fish harvested, one to environmental compliance and one from the owner of the shoreline, who has jurisdiction over activities up to 300m offshore. In Norway the situation is similar, but the defining distance is only 1.5m.
8. Although it is difficult to make precise comparisons since local circumstances are so variable, chemical nitrogen removal costs in the range of 150–250 SEK/kilo whereas biological removal is estimated to cost in the range of 25–40 SEK/kilo (€1≈ 9SEK).
9. The licence is for 9000MT of mussels to be harvested at Lysekil. The effective production capacity of the existing site is nearer to 7000MT. In 2005, 40MT of mussels were harvested as part of the experimentation on site. In 2006 a 'real' harvest of 900MT was extracted, with inventory then standing at 3000MT. This was enough for sales development to begin. In 2007 the harvest is projected to be 3500MT, rising to 6000MT in 2008.
10. They do not pay for this phosphorus removal, although Nordic Shell may seek to charge clients for this, too, in future. By using mussels, some phosphorus is removed along with the nitrogen since the ratio in the bivalve's body mass is constant at 40:16:1 for C, N and P, respectively.
11. Kollberg (2000).

6. The third sector in action: a cross-border partnership in the Western Balkans

Jovo Ateljevic

INTRODUCTION

This chapter explains how an NGO (non-governmental organization) engages in activities of social and institutional entrepreneurship. In this study, tourism provides the empirical context in the cross-border regional tourism development of the eastern part of the Republika Srpska[1] (RS), BiH (Bosnia and Herzegovina) and western Serbia. The region, known as the Drina Valley Tourism Region (DVTR), encompasses eight municipalities, four from each side of the Drina river, which forms the border between the two countries. The regional economy is strongly dependent upon agriculture and a few tourism activities with good prospects for innovative tourism development. One of the main problems facing all the municipalities is negative population growth and an increasing number of younger people permanently leaving the region. The area also provides a specific political and historical context due to its dynamic history associated with perpetuated ethnic and religious struggles amongst the communities[2] along the river since the Ottoman invasion in the fifteenth century. The dissolution of the former Yugoslavia followed by the civil war in the early 1990s revived the historical tensions that had been controlled in the former Yugoslavia. In such a context, BiH and Serbia, and particularly their periphery, which is characterized by parochial thinking combined with the legacy of the former system in which everything was centrally planned, any new initiative or disturbance of traditional thinking is an increasingly challenging task (see for example, DiMaggio, 1988). In this light, any major changes would require a large amount of both entrepreneurial and social skills. Creating new practice and institutional infrastructure is essentially an example of institutional and social entrepreneurship as it relates to alteration of existing practices (see, for example, Maguire et al., 2004) in order to add economic and social values to the local communities through tourism development. The process of a sustainable regional tourism development in complex socio-political contexts is not well understood; therefore a number of questions need to be asked. Who instigates the process? How is the process negotiated and maintained? Who gets involved in the process and how are decisions made? In this study, apart from addressing these questions, the author has been particularly interested in the role played by the international NGO, Social Solutions, and its ability to facilitate the process of this cross-border sustainable tourism development.

Our empirical investigation is limited to the international NGO sector that is regarded as the main force in institutional capacity-building (ICB) (Thomson and Pepperdine, 2003). ICB refers to a provision of technical or material assistance to strengthen one or more elements of organizational effectiveness, including governance, management capacity, human resources, financial resources, service delivery, external relations and sustainability. The concept of ICB is also associated with building civil society or democratization. Building organizational and institutional capacity is an essential development intervention towards the strengthening of civil society. Indeed, it is the heart of development practice. International and indigenous NGOs and many governments in developing countries recognize the importance of capacity-building for development (James, 1994). Collectively and separately, the elements of capacity are often thought of as assets, or 'capital', which, in the context of capacity-building, refers to 'human capital', the knowledge and skills of people (as individuals) (Thomson and Pepperdine, 2003). Thus, capacity-building relates to a range of activities by which individuals, groups and organizations improve their capacity to achieve sustainable development, which is often associated with the empowerment and mobilization of local communities.

The ultimate aim of this chapter is threefold. First, the chapter explains how NGOs engaged in entrepreneurship through social capacity-building (SCB) help local communities to convert their economic and social weaknesses into strengths. Secondly, it provides essential conceptual understanding of social and other capacity-building, regional (tourism) development and institutional/social entrepreneurship through negotiation between a multiplicity of stakeholders within a complex political structure from both sides of the Drina river. And thirdly, the chapter identifies and explains the complexity of the regional development process burden by various internal and external political influences as well as personal interests by the key actors.

METHODOLOGY

The chapter is based on empirical material collected during the process of the cross-border tourism development, initially named the Drina Valley Tourism Region (DVTR).

Tourism development, which provides the context for this study, has particular significance and it presents methodological opportunities since its development generally involves an array of stakeholders. In addition, tourism development often serves as a vehicle for overall economic development and a boost for local entrepreneurship activities. The sector also has the potential to bring more equitable, sustainable, and net benefits to local people. In the context of the former Yugoslavia, tourism also has political significance in bringing together people from different ethnic/ religious groups. Therefore, in our study the strategy adopted by the NGO was a community approach to regional tourism development through discourse, as an analytical framework to accommodate the complexity of the two countries' (Serbia and BiH) 'distance' context. By the notion of distance or distal,[3] we mean a multiplicity of social structures in terms of class, culture, religions, ethnic composition and institutions (Fairclough, 1995). By using discourse analysis we are able to explore and explain the process of social movement and its (re)construction. In our study, discourse ascertains the role, position and actions (discursive) of different actors involved in the process of building social capacity infrastructure in the given context. Moreover, the intrinsic reason for the existence of most of the NGOs is related to their role in changing civil society. Therefore, discourse analysis is not only able to explain how social reality is constructed, but 'how it is maintained and held in place over time' (Phillips and Hardy, 2002, p. 6). In other words, we focus on (in)ability of individual actors, involved in the process of institutional capacity-building through discourse, to act as a resource to bring about sustainable changes. Discourse analysis is also an interrelated set of texts and the practices of production, dissemination and consumption that bring an object into being (Fairclough, 1992; Phillips and Hardy, 2002).

Empirical data was obtained during the three-year-long fieldwork in the DVTR. The fieldwork began with initial interviews conducted with a number of key individuals, including three managing directors of Social Solutions, local NGOs and the tourism development project. The managers provided a useful background for the project and gave us an opportunity to obtain all the data we needed. Unstructured interviews were also conducted with eight mayors of the municipalities (four from each side of the Drina river) at different stages during the fieldwork. During this time the author (he was employed by Social Solutions) attended a number of formal and informal meetings, workshops, seminars and social events organized in different settings; municipal buildings, community centres, local business centres, pubs, hotels and other social settings including special tourism events such as white water rafting, regattas on the Drina river and fishing. In most of these meetings and events the NGO (Social Solutions) was an active participant. The collected data helped us to uncover the various layers of the reality in the eight municipalities that emerged from the negotiation and struggles between the various actors.

THE GEOPOLITICAL CONTEXT AND REGIONAL PROLIFE

In order to understand the process of economic and social change in the former Yugoslav states including BiH and Serbia, it is necessary to understand the Balkan context in which external influence is one of the main characteristics in the process of political and economic transformation known as the transition process. The transition process is a concept coined in the early 1990s after the dissolution of the Soviet Union and its republics and defines the replacement of the centrally planned socialist economic system by the market economy (Blanchard, 1997). The economic and political model of the former Yugoslavia was significantly different from the mainstream model of communism exercised in the former Soviet bloc. Essentially, Yugoslavia was a non-aligned, socialist state with less strict government intervention. The command economy was looser, allowing different forms of private ownership, although on a smaller scale and mainly in the service sector (tourism, hospitality and craft industries). Thus the process of transition from a socialist economy to a market economy could not be viewed as entirely novel for the Balkan successor states which emerged after the Yugoslav civil war, and arguably they should have had a much easier transition than the remainder of the former Soviet bloc (Ateljevic et al., 2004). However, the process of transition has frequently been seriously hampered by stubborn remnants of the former ideology and a new set of institutions created in the aftermath of the civil war.

The economic and political transformation in the context of the former Yugoslavia that has often been solicited by various international actors, has created a specific political and socio-economic environment in some of the newly formed countries in the former Yugoslavia, including BiH. Due to its complex ethnic/cultural structure as well as geopolitical significance, BiH has attracted a considerable international presence in the region (Papic, 2003). In spite of the extensive external help which has continued well after the peace agreement signed in 1995,[4] the country is still somewhere half-way between transition and economic and political consolidation. The effectiveness of the intervention of the foreign actors is strong, not only in the light of its financial significance, but also of its concepts and strategies. In both countries the lack of an adequate institutional infrastructure has been regarded as the main obstacle in the transition process. Particularly in BiH, economic and social development has been undermined by an increasingly slow process of political consolidation amongst the constituencies. Thus, building institutional and social capacities in such a complex environment is not a straightforward process; it requires significant resources and diplomacy to negotiate many interests between an increasing number of stakeholders (Strauss and Corbin, 1990).

DRINA VALLEY TOURISM REGION

The region (see Figure 6.1), situated in the Drina river valley, comprises fragile ecosystems and equally fragile open economies facing unique sustainable development problems and opportunities. The economy is strongly dependent upon agriculture and a few tourism activities with good prospects for tourism rejuvenation and development. A sizeable influx of concessionary finance, official grants and net private transfers from abroad sustain development programmes in some parts of the region, particularly in Srebrenica and Bratunac. Diverse natural resources provide a broad economic base for the region. These are: fertile agricultural land; high-quality forestry resources; considerable reserves of several valuable ores and minerals; and attractive nature and landscape, including the Drina river. The Drina river (over 100km), consisting of 14 additional small streams and rivers, is indeed one of the key regional assets suitable for a number of economic activities including: tourism, fishing and fish farming, drinking/industrial water supply and electricity generation.

Despite an increasing number of people returning to the war-affected areas a negative population growth remains one of the main concerns for all eight municipalities, as an increasing number of younger people are leaving the region on a permanent basis. The total population in the eight municipalities (an area of 3861km²) is about 215000. In RS-BiH the population is 56000, comprising: Bratinac (22000); Srebrenica (11000); Rudo (10000) and Visegrad (13000) (Repubika Srpska Institute of Statistics, 2009), and in Serbia it is 159000, comprising: Ljubovija (17000); Bajina Basta (30000); Uzice (83000) and Priboj (30000) (Statistical Office of the Republic of Serbia, 2009).

Recent indicators suggest that there are serious skill shortages in a

Source: Ateljevic et al. (2004).

Figure 6.1 Drina Valley Tourism Region

number of sectors (primarily services, construction, high-tech manufacturing) in most of the municipalities, and that these shortages are most apparent in the areas of foreign investment growth. The quality of available human resources falls below the minimum required for industrial standards, and the qualifications and skills already attained are of lesser value (Ateljevic, 2008).

Due to its geopolitical significance as well as its natural resources (minerals in Srebrenica), BiH has a long history of settlement with different occupants (Roman, Turks, Germans, Hungarians, Slavs), evident from the third century onwards. The region has always created major gateways for both people and goods. For example, during the fourteenth century, Srebrenica was one of the largest mining centres in the Balkans with a total population of over 10 000 people (compared to Rome, which at the time had a population of 20 000). As a result, the region has a rich historical and cultural heritage (CARE, 2005).

Tourism has excellent potential to generate income and jobs, and is an important tool to assist in achieving sustainable economic development in the region. Currently, main tourism activities are concentrated around the river Drina and Tara mountain in Bajina Basta. With the exception of Bajina Basta (which attracted about 100 000 visitors in 2004) in the other seven municipalities tourism activities are not so visible, apart from a few organized events. However, before the disintegration of the former Yugoslavia, Srebrenica used to attract more then 10 000 domestic visitors annually, because of its very rare mineral springs in the Crni Guber spa (CARE, 2005).

The Drina Valley Tourism Region reflects both global tourist trends and the development and direction of tourism. As a result, sustainable development is the key to the future of tourism development in DVTR. It is not enough simply to benefit local people economically; they must also have the ability to have some input into the development and management of the tourism industry. Institutional support for tourism and growing interests in its development in the region are not in place. Currently there are only two tourism-related organizations in the entire region, Turisticko-sportski Centar in Bajina Basta (Centre for Tourism and Sport) and the newly established Tourist Organization in Srebrenica. To increase national and regional institutional capacities for sustainable tourism development, the municipalities must now make collaborative efforts, gaining strength and innovation in numbers.

SOCIAL SOLUTIONS: AN INTERNATIONAL NGO

Non-governmental organizations, collectively described as the independent sector, vary greatly in scope, size, resources and impact. Often referred to as the third sector,[5] NGOs can be community-based or multinationally organized grassroots-oriented or policy-oriented. They have proven to be effective in mobilizing the support of the international community for many creditable causes in the public interest. Their missions involve a range of different activities: research-based, service-oriented, geographically focused, educationally driven, faith-based, ideologically focused or engaged in public advocacy. Regardless of such a wide focus, their funda-mental principles are more likely to be consistent with the objectives for which they receive funds.

Donations are the main source of NGOs' funding, which can come from governments, the UN, private trusts, individual donors, religious institu-tions and other NGOs. NGOs are non-party/politically affiliated organi-zations and have no explicit political missions; however, given the nature of their activities and funding, the dependency and political significance of NGOs should not be underestimated (Bossuyt and Develtere, 1995). They often have a strong influence on policy decisions and shaping politi-cal perspectives on various social and economic issues. It is believed that NGOs are capable of leveraging their influence through strategic alliances with other NGOs and government authorities. One of the major avenues through which NGOs exercise their political role is the media. They tend to establish broad and deep relationships with local communities, which is increasingly common for most NGOs. Establishing close relationships with local communities with a strong sense of mutual trust and respect is one of the key priorities for any NGO.

The effectiveness of NGOs is largely dependent on their leaders, who have the right skills in public policy negotiations, building social alliances, strategic planning, and other competencies that enhance their capacity to bring about change (Doh et al., 2006). In order to bring about change, NGOs need to be in the forefront of many innovations that have pro-vided ideas and models replicated or adapted in other settings and situa-tions. Generally non-profit organizations are seen as a growing source of solutions to issues facing today's society, such as poverty and pollution (Amankwah and Anim-Sackey, 2003). This is very much associated with the concept of social entrepreneurship which is often (but not exclusively) related to not-for-profit organizations with strong social missions as well as the individuals who manage and work in such organizations (Dees et al., 2002).

Social Solutions is an international NGO that operates in a number of countries and is one of the world's largest of its kind. In north-west Balkans the NGO has existed since 1994 with an aim to contribute to post-war recovery and the socio-economic development of Bosnia & Herzegovina, Croatia, and Serbia & Montenegro. Social Solutions was one of the first NGOs to operate during the wars in the former Yugoslavia. The organization is working to increase economic opportunities by support-ing the establishment and growth of small and medium-sized businesses. Another major focus of their work is promoting peace and democracy in the region. Social Solutions works with forward-thinking local organiza-tions and student associations to help them influence decision-makers to become a positive force for change. One of the organization's missions is to strengthen local organizations and capacity-building by strengthening networks between organizations from different communities and through development projects that benefit members of all ethnic groups. One of the current Social Solutions projects in BiH is strengthening democracy in eastern BiH by supporting local organizations. Social Solutions provides local organizations with training and resources in order to help them increase their influence over decision-makers and promote democratic values. Part of this project is tourism development in the region.

One of the reasons for selecting an international NGO as a research site was its increasingly important role in building social capacities in the Balkans in the last 10–15 years. In so doing, the organization has established an extensive network with various government and non-government institutions and individuals in the country. It has particularly developed strong links with local NGOs that are commissioned by the organization for specific tasks. The organization also attracts some of the best local employees who seek international experience and good learning environments combined with a significant monetary reward (the salary package is approximately five times the average salary in BiH).

TOURISM DEVELOPMENT: SOCIAL SOLUTIONS IN ACTION

The programme was led and managed by Social Solutions (an international NGO) and was based in their local office in Bratunac, RS. Local professional staff, plus administrative and liaison officer support, were also based there and were supervised by an NGO manager based in Sarajevo. Additional international and local expertise was deployed in line with the demands of the programme.

The ultimate goal of the project Drina Valley Tourism Region (DVTR) was to provide the groundwork for the development of a decision support system that can assist community, industry and government stakeholders in planning and developing future tourism and other economic initiatives in the region. The aim of this study is twofold: first, to propose a constructive study for tourism planning and development, a project that can assist in maximizing the performance of tourism as a means of achieving sustainable community development in the cross-border Drina Valley Tourism Region (DVTR) and secondly, to propose the establishment of a regional tourism organization and to make recommendations for its possible governance structure and best practice policies.

The project conducted by Social Solutions is based on the community

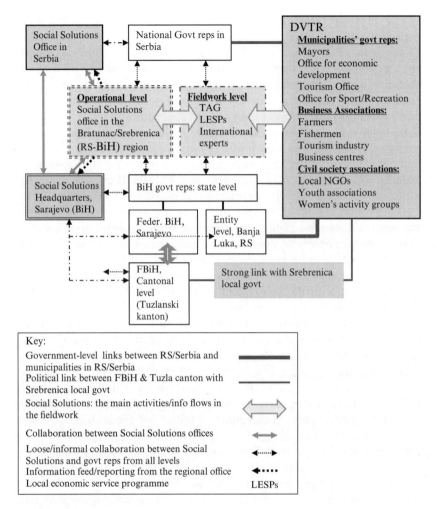

Source: The author.

Figure 6.2   Social Solutions strategic framework

and multi-stakeholder approach which required the need for intense negotiation with various stakeholders on local, regional and national levels (see
Figure 6.2). The process involves various formal and informal activities,
including a number of workshops, with the intention of bringing together
representatives from the eight municipalities with an ultimate objective
of establishing institutional mechanisms to achieve long-term sustainable
tourism development.

The tourism development project, of which building institutional capacity is the essential pillar, began with the formation of an Action Development Plan which included a number of strategic steps carried out by a Tourism Action Group (TAG) consisting of 16 people (two representatives from each municipality) whose activities were coordinated by a Liaison Officer (LO) appointed by Social Solutions. The LO ensured full participation of and transparency of activities within the TAG while the TAG members extended these concepts to their municipalities through engagement of the key stakeholders. Actions undertaken by the TAG and other interest groups representations were translated into consumer-friendly and accessible texts. The participants would receive the contextualized material and had the opportunity to contribute their opinions.

For an NGO like Social Solutions, whose focus leans mainly towards marginalized people's rights, the implementation of an economic development programme that emphasizes entrepreneurship and job creation was always going to be a challenge. But the key to this challenge was not only economic regeneration of an extremely poor region, across international borders with the subsequent creation of community jobs within the tourism supply chain, but included the issue of building sustainable institutions. This implies cooperation and partnerships (both between ethnic groups and across borders in the context of the aftermath of a bitter war in the 1990s), the development of a common tourist product based around a common natural resource – the Drina River Valley – and the equal involvement of the local state (municipalities), the private sector (SMEs) and the communities targeted (community groups, associations and NGOs), through multi-stakeholder entities (see Figure 6.2).

This project was designed to assist the economic regeneration of the Drina Valley by fostering and promoting a quality and sustainable visitor industry in the region. In practice, this meant that the state – at national, regional and local (municipal) levels – would invest in the infrastructure needed (roads, signing, nature trails, river clean-up, solid waste disposal, municipal tourist associations). The private sector would help develop SMEs within the tourism supply chain (accommodation, restaurants, internet cafes, hiking trails, rafting enterprises, river boating). Community associations would look to coordinate the efforts of fishing, hunting (photo safaris), hiking and rafting associations and employment opportunities for community members (ideally the most marginalized – single mothers, women more generally, young people). Associations would look at common licensing, monitoring, and so on, whilst environmental groups would look at possibilities for river clean-up (working in cooperation with dam operators), solid waste disposal and vital environmental education.

Given the multidimensional nature of the tourism industry, the project emphasized the need to view tourism from a number of different perspectives.

For the producers of tourism goods and services, the project offered enhanced promotion, increased yield, better access to services and information, and greater responsiveness from the eight municipalities. For the municipalities and those that plan tourism-related activities and infrastructure, there was the prospect of a coordinated approach between different stakeholder groups to develop a crucial component of the economy through a strategy focused on economic yield and environmental, social and economic sustainability. For the community there was the opportunity to play an increased role in the planning of future tourism development, in order to be more aware of the issues associated with the industry and to benefit from extra revenue and job creation.

The Process

Whilst the Social Solutions approach is bottom-up and participatory, it was clear that, given recent history, it was necessary to first acquire the main political actors on board, in both countries. In order to begin this educational and advocacy process, a multi-stakeholder workshop was held to develop a Strengths, Weaknesses, Opportunities and Threats (SWOT) analysis of the situation. Given the nature of the tourism sector and its wider geographical and political significance, this analysis was not limited to the DVTR but placed in the broader context of Serbia and BiH. The analysis confirmed that the two countries are blessed with a treasure of natural diversity, historical and cultural heritage and traditions that reflect the new trends of market travel. As a result, tourism in both countries has a strong potential for development and, if adequately planned, can play a significant role within the two economies and will become increasingly important over the next ten years. Moreover, tourism occupies centre stage of both countries' economic strategy.

BiH and Serbia have major tourist assets to offer people who seek contact with nature, away from crowds, whether they are lovers of quiet walks or whether they enjoy skiing, rafting, hunting or bird-watching. Those in search of more cultural tourism will be able to relive centuries of history by visiting the very many heritage sites, dating back to Roman times. Within the context of tourism, the Drina Valley tourist project, as a cross-border tourism entity of BiH and Serbia, represents a blend of the best features of the two countries. This was an important phase of the development process in raising awareness about the tourism opportunities amongst the stakeholders. More importantly, the outcomes of the SWOT analyses were used as an effective and convincing tool during the process of negotiation.

Apart from many opportunities, the exercise addressed a number of regional weaknesses and external impediments that were subsequently translated into actions to be undertaken within an agreed and realistic timeframe of three years.

These actions were to:

- identify the key stakeholders from the eight municipalities;
- build for tourism development institutional capacity starting with the Tourism Action Group;
- tourism planning and strategy;
- lobby for infrastructure improvement at all government levels;
- identify the most effective mechanism for education and training;
- identify those with most tourism and marketing knowledge and experience in the eight localities;
- provide recommendations to government (local, regional, national) to develop a simulative regulative and policy framework for sustainable tourism development and to provide incentives to outside investors.

STATE STRUCTURES

These findings were presented to the Ministry of Tourism in Serbia and in Bosnia & Herzegovina (Serb Republic entity in whose territory the project lies), emphasizing not only the potential for economic regeneration and the encouragement of entrepreneurship, but also the aspect of political and social reconciliation. The discussion emphasized the necessity for multi-stakeholder partnerships (state, private sector, civil society) and the need for political and financial input from the state. Both ministries reacted positively with promises of high involvement.

Municipalities

With this endorsement, the next set of workshops gathered together the eight municipalities (they are Ljubovija, Bajina Basta, Priboj and Uzice in Serbia, and Bratunac, Srebrenica, Visegrad and Rudo in BiH); this included the mayors, economic departments and municipal tourist associations. Each had been approached individually already. Again the SWOT analysis, the emphasis on partnerships, reconciliation and commitment of time and resources was made. The results of the workshop led to a

Memorandum of Understanding (MOU) on support, commitment of key personnel and cooperation, signed by all eight mayors in the presence of high media coverage. Initially, the media based in the Federation of BiH (Bosniac and Croat entity), were sceptical, especially given that Srebrenica was an integral part of the arrangement, and that the role of the international community had been less than positive over the past 10 years. Social Solutions dedicated a lot of time to the media subsequently and, although there are still sceptics, we managed to drive the point across that economic regeneration and reconciliation were keys to the future of this depressed region and that the local state, local businesses in the tourism supply chain and community groups were in favour of moving forward.

Meanwhile, the eight mayors each designated a representative to sit on a committee that would become the overall strategic board (with Social Solutions as managers) of the initiative from the municipal side, meeting monthly and agreeing (by majority vote) on all strategic directions. This became known as the Tourist Action Group (TAG). In order to unlock the economic potential of tourism development in the Drina Valley, the major challenge was to stimulate and harmonize tourism development and marketing strategies to meet the changing needs of the consumer, while at the same time creating a sustainable industry – one which maximizes economic benefits while reducing socio-environmental costs. It was also vital to achieve some form of balance between the potentially conflicting uses of common pool resources in a cross-border context encompassing the eight municipalities. For the municipalities and the state tourism ministries, this worked very well. Strategies were developed along common lines in each municipality, financial input for infrastructure was forthcoming and overall parameters for the common Drina Valley product development were made and put out to tender. It is interesting to note that, during a stakeholder analysis workshop carried out with all stakeholders, the state actors were at the top of the scale in terms of potential investment, since FDI and even local private investment was seen as only potentially forthcoming once the product and marketing of the Drina Valley Tourist Region was up and running (envisaged for 2009/10).

Entrepreneurs

Following the high-profile signing of the MOU, Social Solutions began a series of both explanatory and more specific workshops with local business people, with NGOs and community groups. During this first six months there were few people in the area that were not aware of the Drina Valley Tourist Project and its potential.

Local or indigenous entrepreneurs are key agents for economic change and regional development in BiH and Serbia. In this context, tourism plays an important role in a number of ways. As a result of the growth in international tourism, small (tourism) enterprises have gained political importance in both developed and less developed countries, as governments have assumed the strategic direction of regional development goals using small firm programmes to target specific geographical or demographic groups. Therefore, in the context of the Drina Valley, tourism and small tourism enterprises were to be used as development tools for the empowerment of the economically and socially depressed communities and were particularly focused on the empowerment of socially marginalized groups (for example women, young people, returnee families).

Social Solutions held a series of workshops, public meetings and training sessions with local entrepreneurs, both from existing businesses and potential SMEs. As a result, some 200 business people were clear about their potential to receive grants from the programme. Workshops were based on five years of experience, in the Balkans, from working with SMEs. Thus, detailed business and financial planning, proposal preparation and presentation, and strategic thinking were highlighted. An important result of these deliberations was that a group of local businesses (agro-business, restaurants and hotels) decided to set up a Business Association. They were assisted by Social Solutions workshops to develop a mission, aims, objectives, a constitution and registration with local authorities plus a small grant for office space and equipment. This was established for eastern BiH (such things already existed on the Serbian side). Over 75 businesses registered and paid membership dues, hired support staff, elected a chair at a general meeting and, after one year of operation, became self-supporting. This is the first of its kind in eastern BiH and serves as a model for other areas. With some help from Social Solutions, the association has become a key player in advocacy and lobbying for better business services from the municipalities, in debates on strategies for SME development and in stakeholder decision-making on SME start-up grants. There has been increasing interest in Bed & Breakfast accommodation in these discussions together with the key idea of using these to display local produce (jams, fruit wines, crafts). This is an area to be explored fully in the next stage (2010).

Community Groups

During the first six months of the initiative, there was much interest and involvement of local NGOs (women's groups, youth organizations, and environmental organizations), local sports associations (fishers, hunters, hikers, climbers, rafters) and community associations that represent villages on the municipal assemblies. Results included a community voice in all deliberations and, more concretely, a unified licensing, fees and calendar for fishing throughout the region through the Drina River Valley Fishers Association. This included a grant to supply boats for policing these agreements. Hunters' Associations are traditionally more organized, with national laws already in place to regulate the sport. Social Solutions introduced the idea of photo safaris and hiking/viewing. Rafting SMEs already exist and are well established. The assistance they needed was related mainly to marketing and river clean-up.

Organizational Forms

The Tourist Action Group (TAG) and the Business Association, along with the Fishers' and Hunters' Associations have, to date, been the strongest participants in the ongoing development of this initiative. However, a mid-term review by Social Solutions pointed to the reality that the TAG had become the key player in terms of strategy development, grant-making and infrastructure funding. In this sense, the Business Association and the NGOs have become rather more recipients of grants than full stakeholders. In 2008, this will be rectified with an expanded TAG to incorporate them.

Grants to Entrepreneurs, Municipalities and NGOs/Community Associations

The TAG decided to combine the concept of grant funding for strategic interventions associated with furthering the goals of a regional tourist product with a fair share of funding for each of the eight areas (municipalities) in order to avoid conflict later on. Also, a decision was made to spread project funds equally between municipalities, SMEs and community initiatives. Thus, at the first round and only for projects within the strategic criteria, there would be three projects per area for a total of 24 projects funded.

Within the context of the Balkans, the jury is still out on the issue of grant funding vs. soft or commercial loans. The fact is that this project has a grant fund (available, in a competitive process, to all stakeholders to enhance knowledge and to increase tourism assets) worth approximately €1 million over three years. Some feel that grants distort the market and promote opportunism from those applicants with better skills in writing proposals, good contacts with municipalities and the like. On the other side, commercial loans from banks and micro-credit organizations are seen as expensive (12–18 per cent) and often impossible to obtain (due to lack of collateral). We did our best to give all potential applicants equal training in business and financial planning – some ten workshops per municipality – and chose a project approval committee from as wide a range of stakeholders as possible. Our experience, in the end, is that whilst grants make for quicker and more visible results (donors tend to favour this), they do distort the market and lead to much social and political disturbance. Given the delicate context of this region, especially on the BiH side (returnees vs. residents, Bosniac vs. Serb, to name only two), we were inundated with complaints when project approvals were posted publicly, and spent much valuable staff time holding commissions and enquiries (none of which resulted in any changes, incidentally). In future, soft loans or administrative subsidies to the lending institutions might be a fairer and less contentious approach than direct grants.

The nature of the proposals received and assessed by an independent business consultant was interesting. Entrepreneurs generally had solid business and financial plans and were, as encouraged in workshops, able to post their own funding (usually as much as 50 per cent) in initiatives that basically called for imported equipment, for example stainless steel tanks for wine-making, furniture and equipment for Bed & Breakfasts, machines for jam-making, irrigation and frost prevention sprays for fruit and vegetable production, vehicles. Social Solutions also encouraged a number of Public–Private Partnerships (one per municipality in the first phase) whereby the municipality would supply land (often beach-front), roads and bulk services to entrepreneurs who would provide buildings, equipment and management staff for tourist initiatives. Municipalities generally asked for equipment (computers) and office furnishings as well as specific staff training for tourism-related activities (economic and spatial planning departments, tourist associations, publications). NGOs and community associations were generally modest in their applications and concentrated on basic equipment such as boats as mentioned above, and publications and supplies for campaigning.

THE MAIN OBSTACLES AND RECENT CHANGES

Tourism and other projects for various capacities-building in the region have identified and revealed many weaknesses in all eight communities.

- *Poor infrastructure and slow infrastructure improvement*: this is a particular problem on the BiH side due, in part, to the war, but there have been improvements. As an example, the Serb Republic government has improved the river road from Bratunac to Skelani/

Baijna Basta, and tourist associations have been set up in all eight municipalities, but progress is slow in other areas of concern (e.g. internet access, signing, nature trails, waste disposal).

- *Poor institutional capacity and linkages between key stakeholders*: the project has greatly assisted municipalities in planning and human resource upgrading and, as a result, the Tourist Action Group (TAG) has developed a strategic plan for the region, and the tourist 'product' has been defined. At the moment, a marketing plan is being developed which entails a series of tours throughout the region as a whole, with key features within each municipality highlighted, for example the bridge on the Drina in Visegrad (over 300 years old), rafting, hunting, fishing, and so on. The TAG, as a new institute, now has a secretariat, and has funding from the state tourism offices of BiH and Serbia and, following the completion of the marketing plan, will focus some of its efforts on investment into the region.
- *Lack of ecological conscience, environmental degradation, litter and waste management*: whilst many workshops and connections with environmental groups have been made, this remains one of the weaknesses of the programme. Municipalities find that the issue of and funds for solid waste disposal are very difficult, and little progress has been made. It's the same with river clean-up campaigns and this is mainly due to the periodic sluicing of the dams and the low consciousness of communities. This is seen as a major design fault in the programme, in that insufficient funds were made available and reliance on local and international environmental groups has proved to be erroneous.
- *Outdated and limited knowledge, skills (marketing in particular)*: this is gradually being addressed by bringing in marketing expertise from outside. The issue for the future is how to get TAG and other players to interact with professional tour operators from target countries in the Balkans and in Europe.
- *Lack of motivation of young people to stay in local areas and general decline of population*: whilst some jobs have been created via the thirty-odd SMEs already in operation, the overall population continues to decline, especially in BiH. This is a general phenomenon as young people move to the cities to seek employment and, ultimately, to emigrate. The consequences of the Dayton Peace Accord (especially around the formation of high-cost entities and cantons) and the continuing ethnic tensions make EU entry a distant prospect. Consequently, the economy generally is not performing well as inflation rises.

- *Lack of distinct brand or identity*: the development of the product and the marketing plan is making this a reality.
- *Legal instability*: *inconsistent and unfavourable legal/policy framework for tourism development, cross-border regulations and services*: this has improved in that regional Drina Valley tours will have much improved cross-border regulations as agreed by both countries. Another positive example is that a common policy framework now exists on fishing licences, seasons, and so on via the integrated Drina Valley Fishing Association.
- *Inadequate privatization of tourism-related business facilities*: this is still a problem issue but gradually, and especially when a facility receives a grant from the project, joint public/private ownership is being consolidated as well as some instances of privatization.
- *Lack of external funding*: as donor funding declines in BiH and Serbia (although most of what is left is designated for economic development), foreign direct investment still tends towards energy, forestry and telecommunications. Once the marketing is launched it is hoped to attract investors, local and foreign, but this is still a way off.

The most recent report (Ateljevic, 2008) demonstrates that many tangible and intangible improvements have been made in all areas largely due to Social Solutions, which has been providing constructive and comprehensive assistance in building economic, social and institutional capacities in the region. This NGO has been effective in mobilizing the support of the national and international community for many creditable causes in the region's public interest. On the BiH side, specifically in Srebrenica and Bratunac, due to their many natural resources, generally improved infrastructure and their modernized institutional structure, the municipalities have attracted an increasing number of businesses in all traditional sectors: manufacturing, agriculture and food processing, and forestry and wood processing (Ateljevic, 2008). These two municipalities are now doing their utmost to erase negative images by focusing on economic development. Both are proactively welcoming investors to benefit from an increasingly favourable business environment. Local authorities in both municipalities are forward-looking and, in recent years, have demonstrated their full commitment to pursuing sustainable economic development in partnership with other municipalities from this part of the country. The two localities continue to foster constructive cross-border collaboration with neighbouring municipalities in Serbia.

THE KEY IMPLICATIONS AND CONCLUSIONS

As the findings and discussion suggest, cross-border collaboration is not a straightforward process, and Figure 6.2 clearly illustrates that complexity in this particular case, DVTR. In hindsight, this stakeholder analysis tended to move the focus more towards the state as the prime mover, and the underdeveloped private and community sectors became more the recipients of resources rather than prime movers in the decision-making process. The result was the separation of activities between the sectors. However, much work was done with the private sector, such as setting up a Business Association for eastern BiH, and with civil society groups, especially those related to fishing, hunting, and bed and breakfast accommodation. However, what is beyond doubt is that an organization is needed as a catalyst for this process to succeed – in this case Social Solutions – and that this is an organization that is not only objective – an outsider if you like, which has no political affiliation – but that is an NGO which keeps the social aspects to the fore whilst, at the same time, encouraging local initiatives, especially those of local entrepreneurs.

Power relations are a key facet of any development initiative anywhere, and this underdeveloped area attempting a cross-border cooperative initiative is no exception. The war in eastern BiH saw many atrocities committed, and the inadequacy of the international community was clearly exposed; this has left deep wounds and suspicions. Add to this the fact that Srebrenica Municipality is essentially run by the SDA (Muslim party) and the rest by a variety of Serbian nationalist parties. However, Srebrenica Municipality officials are masters at donor relations and they quickly endorsed the project. The point here is that municipalities in Republika Srbska (BiH) and in Serbia itself are directly linked to line ministries in Banja Luka (administrative centre of RS) and Belgrade, but also to the political parties in Sarajevo, Banja Luka and Belgrade so that their propensity to seek power in a project arrangement like this is strong. They will cooperate among themselves and see to it that project resources are shared equally among them but, perhaps because of the continued mentality of socialism, they are reluctant for community associations and NGOs to obtain much power in the arrangement. The problem with this is that most elected local officials and bureaucrats have an expectation of some personal gain wherever there are outside resources at play. This usually translates into friends and relatives receiving entrepreneurial grants. Social Solutions was very aware of this and built the necessary selection criteria, capacity-building and equality into workshops, meetings, conferences and grants.

In eastern BiH, there has been a large transfer of foreign funding since the end of the war in 1995. So you have this strange mentality, mentioned above, of entitlement amongst all groupings: state, business and civil society.

Local NGOs are sons and daughters of international NGOs (INGOs) and are thus extremely competitive, tending to follow INGO trends – young people, women's rights, anti-trafficking, violence against women, and so on. These, though laudable in themselves as issues to be faced, tend to link them nationally and internationally into UN statistics rather than focusing on local issues of employment, education and health care. Thus, in this tourism project, the local NGOs seemed interested only in possible grants related to their salaries and were therefore not a force within the overall power relations. This was left to the community groups and community-based organizations (CBOs) who were not only much more representative of people in the area, but were forceful and creative in workshops and meetings. Those community organizations that were organized around specific activities – fishing, hunting, rafting, hiking – were especially active and pertinent to the tourism focus. Entrepreneurs and local business people in general, whilst fulfilling their mandate to get profitable businesses going and to make money and indeed invest their own money, were also very active in enhancing the 'contact sport' of influencing municipal officials in order to acquire the grants.

There can be no doubt, from experiences to date, that a neutral, creative, participatory-oriented organization like Social Solutions is essential, given the political context and the potential for power imbalances. However, it must be said that the prevailing entitlement attitudes, the power of the local state and the virtual non-existence of relevant local NGOs presented a high potential for failure. But consistent efforts towards maximum participation and transparency have borne some fruit, and the process continues quite successfully, even though setting up the TAG (see the above section on municipalities) to the exclusion of other stakeholders was a mistake. This will be rectified in the future to improve more inclusivity.

The DVTR model is specific in a number of ways; however, it helps to enhance our general understanding of the process of local/regional development – beyond BiH and Serbia or the Balkans' context – by emphasizing two key issues. The first is related to the participatory approach of multiple stakeholders from the state, the private sector and civil society and giving them equal weight in discussion and planning (this latter a good lesson learned by Social Solutions). The other relates to donors, and it is important that they be persuaded towards loans rather than quick-fix grants. Both the stakeholders and donors have a better chance of enhancing the sustainability of the initiative.

NOTES

1. The state of BiH has a highly complex political system – it consists of a confederal government in which power is rotated between three ethnic communities (Bosniacs, Croats and Serbs). Within this, there are two political entities: one is the Bosniac–Croat Federation (FBIH), mainly made up of Bosnian Croats and Bosnian Muslims (the latter now termed Bosniacs). The other is Republika Srpska (RS), a state in which Bosnian Serbs form the majority.
2. The local communities are divided by religious beliefs: Christian Orthodox (the Serbs living on both sides of the river); and Islam (the Muslims living on the left bank of the river, the BiH territory).
3. As opposed to distal proximate, the context refers to 'immediate features of the interaction, including the participants taking part in an episode to be (e.g., a consultation, an interrogation, a family meal-time) the sequences of talk in which particular events occur and the capacities in which people speak. . .' (Phillips and Hardy, 2002, p. 19).
4. The General Framework Agreement for Peace in Bosnia and Herzegovina, also known as the Dayton Agreement, Dayton Accords, Paris Protocol or Dayton–Paris Agreement, is the peace agreement reached in Dayton, Ohio in November 1995, and formally signed in Paris on 14 December, 1995. These accords put an end to the three and a half year-long civil war in BiH, one of the armed conflicts in the former Yugoslavia. According to the agreement, BiH became a confederation consisting of two Entities, the Federation of Bosnia and Herzegovina (FBH) and the Republika Srpska (RS).
5. The third sector refers to those organizations that are not-for-profit and non-government, together with the activities of volunteering and giving which sustain them. These include non-profit, non-government, community, voluntary, club, society, association, cooperative, friendly society, church, union, foundation and charity.

REFERENCES

Amankwah, R.K. and C. Anim-Sackey (2003), 'Strategies for sustainable development of the small-scale gold and diamond mining industry of Ghana', *Resources Policy*, **29**, 131–8.

Ateljevic, J. (2005), 'Drina Valley Tourism Region: a cross-border partnership', (the project proposal), CARE International, Sarajevo, BiH.

Ateljevic, J. (2008), 'Srebrenica and Bratunac region: an ultimate location for industry and commerce', a generated research on investment potentials in Srebrenica and Bratunac municipalities, CARE International North West Balkans, Sarajevo, BiH.

Ateljevic, J., T. O'Rourke and Z. Todorovic (2004), 'Entrepreneurship and SMEs in Bosnia and Herzegovina: building institutional capacity', *The International Journal of Entrepreneurship and Innovation*, **5**(4), 241–54.

Blanchard, O. (1997), *The Economics of Post-Communist Transition*, Oxford: Clarendon Press.

Bossuyt, J. and P. Develtere (1995), 'Between autonomy and identity: the financing dilemma of NGOs', *The Courier ACP-EU*, No. 152, July–August: pp. 76–8, available at www.hiva.be/docs/artikel, accessed on 29 May, 2006.

CARE (2005), 'Regional economic development: a cross-border partnership between Bosnia and Herzegovina (BiH) and Serbia and Montenegro (SCR)', Sarajevo: CARE International for the Balkans.

Dees, J. Gregory, Peter Economy and Jed Emerson (eds) (2002), *Strategic Tools for Social Entrepreneurs: Enhancing the Performance of Your Enterprising Non-profit*, New York: Wiley and Sons.

DiMaggio, P.J. (1988), 'Interest and agency in institutional theory', in L.G. Zucker (ed.), *Institutional Patterns and Organizations: Culture and Environment*, Cambridge, MA: Ballinger, pp. 3–22.

Doh, P. Jonathan and R. Terrence Guay (2006), 'Corporate social responsibility, public policy, and NGO activism in Europe and the United States: an institutional-stakeholder perspective', *Journal of Management Studies*, **43**(1), 47–73.

Fairclough, N. (1992), *Discourse and Social Change*, Cambridge: Polity Press.

Fairclough, N. (1995), *Critical Discourse Analysis*, Boston, MA: Addison-Wesley.

Fligstein, N. (1997), 'Social skill and institutional theory', *American Behavioural Scientist*, **40**, 397–405.

James, R. (1994), 'Strengthening the capacity of Southern NGO partners: a survey of current northern NGO approaches', International NGO Training and Research Centre, *INTRAC Occasional Paper Series*, **1**(5), Oxford: INTRAC.

Maguire, S., C. Hardy and T. Lawrence (2004), 'Institutional entrepreneurship in emerging fields: HIV/AIDS treatment advocacy in Canada', *Academy of Management Journal*, **47**(5), 657–79.

Meyer, J. and B. Rowan (1977), 'Institutionalized organizations: formal structure as myth and ceremony', *American Journal of Sociology*, **83**, 340–63.

Papic, Z. (2003), 'From dependency towards politics of sustainable development', paper presented at the conference, 'Business Activities in Bosnia and Herzegovina in Association with Development and Cohesion in SE Europe: Strategic and Politics in a Fragmented Region', Sarajevo, 10–11 November, organized by Victoria University, Melbourne.

Phillips, N. and C. Hardy (2002), *Discourse Analysis: Investigating Processes of Social Construction*, Thousand, Oaks, CA: Sage.

Repubika Srpska, Institute of Statistics (2009), 'Demography', available at http://www.rzs.rs.ba/, accessed on 12 May, 2009.

Statistical Office of the Republic of Serbia, (2009), 'Population', available at http://webrzs.statserb.sr.gov.yu/axd/en/index.php, accessed on 10 May, 2009.

Strauss, A. and J. Corbin (1990), *Basics of Qualitative Research: Grounded Theory Procedures and Techniques*, London: Sage Publications.

Thomson, D.M. and S. Pepperdine (2003), 'Assessing community capacity for riparian restoration', *National Riparian Lands Research and Development Program*, Canberra: Land & Water Australia.

PART II

Micro-economic Factors in Nurturing High
Potential SMEs

7. Board network characteristics and company performance in Sweden: the case of Gnosjö companies and their board members in southern Sweden

Ossi Pesämaa, Johan Klaesson and Antti Haahti

INTRODUCTION

When managers of entrepreneurial companies typically talk about strategies, they first consider what products to make and secondly where to locate the business. The entrepreneurial companies locate in rural areas because of a wish to maintain a certain lifestyle, or because they can combine a resource available there with certain knowledge or interest that they have (Getz and Nilsson, 2004). In addition, many managers of entrepreneurial companies are confident in locating in a rural area, because there often is economic and social structure supportive of local corporate governance. The most central part of corporate governance is the board of directors. In an entrepreneurial company in a rural area, such members of boards are most likely to be individuals in dominant positions influential in the local economy.

A board is thus an important forum for entrepreneurial companies to conceive, discuss and establish strategies (Randøy and Goel, 2003). Most boards reflect different combinations of ownership (Chuanrommanee and Swierczek, 2007). Some small entrepreneurial companies have a 'paper board', which consist of the entrepreneur and his/her spouse as well as an auditor. Others use the group dynamics of a board more fully, by including special expertise in combination with a required auditor and minority ownership (Bedard et al., 2004). Finally, there are other constellations where local friendships reflect the board structure (Ingram and Roberts, 2000).

We know that social capital in a local setting can be a beneficial force for local companies (Piore and Sabel, 1984). Gnosjöregion is a rural area, known for its entrepreneurial 'spirit', and probably one of the most well-known regional clusters in Sweden (Karlsson et al., 1992; Karlsson and Larsson, 1993; Johanisson, 1996). The region is in south Sweden. The local population is known for strong religious traditions and high church attendance, a low level of education, a strong focus on manufacturing industry, strong local cohesiveness, high number of small family companies and domination of men in the industry (Wigren, 2003). The Gnosjöregion has created many legends and myths that circulate in both academia and practice. Their closeness to each other has created a view that there is an in-group, which makes it difficult for outsiders to become accepted by the locals. One of the arguments heavily highlighted is that membership to any of the local churches will give people entrance to the local structure. This would thus make it rather difficult for individuals in the out-group to enter.

This region is also reported to have very high-performing, small manufacturing companies. For instance the small municipality of Gnosjö has less than 10 000 residents and approximately 250 small companies, which makes the density of companies to residents one of the highest in Sweden. In this town the companies have a total sales of approximately 6 billion SEK (approximately $1 billion). This success has also created a heightened awareness in Gnosjö. On their website this is indicated by 'the spirit of Gnosjö', which reflects the professional skills, hard work, economic practice, humility, respect, networks, cooperation, entrepreneurship, no elitism, no barriers to overcome difficulties that arise, flexibility, artfulness and holistic thinking (see www.gnosjo.se).

Lately Gnosjö people have become more aware of opportunities in the development of new emerging service industries such as tourism. This development of new service industries is focused on cooperation among the regions of Gnosjö, Gislaved, Vaggeryd and Värnamo. This cooperation is an effort to develop destination management practices in order to build a coordinated approach to the strategic management of tourism and design of tourism experiences. Cooperation within and between organization aims to raise awareness and thereby strengthen overall region (when considered as a destination) in national and international markets. Their initiatives include cooperating in marketing to build a strong presence, for example in travel expos and exhibitions and various events, and to develop a common web portal (www.gnosjoregionen.se) to promote the whole region as a tourist destination.

Considering what is publicly stated and the stories created and told about this region, one may expect that this networking would also be reflected in the existing structures in the region, such as enterprise boards. On the basis of the Gnosjö regional spirit, we would expect a high level of cohesiveness among entrepreneurial families and their friends. Therefore, it may be expected that this should also be reflected in the board structures developed in the public limited companies (PLC) in tourism.

To explore, elaborate and test these propositions we designed a model and collected data from the boards of public companies. We collected information about all companies with publicly reported financial information operating in the tourism industry. We found a total of 95 companies, which had 379 board members among them. These companies were examined closely with a focus on selected independent variables that were likely to influence fluctuations in company performance.

The research objective was based on the following question: does higher social capital, as indicated by the number and efficiency of relations, in combination with company continuity, build and influence the performance of the company? In order to propose an answer to this question we developed a model based on earlier theory on board characteristics (see, for example, Kim, 2005).

THE FUNCTION OF A BOARD

First of all, Swedish limited companies are required to have a board, an independent auditor and at least two ordinary members on the board. With the auditor included, the typical Swedish company board consists of at least three members: two ordinary members and one auditor. The auditor can be selected by the company even though their function is to ensure that all financial reporting reflects a standardized way to report financial information and that the numbers give a *true and fair view* of the company (Choi, 1997). The auditor is typically a very important individual for a small company (Bushong, 1995). Their authority involves control (Bushong, 1995) so that the stakeholders, that is the bank, the suppliers, the customers, the employees, the state, the employee organizations, and other organizations (Frooman, 1999) may have confidence in agreements. The auditor is also allowed to work proactively to prepare for new emerging situations and to use his or her competence to advise and make recommendations to steer the small company away from potentially difficult situations. Companies therefore generally select auditors that operate proactively. It is even likely that companies may select an auditor who uses her/his expertise to operate on the border line of what is allowed, and may also evaluate the auditor and renew his contract based on his performance as, in Sweden, an auditor is paid by the client that he is assessing. Auditors can be very expensive. This expense can often be justified because of the expertise they have on tax and experience working with other companies. They have therefore typically gained a highly respected position as the main advisor. Together with the rest of the board, the auditor is a crucial part of small companies' strategic corporate governance.

A BOARD, ADMINISTRATION AND PERFORMANCE MODEL

A literature study was conducted on strategies that link entrepreneurship to corporate governance, board characteristics and its relationship to performance. Our literature search in the Social Sciences Citation Index from 1945–2008 on 'corporate governance' generated 2208 studies in peer-reviewed journals. One of the most cited in this area (560 citations) and relevant to our study was Shleifer and Vishny (1997), which offered different directions for conducting studies in this field. Our next search performed on 'board characteristics' yielded in 1690 studies, and the most cited work relevant for this study (111 citations) was Johnson et al. (1993). Their work included an empirical demonstration of a classical regression on performance including ten independent variables reflecting different strategic dimensions as well as seven control variables. Even though this is a rather subjective literature overview it captures the cutting edge of the literature that has been published so far on the relevant topics of interest in this study. Table 7.1 demonstrates the directions these studies take in extant research.

Kim (2005) suggests that 'board external social capital can be defined as the degree to which board members have outside contacts within an institutional environment' (p. 802). Lefort and Urzúa (2008) explicitly recommend independence of directors, whereas Black et al. (2006) demonstrate that the structure is affected by financing and then current position of the company. Randøy and Goel (2003) point out the important role played by the founder in corporate governance and Zahra et al. (2000) demonstrate the need to differentiate responsibilities so that the chief executive and chairman are not one and the same person. Finally, Wan and Ong (2005) claim that structure does not matter, but that process has an effect on performance. Table 7.1 also shows a glimpse of the traditions of research design in this area and how different regressions are typically designed.

This chapter outlines a model that reflects how board characteristics, in combination with proper administration and company age, can have an effect on performance.

The model proposes that social capital, measured by number of

Table 7.1 Literature overview of three selected studies recently published and targeting boards with regression analysis

Author	Data access	Sample	Unit/level of analysis	Dependent variable	Independent variables	Controls – interaction variables	Findings
Zahra, Neubaum and Huse (2000)	Secondary data and survey	239 medium sized firms and responses from 94 executives	US manufacturing firms and second senior executives in each firm	Five dependent variables: of corporate entrepreneurship: (1) product innovation; (2) process innovation; (3) organizational motivation; (4) domestic venturing; (5) international venturing	(1) executive ownership; (2) ownership by pension funds; (3) ownership by insurance companies; (4) ownership private companies; (5) board size; (6) board size squared; (7) outsiders ratio; (8) outsider director stock; (9) CEO and chair separated; (10) technological opportunities; (11) past ROA; (12) company size; (13) company age		'Corporate entrepreneurship is high when: (1) executives own stock in their own company; (2) the board and chief executive are different individuals; (3) the board is medium sized; (4) outside directors own stock in the company' (Zahra, Neubaum and Huse, 2000, p. 947)

Table 7.1 (continued)

Author	Data access	Sample	Unit/level of analysis	Dependent variable	Independent variables	Controls – interaction variables	Findings
Randøy and Goel (2003)	Archival sources (annual reports)	204 Norwegian firms	Founder leadership in large public firms in Norway	One dependent variable: Q-value (ratio of market value equity to book value of liabilities)	Four independent variables: (1) Founder leadership; (2) board inside ownership; (3) Blockholder ownership; (4) foreign ownership	Four controls tested: (1) asset tangibility debt ratio (2) firm size; (3) firm age; (4) industry effects. Interaction variables tested: (1) Founder leadership × board inside ownership; (2) Founder leadership × Blockholder leadership; (3) Founder leadership × Foreign leadership	*'Founder led firms can exploit their low agency cost status to use their board and insiders for strategic purposes'* (Randøy and Goel, 2003, p. 634)

Study	Data source	Sample	Context	Dependent variables	Independent variables	Controls	Findings
Kim (2005)	Archival sources	4000 different board members in 10 years	Large publicly traded firms in Korea	One dependent variable: Return on assets	Four independent variables: (1) density (proportion of links relative to possible ties); (2) square of network density; (3) degrees from elite institution (graduated from top schools); (4) membership in economic association	Nine controls tested (1) lagged ROA; (2) age of firm; (3) log of assets; (4) depth to equity ratio; (5) board age, (6) affiliation dummy; (7) board education level; (8) board average age; (9) board size	*Dense and cohesive networks at boards can add value to corporations.* (Kim, 2005, p. 806). In addition external capital has an effect on performance
Wan and Ong (2005)	Survey (sample 424 firms)	212 firms and 299 directors. Self-reported responses on board structure (controls) board process (summated scales) and board performance (self-reported data)	Large firms in Singapore	Two dependent variables. (1) Monitoring scale which seeks their ability to fully pursue their professional role (10 items); (2) An index which seeks transparency of company to public	Four independent variables: (1) effort norms (five item scale); (2) cognitive conflict (five items); (3) affective process conflict; (4) knowledge and skills	Two groups of controls A and B: (A1) Board size; (A2) Industry; (A3) Market; (A4) Revenue; (B1) Chairman duality; (B2) Number of non-executive directors (NED); (B3) Proportion of NED; (B4) Number of independent directors; (B5) Proportion of independent directors	*Board structure does not matter, while board process does. Board structure does not influence board process or board performance* (Wan and Ong, 2005, p. 285)

Table 7.1   (continued)

Author	Data access	Sample	Unit/level of analysis	Dependent variable	Independent variables	Controls – interaction variables	Findings
Black, Jang and Kim (2006)	Survey with 39 different governance elements	453 large firms	Large firms in Korea	Company value index (KCGI)	(1) Assets; (2) sales growth; (3) profitability; (4) equity finance need; (5) sole ownership; (6) chaebol, which is part of a fair business association in Korea; (7) leverage, which is a ratio of depth to market value; (8) firm age; (9) market share; (10) ratio of exports to sales; (11) ratio of capital expenditure to sales; (12) ratio of advertising to sales; (13) ratio of property, plant and equipment to sales; (14) asset size; (15) bank dummy	Three control variables: (1) firm size; (2) no/ yes association to fair trade association; (3) financial	Concludes that *'larger firms are better governed'* . . . *'riskier firms are better governed'* . . . *'more profitable firms are worse governed'* . . . *'firms with higher equity finance need are better governed'* (Black, Jang and Kim, 2006, p. 690)

| Lefort and Urzúa (2008) | National database | Four year 160 company panel data in Chile | Large firms in Chile | Two dependents tested: (1) Tobins Q (ratio of market value equity to book value of liabilities) (2) Return on assets | Five independent variables: (1) Proportion of independent directors; (2) proportion of professional directors; (3) proportion of outside directors; (4) board size; (5) external financial needs | Two groups of controls A and B: (A1) ownership concentration; (A2) degree of coincidence; (A3) group affiliation; incentive programme; (B1) firm size; (B2) leverage; (B3) weekly returns; (B4) industry; (B5) time dummies | 'Proportion of independent directors affects companies' value' (Lefort and Urzúa 2008, p. 621) |

ties, efficiency or strength of ties, can make companies perform better (Granovetter, 1973; Krachhardt, 1992). Our second assumption is that companies typically use their board of directors to clarify different strategic situations. The two first assumptions together form the first *postulate* for this theory, namely that if a board and social capital are of significant importance for a company, then the board is composed of board members with strong relationships to each other. Our next assumption is that companies select their board members exclusively from those who also have a strong influence over the operations of the business. Some of those who know the business best are the ones who are close to the business either in relation to its products or in a local economic sense. These latter arguments are important to interlocking boards (Westphal et al., 2001). Our next argument is that rural entrepreneurial companies develop their contacts from local friendships, which also reflect their performance (Piore and Sabel, 1984; Saxenian, 1994) especially in industrial districts such as Gnosjöregionen (Johanisson, 1996). Finally we believe that the board (structure) is sometimes only an administrative group which works closely to keep the books in order, as Swedish law requires a company to have a board. The next argument for the model is that the board reflects continuity and longevity of working together, which is reflected by the company's number of years in business (company age) and the average age of the board members.

All of this input is considered important in the composition of a board that has to face different strategic tasks. That said, every individual must be carefully selected as they need to meet to discuss sales strategies, market strategies, employment strategies, strategies that concern new administrative control systems, new strategies for location or strategies that concern totally new products. Each strategy may need a new individual with a specific competence.

Apart from the strategic role, many boards are formed to serve institutional interests such as a disciplinary role, a figurehead role, an auditing role or ethical roles (Gabrielsson and Huse, 2005). The roles of members differ just as the way they are selected. Typical members are part of the owner family, friends, or a network of specialists who listen to the advice of an auditor. Therefore, the core of the model proposed does not ignore the experience of an auditor, but accepts that the social capital of the auditor is critical for company performance. Similarly, we argue that ordinary board members who have many contacts are also important for company performance. In addition we argue that factors such as fewer problems highlighted by the auditor, continuity (company age) and the average age of board members will affect the performance of the company. Performance is reflected by two indicators: sales and sales per employee (see Figure 7.1).

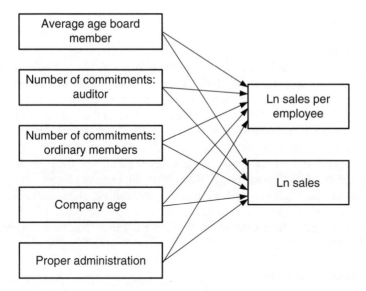

Figure 7.1   Board characteristics and their relationship to performance

Hypothesis

H1   There is a positive relationship between the board members' average age and sales per employee.

H2   There is a positive relationship between the board members' average age and sales.

H3   There is a positive relationship between number of relationships an auditor has and sales per employee.

H4   There is a positive relationship between number of relationships an auditor has and sales.

H5   There is a positive relationship between number of relationships an ordinary board member has and sales per employee.

H6   There is a positive relationship between number of relationships an ordinary board member has and sales.

H7   There is a positive relationship between company age (continuance) and sales per employee.

H8   There is a positive relationship between company age (continuance) and sales.

H9   There is a positive relationship between proper administration (number of accepted audit statements) and sales per employee.

H10   There is a positive relationship between proper administration (number of accepted audit statements) and sales.

Dependent Variable

Performance

Performance is one of the more traditional measures in company-related studies. Ittner and Larcker (1998) examined many different performance measures and their implications on innovation. Others have focused on market share (Greve, 1998); profit share of sales (Audia et al., 2000); assets (Miller and Chen, 2004); and investments (Luo, 1997). In corporate governance many have focused on market value; Q-value (Randøy and Goel, 2003; Lefort and Urzúa, 2008); value indexes (Wan and Ong, 2005; Black et al., 2006); or return on assets (Kim, 2005; Black et al., 2006).

This chapter reflects performance by examining sales and sales per employee. All sales data were accessible from public sources in Sweden and represent a four-year mean, which we calculated from the years 2003–2006.

Independent Variables

Average age

Next we examined average age of the board members. The assumption here is that either seniority or newness would have an impact on performance. This assumption is also consistent with earlier theory (Kim, 2005).

Number of auditor–client relationships

We downloaded the number of clients an auditor has. This indicator is based on the assumption that more clients would form a basis for the creation of a stronger social capital formation, which we assume to have a direct influence on performance.

Number of board member contacts

We also downloaded the number of contacts each ordinary board member has. The same assumed logic should be valid in this case, too; that is, a higher number of contacts in active relationships should enrich the content of stronger ties influencing social capital formation. This should be beneficial for the company, and thus be reflected in the company performance.

Company age

One way to get a picture of continuance, and some indication of resiliency for that matter, is to look at the age of the company. We share the view introduced in the model by Kim (2005). The argument in using age of the company as a predictor for performance is that long-term orientation and resiliency is also beneficial for sustained performance. We therefore examined the number of years the company has been in business as an indicator of continuance.

Administration

To develop an estimate of the quality of administration we downloaded the number of remarks made by auditors in their published audits during the years 2003–2006. The assumption here was that 'clean' books would also breed good performance. The fewer remarks, the more proper the administration.

METHOD

This chapter uses linear regression to estimate the effects each proposed predictor has on performance (Hair et al., 2006). Linear regression typically estimates which independent variables best predict the value of the dependent variable.

Sample

The sample consists of 95 companies selected from a number of national industrial classification (NIC) codes within Gnosjöregionen (www.gnosjoregionen.se), which includes four municipalities: Gnosjö, Gislaved, Vaggeryd and Värnamo (GGVV). The NIC codes used in this study are assumed to reflect tourism and are selected from the following main categories: transportation sector (passenger); housing (e.g. hotels, camps, cottages); food (e.g. restaurant businesses); tourist equipment (e.g. rental of sports equipment); tourism sales bureaux (e.g. travel agents), tourism attractions (e.g. museums, cultural attractions, historical places, man-made attractions (entertainment parks); event and activity providers (e.g. sport and leisure attractions/facilities); peripheral attractions (e.g. retail businesses with a high likelihood of souvenir business). Further details can be provided upon request.

All of the selected municipalities GGVV belong to a functional region, which is also considered as a typical countryside area. According to the national encyclopedia (www.ne.se) Gislaved has 29 327 residents in an area of 1143 km², Gnosjö has 9598 residents in an area of 423 km², Vaggeryd has 12 816 residents in an area of 831 km², and finally Värnamo has 32 841 residents in an area distributed of 1224 km². Following the guidelines about Swedish geographical classification, areas with fewer than 3000 residents and that are more than 45 minutes by car from an urban area are typically considered to be rural. Areas that are 5–45 minutes to a larger

Table 7.2   Descriptive statistics of Gnosjö region

	Residents	Area, km²	Households	Residents/ km²	House- holds/km²
Gislaved	29 327	1 143	11 843	25.7	10.4
Gnosjö	9 598	423	3 631	22.7	8.6
Vaggeryd	12 816	831	5 087	15.4	6.1
Värnamo	34 841	1 224	13 755	26.8	11.2
GGVV region	84 582	3 621	34 316	23.4	9.5

Sources: http://www.ne.se; http://dagspress.se.

city with more than 3000 inhabitants are classified as countryside. Remote countryside areas are characterized by households that are located at least 200 metres from each other, and with fewer than five inhabitants per square kilometre. We therefore consider these as companies inside a remote countryside area. Our example, the GGVV region, has an estimated 10 inhabitants per square kilometre. This would mean that there are roughly more than 100 metres between the households (see Table 7.2).

The sample consists of 95 Swedish limited companies, which means that the owner has stocks in the company but the company is in itself authorized to complete agreements and contracts. These companies are also obligated to report their financial status and to select an auditor to ensure that the financial information, leadership and other control systems reflect a true and fair view of the company (Choi, 1997). In addition, the auditor declares whether or not the principles used to report follow standard principles and practices to report financial information. If these are not followed, the auditor will have to declare this as a remark in a public statement. Finally, these companies also have a board for which they can select any member. Typically the board reflects a structure of ownership, the executive (CEO), the auditor and his/her assistants.

When looking closely at all board members we can say there is a total of 379 members. Out of these members, 129 are auditors, 31 per cent are female and the average age is 49.45 years. Twelve out of the 95 boards were completely dominated by men with no women, and one board was dominated by women, with no males. Most of the boards, however, contained a mixture of men and women. The auditors had on average 214 commitments to other boards, and regular board members had 2.95 commitments to other boards outside tourism and including other regions. There was no difference between the characteristics of boards among the four municipalities.

RESULTS

Results from Hypothesis

We used AMOS software, because we wanted to run two dependent variables simultaneously. This means we also received an extensive report for the overall model. The model was acceptable according to the criteria used by Hair et al. (2006). The model had 10 degrees of freedom in total and a chi square of 12.801 (Chi square/DF=1.280), which also indicate the theoretical model and the sample fit. Typically, AMOS software is used for path analysis or structural equation models, but we used this software in order to run two dependent variables Our test reported that hypotheses 1–5 and 9–10 received no support. The remaining hypotheses, 6–8, received strong support. Social capital and proper administration thus has no support for sales per employee. Social capital is also of limited importance for sales, with the exception of number of commitments from ordinary members which received strong support on sales (H6) ($r = .292$, $p < .005$). The majority of the explanatory power in the model instead seems to emerge from company age, which exhibits support for both sales per employee (H7) ($r = .301$, $p < .005$) and sales (H8) ($r = .246$, $p < .05$).

DISCUSSION

This chapter asked if social capital, as indicated by the number and efficiency of relations in combination with company age, build and influence the performance of a company. Our question was approached by proposing and testing a model based on earlier theory on board characteristics (for example Kim, 2005). The model receives strong support, which indicates that this theory is worthy of further testing and refinement. Our model included 10 hypotheses. Three hypotheses were significant and supported. Based on our findings, company age seems to strongly predict performance (sales and sales per employee). This message might be of considerable importance since many entrepreneurship and innovation programmes focus more on the early period of business start-ups rather than young firms that have survived around five years. The implication for further studies could be that they should focus on programmes in established companies. Our model also strongly considers characteristics in board of directors. Among these characteristics we expected first that average age as a measurement of diversity would have an effect on performance, which was not true in our case. Next, we expected that the auditors' social capital (that is, number of commitments) would affect performance, but auditors' social capital was of a limited importance. However, network characteristics of ordinary members (that is, number of commitments of ordinary members) seemed to influence sales. There is a great deal of variety in our sample in terms of how boards are formed.

One implication could thus be that companies may consider hiring external expertise for the board. Our results were tested in the context of Gnosjöregion, known for its strong social capital. It is therefore somewhat surprising that tourism companies did not have the strong social overlaps that we expected to find on the basis of earlier studies. We may consider this finding a hypothesis for further study. There is a need to elaborate the concept of social capital in such research settings, and to test further for possible contextual and methodological influences that may have limited us to only seeing part of the full picture.

REFERENCES

Audia, P.G., E.A. Locke and K.G. Smith (2000), 'The paradox of success: an archival and a laboratory study of strategic persistence following radical environmental change', *Academy of Management Journal*, **43**(5) 837–53.

Bedard, J., S.M. Chtourou and L. Courteau (2004), 'The effect of audit committee expertise, independence, and activity on aggressive earnings management, *Auditing: A Journal of Practice & Theory*, **23**(2), 13–35.

Black, B.S., H. Jang and W. Kim (2006), 'Predicting firms' corporate governance choices: evidence from Korea', *Journal of Corporate Finance*, **12**(3), 660–91.

Bushong, J.G. (1995), *Accounting and Auditing of Small Business*, New York: Garland Publishing Inc.

Choi, F.D.S. (1997), *International Accounting and Financial Handbook*, New York: John Wiley & Sons.

Chuanrommanee, W. and F.W. Swierczek (2007), 'Corporate governance in ASEAN financial corporations: reality or illusion?', *Corporate Governance: An International Review*, **15**(2), 272–83.

Frooman, J. (1999), 'Stakeholder influence strategies', *Academy of Management Review*, **24**(2), 191–205.

Gabrielsson, J. and M. Huse (2005), '"Outside" directors in SME boards: a call for theoretical reflections', *Corporate Board: Roles, Duties and Composition*, **1**(1), 28–37.

Getz, D. and P-Å. Nilsson (2004), 'Responses of family businesses to extreme seasonality in demand: the case of Bornholm, Denmark', *Tourism Management*, **26**(1), 17–30.

Granovetter, M. (1973), 'The strength of weak ties', *American Journal of Sociology*, **6**, 1360–80.

Greve, H.R. (1998), 'Performance, aspirations, and risky organizational change', *Administrative Science Quarterly*, **43**, 58–77.

Hageback, C. and A. Segerstedt (2004), 'The need for co-distribution in rural areas: a study of Pajala in Sweden', *International Journal of Production Economics*, **89**, 153–63.

Hair, J.F., B. Black, B. Babin, R.E. Anderson and R.L. Tatham (2006), *Multivariate Data Analysis*, 6th edn, London: Prentice-Hall.

Ibarra, H. (1993), 'Personal networks of women and minorities in management: a conceptual framework', *Academy of Management Review*, **18**(1), 56–87.

Ingram, P. and P.W. Roberts (2000), 'Friendships among competitors in the Sydney hotel industry', *American Journal of Sociology*, **106**(2), 387–423.

Ittner, C.D. and D. F. Larcker (1998), 'Innovations in performance measurements: trends and research implications', *Journal of Management Accounting Research*, 205–38.

Johannisson, B. (1996), 'Personliga nätverk som kraftkälla i företagandet', in B. Johannisson and L. Lindmark (eds), *'Företag, Företagare, Företagsamhet'*, Lund: Studentlitteratur.

Johnson, R.A., R.E. Hoskisson and M.A. Hitt (1993), 'Board of director involvement in restructuring: the effects of board versus managerial controls and characteristics', *Strategic Management Journal*, **14**, Special Issue: Corporate Restructuring, pp. 33–50.

Karlsson, C. and J. Larsson (1993), 'A macro-view of the Gnosjö spirit', *Entrepreneurship & Regional Development*, **5**(2), 117–40.

Karlsson, C., J. Larsson and J. Wiklund (1992), *Gnosjöfenomenet*, Stockholm: Allmänna Förlaget.

Kim, Y. (2005), 'Board network characteristics and firm performance in Korea', *Corporate Governance: An International Review*, **13**(6), 800–808.

Krackhardt, D. (1992),'The strength of strong ties: the importance of philos in organizations', in N. Nohria and R. Eccles (eds), *Networks and Organizations: Structure, Form, and Action*, Boston, MA: Harvard Business School Press, pp. 216–39.

Lefort, F. and F. Urzúa (2008), 'Board independence, firm performance and ownership concentration: evidence from Chile', **61**(6), 615–22.

Luo, Y. (1997), 'Partner selection and venturing success: the case of joint ventures with firms in the people's republic of China', *Organization Science*, **8**(6), 648–62.

Miller, K.D. and W-R. Chen (2004), 'Variable organizational risk preferences: tests of the March–Shapira model', *Academy of Management Journal*, **47**, 105–116.

Piore, M.J. and C.F. Sabel (1984), *The Second Industrial Divide: Possibilities for Prosperity*, New York: Basic Books.

Randøy, T. and S. Goel (2003), 'Ownership structure, founder leadership, and performance in Norwegian SMEs: implications for financing entrepreneurial opportunities', *Journal of Business Venturing*, **18**(5), 619–37.

Saxenian, A. (1994), *Regional Advantage: Culture and Competition in Silicon Valley and Route 128*, Cambridge, MA: Harvard University Press.

Shleifer, A. and R.W. Vishny (1997), 'A survey of corporate governance', *The Journal of Finance*, **52**(2), 737–83.

Wan, D. and C.H. Ong (2005), 'Board structure, process and performance: evidence from public listed companies in Singapore', *Corporate Governance*, **13**(2), March, 277–90.

Westphal, J.D., M.-D.L. Seidel and K.J. Stewart (2001), 'Second-order imitation: uncovering latent effects of board network ties', *Administrative Science Quarterly*, **46**, 717–47.

Wigren, C. (2003), 'The spirit of Gnosjö: the grand narrative and beyond', JIBS Dissertation Series No. 017, Jönköping, Sweden: Jönköping International Business School.
Zahra, S., D. Neubaum and M. Huse (2000), 'Entrepreneurship in medium-size companies: exploring the effects of ownership and governance systems', *Journel of Management*, **26**, 947–76.

Other Sources

www.dagspress.se
www.gnosjo.se
www.gnosjoregionen.se
www.ne.se.

8. Knowledge creation and management in an Italian biotech startup

Massimo Merlino and Stefania Testa

1 INTRODUCTION

In today's markets, characterized by high levels of dynamism and complexity, both academics and practitioners appear to agree that the firm's most important asset is knowledge (King and Zeithalm, 2003), since it is the basis for generating innovation (Basadur and Gelade, 2006). Thus it is not surprising that Knowledge Management (KM) (that is the discipline aimed at investigating processes, systems and behaviours that allow companies to nurture and enhance their organizational knowledge) has become one of the hottest issues of management research and practice.

Although KM is important for all industries, it is particularly relevant to the so-called knowledge-intensive sectors (for a definition of knowledge-intensive sectors, see Smith, 2002) due to a need for high innovativeness (see, for example, Ruiz Mercader et al., 2006). The biotechnology industry is among these and, due to its high growth rate and impact on economic output, it has alerted the attention of the managerial and academic communities. Biotechnology commonly refers to the application of biological and biochemical science to large-scale production for the purpose of modifying human health, food supplies, or the environment (Standard & Poor's, 2002). About 50 per cent of the world's turnover in the biotech industry is derived from the healthcare sector, while the remaining 50 per cent is derived from agricultural/foodstuff, environmental and industrial biotechnologies. There are essentially two types of companies within this industry: integrated companies (pharmaceutical, food and agricultural, chemical, and so on) which utilize biotechnologies for production or research purposes and which are mainly based on products; and specialized biotechnology companies, which are mainly based on technologies (for highlights on the Italian biotech industry see Bigliardi et al., 2005). Specialized companies are usually small, young companies and play a very important role in the development of biotechnologies. In the United States and Europe, they comprise more than 60 per cent of all the companies in the sector. According to the existing literature, the main features and roles of the small biotech enterprises can be summarized as follows: high levels of technical-scientific content; close basic research relationships with universities and research centres; a willingness to enter into flexible relationships with integrated companies (joint ventures, research on commission, and so on); an aptitude for discovering new products and new processes; an involvement in the transfer of basic research to large-scale manufacturing. The survival and growth of such firms depend mainly on their ability to absorb and exploit new technological advancement, and this creates an incentive to enter networks at a faster pace than other less knowledge-intensive companies (Pena, 2002; Baum et al., 2000). As noted by Nosella et al. (2005), small firms in the biotech industry represent the *trait d'union* between the academic and the industrial world, because they link the scientific community (depository of knowledge) and the technological community (oriented to industrial exploitation of scientific knowledge). Furthermore, few biotechnology firms own manufacturing and distribution assets to market their knowledge-intensive products, thus they need to form agreements with other companies owning such assets. Such new inter-organizational arrangements ask for an integrated KM approach that mixes together internal core competencies with inter-organizational extensions in order to understand how to create and effectively handle knowledge-based resources.

It is worth noting that, paradoxically, despite the fundamental importance of knowledge for biotechnology companies, it often appears to be a highly undervalued asset. A survey of UK life science companies carried out in 2001 indicated that although many recognized the importance of effective KM, few considered that a deficiency in KM would pose a business risk (see Arthur Andersen, 2001). Ironically, younger companies were prone to holding this attitude, perhaps because at this stage of their development other matters (for example, financing and staffing) seem more pressing. The present chapter focuses on an Italian biotech startup with a twofold aim:

- investigating its awareness/unawareness on the importance of KM;
- identifying the KM practices through which it creates, manages, exploits and nourishes its knowledge, taking into consideration the assumption that, in such an industry, knowledge is the result of continuous collaboration inside a knowledge network.

The rest of the chapter is organized as follows. In section 2, we present a brief theoretical background on KM and knowledge networks as well as on knowledge types: technology, organizational and marketing knowledge. Section 3 describes the methodology, while section 4 describes our case study, a biotechnology company in the startup phase with its knowledge network. Empirical evidence is described and discussed in section 5, and we conclude with section 6, which discusses the implications for practice and research.

2   THEORETICAL BACKGROUND

A Framework for KM

In order to investigate how organizations manage, exploit and nourish their knowledge, this chapter uses a framework for the analysis of organizations as knowledge systems (Holzner and Marx, 1979) composed of a collection of four knowledge processes: creation and/or acquisition (hereafter creation/acquisition); storage and retrieval; transfer and sharing; and application. The model, even though it dates back to the late 1970s, is still considered as a reference point for the knowledge management literature and provides a starting point for more recent models (for example Pentland, 1995; Alavi and Leidner, 2001). In fact, many of the frameworks developed overlap widely.

The knowledge processes introduced above are briefly described here.

Knowledge creation/acquisition is the process of generating knowledge internally and/or acquiring it from external sources. It is worth noting that the effective acquisition of knowledge from external sources depends on the ability of the firm to recognize the value of new external knowledge, assimilate it and apply it for commercial ends. Cohen and Levinthal (1990) label this capability as a firm's absorptive capacity, which is largely a function of the firm's level of previous related knowledge. According to this perspective, what is of no value for some constitutes valuable knowledge for others, and vice versa.

Knowledge storage and retrieval refers to the processes of structuring and storing knowledge in order to make it more formalized and accessible.

Knowledge transfer and sharing refers to the processes of transferring, disseminating and distributing knowledge in order to make it available to those who need it.

Knowledge application is the process of incorporating knowledge into an organization's products, services and practices to derive value from it.

As noted by Wong (2005), most discussions on KM concern large organizations and little attention is paid specifically to SMEs and startups even though the balance of KM requirements changes as a company develops.

In the case of startups, knowledge creation/acquisition seems to be the most critical phase, together with application.

As regards creation/acquisition, Nonaka (1994), Nonaka and Takeuchi (1995) and Nonaka and Konno (1998) articulated the most comprehensive model. These authors, according to Polanyi (1966), identify two dimensions of knowledge: tacit and explicit. Tacit knowledge is personal, context-specific, difficult to formalize and communicate. It includes mental models and schemata, skill-related know-how and subjective insights. Explicit knowledge, in contrast, is transmittable in formal, systematic language (symbols, words and/or numbers). According to these authors, new knowledge is created when there is continual cycling from one dimension of knowledge to another, from tacit to explicit and from explicit to tacit. Andriani and Hall (2002) extended the model, adding elements related to the environment outside the company boundaries: 'locating and acquiring external explicit knowledge new to the group' and 'locating and acquiring external tacit knowledge new to the group'. It is worth noting that explicit and tacit are two coexisting dimensions of knowledge (Polanyi, 1966), and introducing them as two distinct kinds of knowledge is an expedient to simplify the modelling of the concept. According to a main current in the literature, in line with Nonaka and Takeuchi (1995), tacit knowledge is the critical knowledge dimension for organizations.

As regards startups specifically, they can acquire knowledge and capabilities they do not possess by means of alliances (Liebeskind et al., 1996) and collaborations, as well as internationalizing (Zahra and George, 2002; Barkema and Vermeulen, 1998). They can draw upon country-specific knowledge-developing international alliances (Almeida et al., 2002) and/ or they can take advantage of geographical proximity in the acquisition of technologies and tacit knowledge. As an example, Gittelman and Kogut (2003) argue that co-location with research centres is a requirement for success in the biotechnology industry. In fact, the proximity to knowledge centres offers a strong potential for innovation (Chiaroni and Chiesa, 2006). On the one hand, it allows critical mass to be gained particularly for pre-competitive activities as basic research thanks to the availability of a qualified labour market. On the other hand, it favours informal networking and other mechanisms to diffuse tacit knowledge among people working within a cluster. Firms can learn from each other both informally, by being a part of the 'localized buzz' of their cluster (Batheld et al., 2004), and by means of formal mechanisms of knowledge acquisition such as licensing, acquisitions and alliances. Nevertheless, Zucker et al. (1998) argue that knowledge (at least technology knowledge) does not transfer via informal mechanisms such as local social and trade meetings, but actually through formal collaboration among scientists.

As regards application, in the case of startups in knowledge-intensive sectors, the patent system represents the most tangible and clear way through which knowledge is applied to generate corporate value.

It is worth noting that knowledge creation/acquisition and knowledge application must follow one another in a continuous cycle.

Knowledge Types

The chapter adopts a threefold classification of knowledge which includes organization, marketing and technology knowledge (uit Beijerse, 2000). According to uit Beijerse (2000, p. 166):

> Knowledge with regard to the organization has to do with things such as management, policy, culture, personnel, career planning, internal processes, cut backs, alliances and teamwork. When thinking of marketing knowledge, one should think of things such as competition, suppliers, customers, markets, target groups, consumers, clients, users, interested parties, sales, after sales, trade and distribution and relation management. When thinking of technological knowledge, one should finally think of knowledge of products, research and development, core competencies, technological development, information and communications technology, product development and assembly.

3 METHODOLOGY

A case study was developed in order to analyse how a biotech startup creates, manages, exploits and nourishes its knowledge, taking into consideration the assumption that knowledge is the result of continuous collaboration inside a knowledge network. Some authors (Blackler, 1995; Miner and Mezias, 1996) suggest that qualitative approaches are the most appropriate approaches in order to thoroughly investigate the issue of KM, mainly in order to detect social dynamics. The qualitative analysis allows the researchers to understand contextual specificities and it is consistent with the knowledge perspective adopted in this work, based on the idea that knowledge is embedded and constructed from and through social relationships and interactions.

Data collection was based on semi-structured interviews with the members of the entrepreneurial team and the management team. Individual interviews lasted from one to two hours. Archival documents have been collected too, respecting the distinct tradition in the literature on social science research methods that advocates that different sources of data (and methods) be used to validate one another (Jick, 1979). In gathering the data, standard techniques were followed (Yin, 2003). After the transcription of the interviews, data was coded in order to identify themes, recurring comments and parameters which could be analysed in relation to the research question.

4   RESEARCH SETTING

The Company

The research setting is the startup company BioMan. It was founded in 2002 and has been operating in Bioindustry Park Canavese since 2004. The company operates in the fields of research, development and production in the biotechnological fermentation sector. It creates innovative products that may become high value-added components of functional foods, dietetic products, dietary supplements and cosmetic products. Such products combine live bacteria with organic oligo-elements, a combination that is not generally available on the market. The main customers are food industries, dietary industries, pharmaceutical industries, large distributors of ingredients for the food industry and big store chains in the sectors of food and drug.

The strategic positioning of the company in these fields has been a result of a six-month study made by the founders together with two well-known Italian biotechnology experts.

Company activities started in collaboration with the Faculty of Agriculture of Milan University, Microbiology Department, where the initial research (on selenium) was commissioned. As a result of the positive initial results achieved, in February 2004 BioMan moved into the Bioindustry Park del Canavese, where a research laboratory equipped with a laboratory pilot plant for fermentation was available.

From 2004 to date, the company has conducted and completed several research projects about organic mineral trace elements. It has tested and patented organic selenium with live lactobacilli and organic zinc with live bifidobacteria and streptococci. Organic copper will be ready by the end of 2008 and organic manganese by the middle of 2009.

In 2005, BioMan expanded its business by moving into the paint industry. A new company has been established, named Biopaint, with a 25 per cent shareholding held by BioMan Srl and the remaining 75 per cent held by Eporgen Venture. Biopaint was established on the basis of contacts with Danish researchers, with the aim of identifying and developing new antifouling agents of chemical but also enzymatic origin, to be added to antifouling coatings for pleasure boating and shipping industries. This company is totally financed by venture capital while the research on non-pollutant antifouling paints is carried out in collaboration with university researchers (Viterbo and Bologna) and paint experts (Trieste).

The Business Model

BioMan has chosen to use a business model that includes: basic research carried out in collaboration with leading universities, pre-industrialization, patent application at both national and international level, process scale-up and industrial exploitation of patents. The last phase of the process can be achieved in two different ways: by granting manufacturing licences to significantly large research-based companies or by selling intermediate or finished products to companies, directly or via distributors operating in the various markets and utilizing the contract manufacturer's capacity (see Figure 8.1).

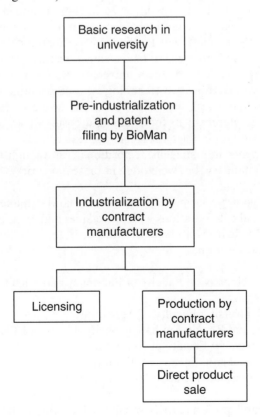

Figure 8.1   The business model

5   EMPIRICAL EVIDENCE

Knowledge Creation

The interviews revealed that the starting knowledge base of the company was not specifically on biotech.

As regards the entrepreneurial team (five founders), member 1 has a master's degree in archaeology; member 2 has a master's in chemical engineering and is a university professor in Innovation Management and Entrepreneurship; member 3 has a master's degree in chemistry and is a director in an R&D department in healthcare; and members 4 and 5 hold masters' degrees in management engineering. Member 1 approached biotech by means of university courses where biotechnologies were applied for restoring and maintaining archaeological remains, and member 2 went into biotech as a result of his long past experience as a consultant for large sugar companies where he was involved in projects aimed at producing amino acids through fermentation of sucrose from sugar beets.

As regards the management team, this is composed of one Managing Director (responsible for general management, research and development and marketing), one Chairman (a university professor heavily involved in development of innovative technologies), one scientific expert (in the field of biotechnologies), and one Operations Manager (with expertise in company development in foodstuffs and cosmetics sectors): some of these people are also in the entrepreneurial team. Many of them had significant experience in management positions even though they were not in the biotech industry, but were often in those industries which are usual markets for biotech.

In order to gain specific biotech knowledge, BioMan makes use of a vast array of external collaborations with universities and research institutions as well as individual researchers. BioMan operates in collaboration with the following institutions:

- Bologna University: Faculty of Pharmacy and Faculty of Chemical Engineering;
- Milan University: Faculty of Agriculture;
- Modena and Reggio Emilia University: Faculty of Biotechnology;
- Pisa University: Faculty of Agriculture;
- Turin University: Faculty of Biology;
- Viterbo University: Faculty of Agriculture.

All the research projects carried out in collaboration with these universities are governed by agreements that guarantee BioMan's full ownership of the research itself, the results obtained and the strains used, while the universities receive royalties, amounting to no more than 1 per cent of the turnover achieved (the research on selenium, completed, and on copper, currently in progress, is carried out on this basis).

This ability to develop a collaboration with university departments is of paramount importance. In fact, earlier studies affirm that relationships with established and reputable organizations such as leading research universities are often related to enhanced enterprise success (for example, Meeus et al., 2004; Mian, 1997). George et al. (2002), in their study on 147 biotechnology enterprises, show that enterprises with university link-ages report lower R&D expenses while having higher levels of innovative outputs. Moreover, linkages with universities give enterprises a window on emerging technologies and scientific discoveries. In general, the rela-tionship seems to be a win–win relationship: on the university side, scien-tists who conduct research in existing and emerging technologies have the opportunity to develop and test their theories, enrich their skills, train and place their students.

Another aspect of collaboration is the relationship with individ-ual researchers from academic research institutions. In the case of BioMan, two members of the management team are academics but their involvement is independent from their departments, due to personal linkages.

According to one interviewee, having contacts with universities gives the enterprise access not only to knowledge resources, but also to prices below market rates: 'Italian academic research centres are cheaper than outsourcing research in a developing country such as India and the benefit is that geographical proximity makes the transfer of (tacit) knowledge easier'.

In terms of money spent on R&D activities, another interviewee com-mented: 'Each year, the company spends an average of 20% of its sales in R&D activities. Despite [the fact that] we do not develop such activities inside the company we coordinate these activities ourselves on the basis of the needs of the company.'

According to all the interviewees, knowledge creation (but also applica-tion) is positively related to the fact that the company is located inside a science park, as the following excerpt clearly shows:

> In early 2005, during some meetings with seed capital companies interested in developing new business activities within the Bioindustry Park Canavese, we discussed a previously discarded project idea (bio-paints) and the interest shown convinced us to consider again the project. The result was the establish-ment of Biopaint. This probably would never happen if we were not inside the Science Park.

Such a location also gives advantages in terms of productivity (a shared dedicated infrastructure reduces initial investments for new ventures).

Knowledge Application

As regards patents, BioMan has gained two patents.

Lacto Bio is patented in Europe (EP 04425408.4), the USA (N. 569935), Canada (N. 2569508), Japan (N. 2007-513919) and Korea (N. 2006-7027696). Such a patent is the conversion of the intellectual activity of a research project that started in the Department of Food Science and Microbiology, University of Milan, and then was developed inside the laboratories of BioMan. The first part of the project was focused on the screening of many intestinal lactobacilli strains and on the isolation of those able to concentrate sodium selenite in organic form. To produce selenium-enriched biomass BioMan worked to optimize: the fermentation protocol; the downstream processing; the product analysis; the scaling up and the final product formulation.

Zinc with live bacteria is patented in Italy (N. TO2007A000555 of 26-07-2007). The patent was extended internationally in July 2008. Such a patent is the result of collaboration between BioMan and the University of Bologna and the University of Modena – Reggio Emilia. The research programme was based on the following experimental areas: setting up of one or more analytical methodologies; selection of strains able to bind and carry zinc; study of a suitable culture medium for the development of the above-mentioned micro-organisms; and development in the laboratory of pilot fermenters.

Concerning products, BioMan does not have any proprietary production plants, so the company operates with the services of outside professional companies to manufacture its intermediate products (as regards foodstuffs) and finished products (as regards dietary supplements). The production plants of partners have been approved by the Ministry of Health and are also GMP and EN-ISO certified in accordance with the provisions of the EU Directives. Nevertheless, BioMan manages all the production planning, quality control and distribution logistics phases, in order to guarantee the customers correct and timely delivery.

6   CONCLUSIONS AND LIMITATIONS

This chapter presented a case study of an Italian biotech startup with a twofold aim:

- to investigate its awareness/unawareness on the importance of KM; and
- to identify the KM practices through which it creates, manages, exploits and nourishes its knowledge, taking into consideration the assumption that, in such an industry, knowledge is the result of continuous collaboration inside a knowledge network.

As underlined in the description of the case study background, the founders of the company do not have any specific biotech training or experience but, driven by their social networks, serendipitous meetings and curiosity towards advances in the biotechnology field, they recognized some market needs and built a venture to exploit that recognized opportunity.

As regards the importance of KM, all the interviewees are aware of that but they underline that the day-to-day workload, challenges and opportunities often relegate KM to a secondary consideration.

Concerning KM practices, it is not surprising that the small group of founders concentrate primarily on R&D (knowledge creation) and usage of results (knowledge application). Nevertheless, what seems to be important for a company is also the ability to learn from failures, that is to learn from those approaches that did not work out as hoped or anticipated, not only during R&D but also in manufacturing and commercial interactions. Furthermore, literature underlines that it is essential for organizations not only to manage what they know but also to activate formal process to acquire what they do not know. In the case under investigation, a formal process to define which kind of knowledge is needed to be acquired is still not being developed. Knowledge is disseminated throughout the organization by means of an informal exchange of information, thus not requiring advanced practices for knowledge transfer and sharing. The compactness of the firm makes it relatively easy to disseminate knowledge among relevant employees.

As regards limitations, the case study approach receives greater scientific approval because it produces results with a high level of validity, from which generalizations can be drawn. However, the narrow scope of this study, which focused on only one startup, does not permit broad generalizations to be made based on our findings. Therefore it may prove useful to conduct quantitative studies in the future, from which generalizations can be derived.

REFERENCES

Alavi, M. and D. Leidner (2001), 'Knowledge management and knowledge management systems: conceptual foundations and research issues', *MIS Quarterly*, **25**, 107–36.

Almeida P., J. Song and R.M. Grant (2002), 'Are firms superior to alliances and markets? An empirical test of cross-border knowledge building', *Organization Science: A Journal of the Institute of Management Sciences*, **13**(2), 147–61.

Andriani, P. and R. Hall (2002), 'Managing knowledge for innovation', *Long Range Planning*, **35**(1), 29–48.

Arthur Andersen (2001), *Managing Risk, Building Value: Risk Management in the UK Life Sciences*, London: Arthur Andersen.

Barkema, H.G. and F. Vermeulen (1998), 'International expansion through start-up or acquisition: a learning perspective', *Academy of Management Journal*, **41**(1), 7–26.

Basadur, M. and G. Gelade (2006), 'The role of knowledge management in the innovation process', *Creativity and Innovation Management*, **15**(1), 45–62.

Batheld, H., A. Malmberg and P. Maskell (2004), 'Clusters and knowledge: local buzz, global pipelines and the process of knowledge creation', *Progress in Human Geography*, **28**(1), 31–56.

Baum, J.A.C., T. Calabrese and B.S. Silverman (2000), 'Don't go it alone: alliance network composition and startups' performance in Canadian biotechnology', *Strategic Management Journal*, **21**, 267–94.

Beijerse, R.P. uit (2000), 'Knowledge management in small and medium sized companies: knowledge management for entrepreneurs', *Journal of Knowledge Management*, **4**(2), 162–79.

Bigliardi, B., A. Nosella and C. Verbano (2005), 'Business models in Italian biotechnology industry: a quantitative analysis', *Technovation*, **25**(11), 1299–306.

Blackler, K. (1995), 'Knowledge, knowledge work and organizations: an overview and interpretation', *Organization Studies*, **16**(6), 1021–46.

Chiaroni, D. and V. Chiesa (2006), 'Forms of creation of industrial clusters in biotechnology', *Technovation*, **26**(9), 1064–76.

Cohen, W.M. and D.A. Levinthal (1990), 'Absorptive capacity: a new perspective on learning and innovation', *Administrative Science Quarterly*, **35**, 128–52.

George, G., S.A. Zahra and D.R. Wood, Jr. (2002), 'The effects of business–university alliances on innovative output and financial performance: a study of publicly traded biotechnology companies', *Journal of Business Venturing*, **6**(1), 577–609.

Gittelman, M. and B. Kogut (2003), 'Does good science lead to valuable knowledge? Biotechnology firms and the evolutionary logic of citation patterns', *Management Science*, **49**(4), 366–82.

Holzner, B. and J. Marx (1979), *The Knowledge Application: The Knowledge System in Society*, Boston: Allyn & Bacon.

Jick, T. (1979), 'Mixing qualitative and quantitative methods: triangulation in action', *Administrative Science Quarterly*, **24**(4), 602–11.

King, A.W. and C.P. Zeithalm (2003), 'Measuring organizational knowledge: a conceptual and methodological framework', *Strategic Management Journal*, **24**(8), 763–72.

Liebeskind, J.P., A.L. Oliver, L. Zucker and M. Brewer (1996), 'Social networks, learning, and flexibility: sourcing scientific knowledge in new biotechnology firms', *Organization Science*, **7**(4), 428–42.

Meeus, M.T.H., L.A.G. Oerlemans and J. Hage (2004), 'Industry–public knowledge infrastructure interaction: intra-and-interorganizational explanations of interactive learning', *Industry and Innovation*, **11**(4), 327–52.

Mian, S.A. (1997), 'Assessing and managing the university technology business incubator: an integrative framework', *Journal of Business Venturing*, **12**, 251–85.

Miner, A. and S. Mezias (1996), 'Ugly ducklings no more: pasts and futures of organizational learning research', *Organizational Sciences*, **7**(1), 88–99.

Nonaka, I. (1994), 'A dynamic theory of organizational knowledge creation', *Organisation Science*, **5**(1), 14–37.

Nonaka, I. and N. Konno (1998), 'The concept of Ba: building a foundation for knowledge creation', *California Management Review*, **40**(3), 40–55.

Nonaka, I. and H. Takeuchi (1995), *The Knowledge Creating Company: How Japanese Companies Create the Dynamics of Innovation*, New York: Oxford University Press.

Nosella, A., G. Petroni and C. Verbano (2005), 'Characteristics of the Italian biotechnology industry and new business models: the initial results of an empirical study', *Technovation*, **25**(8), 841–55.

Pena, I. (2002), 'Knowledge networks as part of an integrated knowledge management approach', *Journal of Knowledge Management*, **6**(5), 469–78.

Pentland, B.T. (1995), 'Information systems and organizational learning: the social epistemology of organizational knowledge systems', *Accounting Management and Information Technologies*, **5**(1), 1–21.

Polanyi, M. (1966), *The Tacit Dimension*, London: Routledge and Kegan Paul.

Ruiz Mercader, J., A. Merono-Cerdan and R. Sabater-Sanchez (2006), 'Information technology and learning: their relationship and impact on organizational performance in small businesses', *International Journal of Information Management*, **26**(1),16–29.

Smith, K. (2002), 'What is knowledge economy? Knowledge intensity and distributed knowledge bases', Working paper 2002-2006, The United Nations University, Institute for New Technologies.

Standard & Poor's (2002), *Biotechnology Industry Survey*, New York: Standard & Poor's.

Wong, K.Y. (2005), 'Critical success factors for implementing knowledge management in small and medium enterprises', *Industrial Management & Data Systems*, **105**(3), 261–79.

Yin, R.K. (2003), *Case Study Research: Design and Methods*, 3rd edn, Applied Social Research Methods Series vol. 5, Thousand Oaks, London, New Delhi: Sage Publications.

Zahra, S.A. and G. George (2002), 'International entrepreneurship: the current status of the field and future research agenda', in M. Hitt, R. Ireland, S. Camp and D. Sexton (eds), *Strategic Entrepreneurship: Creating A New Integrated Mindset*, Oxford: Blackwell.

Zucker, L.G., M.R. Darby and J. Armstrong (1998), 'Geographically localized knowledge: spillovers or markets?', *Economic Inquiry*, **36**(1), 65–86.

9. The international product venturing of a biotech SME: knowledge combination in upstream and downstream networks

Daniel Tolstoy

1 INTRODUCTION

In the global marketplace, where product life cycles are becoming increasingly shorter, firms need to be constantly prepared to re-assess their core activities of business. Recent studies on international small- and middle-sized enterprises (SMEs) have demonstrated that the overall prosperity of these firms hinges on their performance in international product venturing (Indarti et al., 2005; Mesquita and Lazzarini 2008; Ruzzier ct al., 2007). Consequently, SMEs that are able to launch new product solutions successfully in foreign markets may expect reinforced competitiveness and stimulated international growth.

The concept of international product venturing is here defined as the undertakings of an existing firm to introduce a new product in a foreign market (cf. Venkataraman et al., 1992). Even though the interest in international product venturing of SMEs is rapidly increasing, we still know little about the predictors behind this phenomenon. To remedy this research deficiency, this study leans on the magnitude of related research in the field of international entrepreneurship that suggests knowledge combination to be a critical driver of business innovation (Cui et al., 2005; De Clercq et al., 2005; Gassmann and Keupp, 2007; Knight and Cavusgil, 2004; Murray and Chao, 2005; Rialp et al., 2005; Yli-Renko et al, 2001; Zahra and Filatotchev, 2004; Zhou, 2007). Because SMEs typically are resource-constrained, it is reasonable to assume that knowledge combination in these firms is not restricted to the boundaries of the firm, but also takes place in external networks. By building on this idea, the study explores how knowledge combination in networks underlies the international product venturing of SMEs. The study outlines that international product venturing requires knowledge input from both upstream networks (suppliers) and downstream networks (customers). This division may help us understand how the mobilization of a diversified scope of network relationships opens up a multitude of avenues for knowledge to flow and intersect. For example, even though knowledge may very well be combined *within* the confinement of either upstream networks or downstream networks (c.f. Handfield et al., 1999; von Hippel, 1988; Lengnick-Hall, 1996), it can be advantageous for firms to also implement knowledge combinations that reach *across* these networks (Ritter et al., 2004). For instance, innovative product solutions may emanate from combinations of technological knowledge in critical supplier relationships, concerning what products *could* be developed, and market knowledge that resides in important customer relationships, concerning what products *should* be developed. Networks are here understood as the connected customers and suppliers in a firm's environment. Knowledge combination, in turn, is conceptualized as the combination of previously unconnected bits of knowledge for the purpose of developing new business (Buckley and Carter, 1999). In the subsequent empirical inquiry of this chapter, a biotech SME serves as unit of analysis. The biotech firm was considered to represent a pertinent case as it belongs to a global knowledge-intensive industry where international product venturing is imperative for survival.

Against this backdrop, the purpose of this study is to examine knowledge combination within and across upstream/downstream networks, within the realm of the international product venturing of a biotech SME. As a result, the study intends to contribute to SME theory regarding the predicting mechanisms of international product venturing. To provide further direction for this study, three investigative research questions are constructed:

1. How is knowledge combination applied within upstream networks in the international product venturing of a biotech SME?
2. How is knowledge combination applied within downstream networks in the international product venturing of a biotech SME?
3. How is knowledge combination applied across upstream/downstream networks in the international product venturing of a biotech SME?

The remainder of this chapter consists of five principal sections. First, the literature related to international product venturing and knowledge combination in networks is reviewed and a theoretical framework is created. Then, the method of an empirical inquiry into the phenomenon is introduced. Findings from this project are subsequently presented and followed by an analysis and discussion. The chapter ends with a conclusion and discussion concerning managerial implications.

2   THEORETICAL PERSPECTIVE

This section provides a theoretical background to the investigated phenomenon – international product venturing of SMEs. Thereafter, it presents theoretical underpinning of the knowledge combination in networks, where a distinction is made between upstream networks and downstream networks.

2.1   International Product Venturing in Networks of SMEs: A Theoretical Background

Research on international SMEs builds on the assumption that these firms are distinct from larger international firms because of several unique traits. For instance, SMEs that are proactively establishing new ventures in foreign markets – from inception or at a later state – are often described as entrepreneurial by nature (Fletcher, 2006). Consequently, international product venturing of SMEs can be largely understood as an ongoing act of entrepreneurship (Spence and Crick, 2006). The bulk of research on international SMEs has considered knowledge as a key driver to identify/ exploit entrepreneurial opportunities in foreign environments (see Rialp et al., Rialp, 2005 for a review). This can be explained by the prevailing conception that knowledge enables firms to cope with specific foreign market conditions and, thereby, paves the way for effective adaptations to preferences of local customers. Throughout the past few decades, underlying SME research has been the notion that SMEs possess inherent advantages over larger firms in pursuit of knowledge-based opportunities. These advantages are explained by observations implying that they carry less bureaucracy and, therefore, have quicker feet in adjusting to emerging knowledge requirements (Liesch and Knight, 1999). However, there is another side to the coin, implying that small size also may hamper SMEs. Hurdles are generally argued to originate from inherent resource constraints that may impose liabilities of smallness (Baum, 1999). Consequently, SMEs often have to compensate for internal resource deficiencies by seeking leverage of knowledge-based resources that are outside their immediate control. In these cases, firms' networks may be extremely important arenas where complementary bits of knowledge can be acquired and leveraged for product venturing (Dowling and Helm, 2006).

Whereas knowledge input from networks varies in content, research alluding to SMEs' product venturing has primarily stressed a critical need for technological knowledge and market knowledge (Wiklund and Shepard, 2003). On the one hand, technological knowledge involves expertise about the core features of the product offering. On the other hand, market knowledge revolves around the knowledge about customer preferences, competitive situations, and emerging customer segments that are related to the product offering. This idea is supported by Yli-Renko et al., (2001) who studied 180 high-tech ventures and discovered that market knowledge acquired in customer relationships is a strong prerequisite for competitive advantages in foreign markets. In addition, in a review of studies on international retail SMEs, Hutchinson et al., (2005) find that supplier relationships are of critical importance for extracting techno-logical knowledge input that can be applied when contriving new product solutions. Hence, SMEs may benefit from participating in knowledge-sharing networks, comprising both customers and suppliers. Deploying knowledge in both upstream networks and downstream networks may present an abundance of business opportunities that may push interna-tional product venturing to new levels. Moreover, in order for knowledge to be acquired and shared in such networks, relationships need to be close, though flexible enough for firms to be able to adjust to the inevita-ble changes in a competitive business environment (Dyer and Nobeoka, 2000). The next section discusses the concept of knowledge combination in networks in closer detail.

2.2 Knowledge Combination in Networks

Recent research on smaller firms indicates that the applicability of knowl-edge combination is not confined to the boundaries of firms, but encap-sulates their external networks as well (Thorpe et al., 2005). However, activities of knowledge combination in networks are challenged by the fact that knowledge is dispersed, meaning that different connected network actors know different things. Hence, to reap the commercial benefits of the knowledge of others, mechanisms of knowledge combination in networks need to be taken into account.

Knowledge combinations materialize when separate bits of knowledge intersect. In the realm of a business context, this implies that distinct bits of knowledge are orchestrated to achieve commercial benefits. The outcomes of knowledge combination – and the means by which they are realized – are to a large part determined by the different types of comple-mentarities that exist between separate bits of knowledge (cf. Thompson, 1967). In line with Buckley and Carter's (1999) classification of knowl-edge complementarities, they may be additive, sequential or complex. Additive complementarity is the most simple form, and means that bits of knowledge in separate locations are of direct relevance to each other and designated to coincide for a common task (for example A's knowl-edge about production costs is relevant for B's knowledge about market

160   *European entrepreneurship in the globalizing economy*

demand when determining a price for a certain product). Also, they may be sequential, which occurs when knowledge flows are directed to follow a certain one-way path so that knowledge at one location functions as input prior to that acquisition of knowledge at another location (for example A's knowledge about product features influences B's knowledge acquisition concerning market-selection tactics for optimal combined outcome). Further, they may be complex, which occurs when separate bits of knowledge interact through spillovers (for example A's knowledge about R&D needs to be adjusted to B's knowledge about areas of customer use – and vice versa – for maximized results). The consideration of knowledge complementarities in networks may make firms better able to combine knowledge in local networks as outcomes may become aligned with market characteristics and local technological requirements (Lee et al., 2008). Moreover, the enactment of knowledge combination is not only circumstantiated by knowledge complementarities, but also by the nature and location of knowledge. In cases where knowledge is more tacit in nature it is more difficult to understand and codify (Polanyi, 1967). In this case knowledge combinations may require intensive interaction and socialization to be implemented (Nonaka, 1991). In the cases when knowledge is geographically remote, firms may need local representation or sophisticated technology to allow for knowledge flows between organizations (Knight and Cavusgil, 2004).

Even though activities in networks may develop from collective movements that are difficult to influence (Jack et al., 2008), studies have shown that individual firms can be able proactively to pursue knowledge-based opportunities in networks. Such conduct may imply that existing networks are extended and new networks are developed (Sullivan Mort and Weerawardena, 2006). The relative freedom that firms may have to pursue their own goals in networks is, according to network theorists, determined by their flexibility and independence towards other network actors (Burt, 1983). Hence, for firms to keep up with the ever-changing business environment they have to maintain this freedom by questioning current premises and continually implement knowledge combinations that differ from competitors (Teece et al., 1997; Eisenhardt and Martin, 2000; Nonaka et al., 2001).

2.3 Theoretical Framework

This study contends that knowledge can be combined both *within* and *across* SMEs' upstream/downstream networks. This division of network categories is considered meaningful as it constitutes a balanced model regarding firms' technological orientations (roughly represented by activities in the upstream network) and firms' customer orientations (roughly represented by activities in the downstream network). Moreover, studies on international product venturing have argued that firms require both input of technological knowledge and market knowledge (Wiklund and Shepard, 2003). Hence, to achieve diversity and richness in knowledge combinations, knowledge input may preferably be acquired from both upstream networks and downstream networks.

Knowledge combination *within* the upstream network can involve a number of suppliers that are recruited for projects of international product venturing. These firms may have to establish different forms of collaboration to provide conduit for the flow of knowledge and to allow it to be combined between actors (Dyer and Hatch 2006). Knowledge combination *within* the downstream network can involve a certain number of customers that provide feedback regarding product features (Schroeder et al., 2002). Knowledge combination *across* the upstream network and the downstream network implies that knowledge input from each of these dimensions has been intersected into knowledge combinations. An example of this is when customer feedback affects suppliers' technological outlining of new product requirements.

In a first step, Figure 9.1 depicts the current set-up of knowledge combination of a firm. In a second step, the firm has identified an opportunity to connect new actors that can contribute with knowledge input in the upstream/downstream networks. In a third step, these knowledge combinations are realized and a new set-up of knowledge combination is formed. This new set-up forms the basis of what is known in a particular network, and influences (filters) the recognition of future opportunities of knowledge combination (Cohen and Levinthal, 1990).

In line with the intrinsic arguments of this study, the implications of knowledge combination may not be delimited to a single network-category. To the contrary, considering the connectedness of networks (Cook and Emerson, 1978), it is likely that knowledge spillovers bring about knowledge combinations across network categories. These knowledge spillovers are typically triggered in cases where the complexity of knowledge complementarity is high, creating a demand for interactivity (cf. Buckley and Carter, 1999).

3   METHODOLOGY

This study investigates a complex and sparsely explored phenomenon. Consequently, a single-case approach is chosen as it serves the purpose of generating rich insights for new theory development (Yin, 1994). The unit

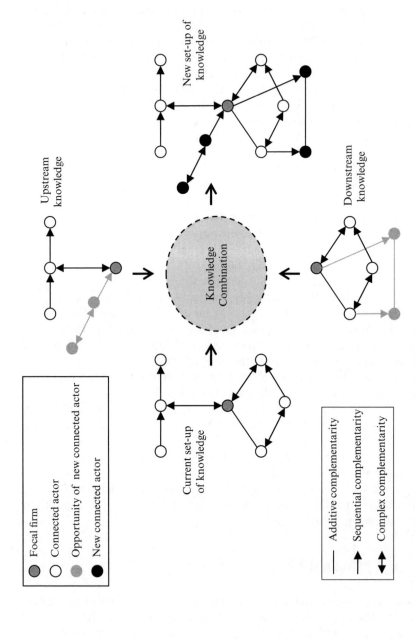

Figure 9.1   Knowledge combination in upstream/downstream networks

Table 9.1   Overview of firm characteristics and collected data

Founded	Employees (2006)	Turnover million euro (2006)	Number of respondents	Number of interviews	Type of Product
1997	22	3.0	4	6	Respiratory devices

of analysis is represented by the international product venturing of a small biotech firm (an overview of firm characteristics is presented in Table 9.1). The analysis focuses on how knowledge is combined within and across upstream/downstream networks in the international product venturing. The investigated biotech firm was chosen on the basis of critical-case sampling: that is, the selected firm is relevant because international product venturing is imperative for its overall competitiveness, a common trait of biotech SMEs.

The firm is located in Stockholm, Sweden, and was singled out by the support of an industry-index in the database Market Manager to make sure that it indeed belonged to the biotech industry. It was also selected on the basis of the criterion that it corresponded to the European Commission's (1996) definition of an SME. Personal interviews were the main form of data collection. In all, six interviews were conducted with four respondents. The study uses a key-informant approach, which is a common practice in marketing research (Phillips, 1981). The individuals we considered as key-informants, and singled out as such, consisted of senior executives who were involved in decisions related to foreign operations. These consisted of the CEO, the sales director, the marketing director, and the technology director. Several measures were taken to guard for quality in the data collection. Attempts were made to interview more than one respondent about each issue. Furthermore, interview data were in all cases substantiated with other forms of data, derived from sources such as annual reports, firm marketing material, newspaper articles, firm website, and financial databases. All interviews were conducted face to face at the site of the firm's head office. The respondents were assured that they and the firm would be treated anonymously in forthcoming studies to make them comfortable about sharing information. Approximately six hours of interview data were collected. Interviews were digitally recorded and transcribed verbatim. Interview data was supplemented with archival data and relevant documents collected from the firms and commercial databases. This data was collected to provide triangulation in validation of interview material (Creswell, 2003). By the support of this data it was possible to structure the interview data chronologically, and evaluate the substance of miscellaneous facts and statements.

The analysis was carried out in several steps. Firstly, a brief outline of the case was presented. Then, by pursuing a replication logic (Yin, 1994), a cross-unit analysis was conducted involving two network categories (upstream and downstream), and three types of knowledge complementarities (additive, sequential and complex). Throughout, literature in the area was consulted for purposes of contrasting and further explaining main findings. In the subsequent discussion findings were tied to the extant literature to reinforce both the internal and external validity of the study.

4 THE INTERNATIONAL PRODUCT VENTURING OF A BIOTECH SME: A CASE STUDY

The empirical inquiry starts out with a short overview of the investigated international product venturing. Thereafter, a cross-unit analysis is conducted to examine how various types of knowledge complementarities (additive, sequential and complex) in different categories of networks (upstream and downstream) constitute knowledge combinations in international product venturing. The cross-unit analysis regarding these dimensions is summarized in Table 9.2.

4.1 Brief Outline of the International Product Venturing

Alpha provides a technologically advanced respiratory device used for clinical research in hospitals and universities. The international product venturing studied had its origin in the fact that the firm believed that the product was becoming outdated and in need of drastic improvements. For that reason, Alpha decided to develop a new generation of the product, which would be launched first in the Dutch market. Because of limited internal resources, the firm was dependent on knowledge input from various sources in the external network – namely, the upstream supplier network and the downstream customer network – to achieve those objectives. The firm began to collaborate with suppliers and customers, and combined knowledge both within and across these networks. Two main objectives were set up to guide the product development process: to design a more usable interface and to make the product significantly smaller. At the end of the project, the initial objectives were met: the device was significantly reduced in size (from 40kg to 0.8kg), and the usability of the interface was improved. The firm even received a prestigious industry award

Table 9.2   Overview of cross-unit analysis

Knowledge complementarity	Knowledge combination within upstream networks	Knowledge combination within downstream networks	Knowledge combination across upstream/downstream networks
Additive	(No observation)	(No observation)	(No observation)
Sequential	Complementary products are ordered from a supplier (calibration gas), and combined with extant technology.	Distributor's knowledge about the Dutch market structure is combined with the firm's internal market knowledge.	(No observation)
Complex	Knowledge regarding sensor technology, software, hardware is combined between the firm and its suppliers in project groups.	Customers' market knowledge is, in iterations, combined with the firm's internal technological knowledge when outlining product specifications.	Customers' knowledge about technology/ application areas is combined with suppliers' technological knowledge through iterative prototype testing.

for the new design. Hence, this case indicates that successful international product venturing rests on the bedrock of various knowledge combinations that reside both within and across upstream/downstream networks.

4.2   Cross-unit Analysis

4.2.1   Knowledge combination within the upstream network
In the realm of the international product venturing, the firm needed to tap the upstream network on knowledge regarding both new sensor technology (to reduce the size of the product) and a new design (to make the product more usable for customers). To obtain access to competencies in the upstream network, the firm instigated three major collaborative relationships involving: (1) an international sensor developing firm (sensor technology); (2) an international software technology firm (new software-based applications); and (3) a domestic hardware developing firm (new

design of product surface). Alpha also ensured that the product met the standards of the customers' supplier of complementary products (which provides a customized gas that is necessary to calibrate the product). For knowledge to be shared and combined between the different participating firms, a project group was formed. Alpha was represented by personnel from R&D, sales, marketing, and service support, whereas the supplier firms were primarily represented by engineers. Parts of the group met weekly in various configurations, depending on the phase of the development. For example, in one phase of the project the supplier of software solutions needed to insert a new complex component in the product. For this, it involved the supplier of this component in project meetings to make sure that the component was compatible with the technology of the other participating firms. Alpha, however, functions as the project leader and has overall responsibility for the project. In the capacity of the organizing node in the upstream network, the firm has daily contact with each participating partner by telephone and email. Alpha has also implemented an intranet to bring together all information and knowledge generated by its project partners, thus enabling all participating parties to get a complete project overview.

4.2.2   Knowledge combination within the downstream network

Knowledge combination within the downstream network primarily involved market knowledge that affected the strategic choices for the design of the product offerings in the Dutch market. Although the firm used a distributor to gain access to customers and to take care of marketing activities, it also ran its own operations in the market. In doing so, the firm strived to not become overly dependent on the distributor and was thereby able to receive first-hand information about particular market conditions. For instance, to gain access to market knowledge input, the firm scanned the Dutch customer network for certain influential customers (researchers and medical doctors) with whom to establish partnerships. From such partnerships, the firm solicited researchers' ideas and preferences about product features and possible application areas. Subsequently, on the basis of this knowledge, the firm learned that there was an unexplored, and possibly lucrative, market in patient care where the product could be applied. By choosing this strategic direction the product had to be equipped with several new features that were required by different types of diagnostic treatments in patient care. The product also had to be drastically reduced in size to be easier to handle for hospital personnel and patients. From its collaborations with customers, the firm was able to distil valuable market knowledge, which was combined with internal knowledge when sketching the initial requirements for how the product should be designed to meet the particular preferences of the customers in the Dutch market. In the realm of the international product venturing, the firm has not experienced any difficulties in making contact and establishing partnerships with influential customers. To the contrary, specialist customers were usually enthusiastic when being invited to work with advanced medical instruments at the cutting edge of technological development.

4.2.3   Knowledge combination across upstream/downstream networks

Knowledge was continually combined across the upstream/downstream network in the investigated international product venturing. The interactions between these two network categories were manifested by processes of prototype testing, indirect customer feedback that was partly mediated by Alpha between its customers and suppliers, and direct customer feedback that was transmitted directly from the customers to the suppliers through joint customer visits comprising representatives from both Alpha and its supplier firms. The product development project was structured as follows:

1.   The product was initially tested on a conceptual level. This meant that ideas were expressed for customers to comment upon. Customer feedback on these initial thoughts was usually addressed in the project group (consisting of representatives of the firm and its suppliers).
2.   Then, the product was tested on a functional level. This meant that initial experiments were conducted to test the technique. Customers were not involved in this phase.
3.   Finally the product was tested on a prototype level. In this phase, the firm and certain members of the supplier firms formed a group where they discussed the viability of the prototypes jointly with customers.

Subsequently, Alpha and the suppliers worked to reach a consensus regarding which product improvements should be implemented. This process included the assessment of several construction proposals. The international product venturing was described as a complex process where single technological modifications or customer comments often had consequences for other connected aspects regarding the technology and usability of the product. Various challenges regarding reaching a final solution could not be overcome simultaneously; therefore, the firm had to interact regularly with both suppliers and customers throughout the course of the project to decide which adjustments to make for the project to move forward. Consequently, the project developed through iterations between and across actors in the supplier network as well as actors in the

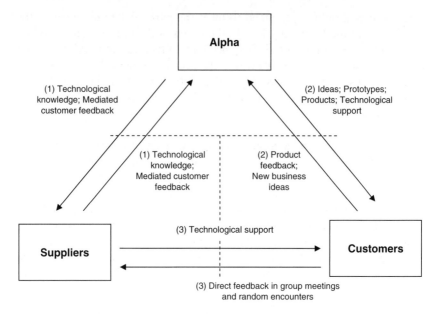

Figure 9.2   Direction of knowledge flows and intersection points for knowledge combination within and across network categories in the case of Alpha

customer network, resulting in new combinations of knowledge across network categories.

Figure 9.2 displays the content and direction of knowledge flows between Alpha and its suppliers (upstream) and customers (downstream). (1) The figure shows that Alpha and its suppliers are engaged in mutual exchange of technological knowledge. Moreover, both Alpha and its suppliers apply the feedback they have previously received from customers in their mutual collaboration. Mediating feedback from customers is complex and requires iterative interaction that is directed both upstream and downstream in the network. The mediation of knowledge allows knowledge to travel across network categories. (2) On the basis of collaboration with suppliers, Alpha is able to derive conceptual ideas and prototypes that are tested on customers. By using the technology, customers can come up with suggestions for product improvements that they communicate to Alpha. (3) On occasions, Alpha arranges group meetings where customers and suppliers can discuss user/technology issues without a middleman. In addition, experts from the supplier firms are occasionally present when customers conduct clinical tests to evaluate the performance of their components. Hence, knowledge flows do reach across network categories. As demonstrated by the case, this may occur through direct encounters or by mediation of a 'broker firm'.

5   DISCUSSION

To gain insights about how knowledge combination is applied in networks in the international product venturing of SMEs, three investigative research questions were formulated. In this section these questions are discussed separately on the basis of empirical findings and theory.

1.   How is knowledge combination applied within upstream networks in the international product venturing of a biotech SME?
In line with Dyer and Hatch (2006), the case shows that the upstream network is of vast importance for generating input for knowledge combination. Further, it is evident that complex complementarities are the ones that are in focus in the firm's upstream network. Hence, the firm seems to allocate most of its personnel, money and time to manage supplier relationships. The reason for this is that these relationships hold a latent potential of generating competitive advantages that can be exploited by knowledge combinations. The relationships that are characterized by complex complementarities seem to be close and cooperative (Dyer and Nobeoka, 2000). Simultaneously, they appear to be flexible in the sense that relationships can dissolve or be programmed on a new course when opportunities for knowledge combination are detected (Sullivan Mort and Weerawardena, 2006). The interaction in these relationships appears to facilitate the exchange of tacit knowledge, which facilitates the implementation of knowledge combinations (Nonaka, 1991). The interaction between actors is, however, somewhat hampered by the geographical distances that divide them. Consequently, as the firm does not have sufficient resources to arrange face-to-face meetings for every occasion in its distant relationships, it relies on technical aids (for example the intranet) to combine knowledge (Knight and Cavusgil, 2004).

2.   How is knowledge combination applied within downstream networks in the international product venturing of a biotech SME?
Consistent with extant theory (for example Schroeder et al., 2002), the international product venturing of the investigated SME appears to be supported by knowledge input from the downstream network. Corresponding to Yli-Renko et al. (2001), certain key customers provide opportunities for knowledge combinations by sharing market knowledge and technological knowledge. Market knowledge is chiefly used by the case firm (1) to

modify the product and (2) to find new application areas for the product. For instance, Alpha learned from its customers that the product had great potential in the area of patient medical care. The proactive strategy to act on this knowledge had implications for the design of the product as well as for which customers the firm decided to target. Hence, these proactive efforts of the firm influenced the construction of the set-up of knowledge combinations in the network (Sullivan Mort and Weerawardena, 2006). Furthermore, many of the knowledge complementarities in the firm's customer relationships are sequential (such as the distributor relationship and relationships with buyers) and do not require much interaction. However, in the network relationships where critical technological/market knowledge is acquired, complementarities seem to be of a higher complexity (similar to the upstream network). Knowledge in these relationships is observed to have the ability to spill over to the firm's strategic decision-making regarding the formation of the international product venture (that is targeted customers, contents of product offering).

3.   How is knowledge combination applied across upstream/downstream networks in the international product venturing of a biotech SME?
An important aspect of network theory is that network relationships are connected across the categories of upstream/downstream networks (Ritter et al., 2004). This notion is prevalent in the case of the investigated SME where there is connection between the upstream/downstream networks that is bridged by knowledge combinations. The importance of combining knowledge across these categories is substantiated by the argument that such conduct can lead to exploitation of a wide diversity of knowledge complementarities, laying the foundation for product venturing that covers the gamut of business considerations (von Hippel, 1988). That is, knowledge from the upstream network may help firms overcome technological constraints, whilst knowledge from the downstream network may help firms to align the product to foreign market conditions (however, the case shows that customers also provide technological knowledge input of immense significance). Even though some of the knowledge complementarities between these networks are sequential, the larger part seems to be of a more complex nature. In practical terms, this means that both suppliers and customers are involved in iterative processes where flows of knowledge either run directly between them, or are mediated by the focal firm. No observations of additive complementarities were found in the empirical data. This is consistent with Buckley and Carter (1999), who claimed that it is unusual with pure forms of addititive complementarities in reality.

6   CONCLUSION

The intended contribution of this chapter was to offer insights into the predictors behind international product venturing of SMEs and, thereby, add to SME research within this field. Leaning on related research in the field of international entrepreneurship, the study sought explanations by focusing on knowledge combination in upstream/downstream networks. The results of the case study indeed show that knowledge combination in upstream/downstream networks is a cornerstone of international product venturing of SMEs. In fact, the findings show that the firm seeks opportunities for knowledge combination by proactively scanning the upstream/downstream for knowledge complementarities. The empirical observations verify the notion that knowledge combination takes place not only within upstream/downstream networks, but also across these categories. Considering all three types of knowledge complementarities, the findings indicate that complex complementarities provide the most critical underpinning for international product venturing. These complementarities seem to involve a broad scope of the network and entail the most innovative outcomes. In the context of the international SME, these findings may have two major implications for theory. The first is that a dichotomous view of the network (i.e. upstream/downstream) may be an advantageous perspective when studying these phenomena. A reason for this is that impetus for new business may accrue in the friction of aligning customer input and supplier input. When the upstream/downstream categories are taken into account, we may be better equipped to recognize the specific intrinsic dynamics that underlie product development. Future studies can preferably adopt this integrated network approach and test whether the external validity of this framework covers a broader spectrum than international product venturings of biotech SMEs. Secondly, the findings suggest that innovation in international product venturing of SMEs is spurred by knowledge combination that is systemized in networks. This implies that firms may need to identify knowledge complementarities in network relationships and apply the proper form of governance to facilitate the subsequent implementation of knowledge combinations. The business relationships that are most critical for knowledge combination often comprise complex complementarities. These complementarities require vast accounts of time and dedication to parcel out viable business acumen and implement new knowledge combinations. Hence, it is crucial that research related to international product venturing of SMEs does not regard relationships in isolation. Rather, more research should study the network at large to generate new knowledge about how to optimize the commercial potential of each knowledge combination. For instance, the observations of the study imply that firms need to allocate time and effort carefully to balance against the knowledge potential of each network relationship. This is important as international SMEs can quickly run out of business as a result of excessive spending and faulty strategic decisions.

7   MANAGERIAL IMPLICATIONS

The findings of this study entail several implications for managers to consider in endeavours of international product venturing. So far, the lion's share of these implications relate to the operations of managers in SMEs, as further research is recommended to substantiate the external validity.

Managers should ceaselessly monitor their business environment and maintain a broad oversight of external business processes. It is imperative to sketch outlines of how business relationships in upstream/downstream networks are connected and what type of knowledge complementarities exist between them. With this information at hand, more effective resource allocation could be achieved and firms will be able to maximize the potential of external knowledge. Effective use of resources in the network steers clear of strategic wrong turns and promotes speed in the configuration of knowledge combination in networks.

Further, it is important for both managers and venture capitalists not only to direct resources to the internal development of technological competence within firms (for example R&D), but also to make explicit plans to develop firms' abilities to tap external competence in upstream/ downstream networks. Such conduct could stimulate cross-fertilization in networks and, thereby, trigger cooperative forms of entrepreneurship that stretch across organizational boundaries.

Finally, to ensure the realization of knowledge combination it is important that managers take action to effectively bridge geographical gaps between their suppliers and customers. For this purpose sophisticated information- and communication tools (intranets, video-conferences, chats, e-meetings) could be helpful. For more complex knowledge combination, face-to-face meetings may still be necessary to push knowledge transfer across organizational boundaries. As interaction strategies that require human involvement are often costly, it is important that they are primarily applied in relationships that have previously been evaluated as potentially profitable.

REFERENCES

Baum, J. (1996), 'Organizational ecology'. in S. Clegg, C. Hardy, and S. Nord, (eds), *Handbook of Organization Studies*, London: Sage, pp. 77–114.

Buckley, P.J. and M.J. Carter (1999), 'Managing cross-border complementary knowledge', *International Studies of Management & Organization*, **29**(1), 80–105.

Burt, R.S. (1983), *Corporate Profits and Cooptation*, New York: Academic Press.

Cohen, W.M. and D.A. Levinthal (1990), 'Absorptive capacity: a new perspective on learning and innovation', *Administrative Science Quarterly*, **35**, 1, 128–52.

Cook, K.S. and R.M Emerson (1978), 'Power, equity, and commitment in exchange networks', *American Sociological Review*, **43**(5), 721–39.

Creswell, J. (2003), *Research Design: Qualitative, Quantitative, and Mixed Methods Approaches*, 2nd edn, Thousand Oaks, CA: Sage.

Cui, A., D.A. Griffith and S.T. Cavusgil (2005), 'The influence of competitive intensity and market dynamism on knowledge management capabilities of multinational corporation subsidiaries', *Journal of International Marketing*, **13**(3), 32–53.

De Clercq, D., H.J. Sapienza and H. Crijns (2005), 'When do venture capital firms learn from their portfolio companies?', *Entrepreneurship: Theory and Practice*, **29**(4), 517–35.

Dowling, M. and R. Helm, (2006), 'Product development through cooperation: a study of entrepreneurial firms', *Technovation*, **26**(4), 483–8.

Dyer, J.H. and Hatch, N.W. (2006), 'Relation-specific capabilities and barriers to knowledge transfers: creating advantage through network relationships', *Strategic Management Journal*, **27**(8), 701–719.

Dyer, J.H., and K. Nobeoka (2000), 'Creating and managing a high-performance knowledge-sharing network: the Toyota case', *Strategic Management Journal*, **21**(3), 345–68.

Eisenhardt, K.M. and J.A. Martin (2000), 'Dynamic capabilities: what are they?', *Strategic Management Journal*, **21**(10/11), 1105–22.

European Commission (1996), 'Commission Recommendation of 3 April 1996 Concerning the Definition of Small and Medium-sized Enterprises', *Official Journal*, No. L 107.

Fletcher, D.E. (2006), 'Entrepreneurial processes and the social construction of opportunity', *Entrepreneurship & Regional Development*, **18**(5), 421–40.

Gassmann, O. and M.M. Keupp (2007), 'The competitive advantage of early and rapidly internationalising SMEs in the biotechnology industry: a knowledge-based view', *Journal of World Business*, **42**(3), 350–66.

Handfield, R.B., G. Ragatz, K.J. Petersen and R.M. Monczka (1999), 'Involving suppliers in new product development', *California Management Review*, **42**(1), 59–82.

Hippel, E. von (1988), *The Sources of Innovation*, London: Oxford University Press.

Hutchinson, K., B. Quinn and A. Nicholas (2005), 'The internationalisation of small to medium-sized retail companies: towards a conceptual framework', *Journal of Marketing Management*, **21**(1/2), 149–79.

Indarti, N., M. Van Geenhuizen and M. Gadjah (2005), 'Knowledge as a critical resource in innovation among small furniture companies in Indonesia', *International Journal of Business*, **7**(3), 371–90.

Jack, S., S.D. Dodd and A.R. Anderson (2008), 'Change and the development of entrepreneurial networks over time', *Entrepreneurship & Regional Development*, **20**(2), 125–59.

Knight, G.A. and T. Cavusgil (2004), 'Innovation, organizational capabilities, and the born-global firm', *Journal of International Business Studies*, **35**(1), 124–41.

Lee, R., Q. Chen, D. Kim and J.L. Johnston, (2008), 'Knowledge transfer between multinational corporations and their subsidiaries: influences on and implications for new product outcomes', *Journal of International Marketing*, **16**(2), 1–31.

Lengick-Hall, C.A. (1996), 'Customer contributions to quality: a different view of the customer-oriented firms', *Academy of Management Review*, **21**(3), 791–824.

Liesch, P.W. and G.A. Knight (1999), 'Information, internationalization, and hurdle rates in small and medium enterprise internationalization', *Journal of International Business Studies*, **30**(2), 383–94.

Mesquita, L.F. and S.G. Lazzarini (2008), 'Horizontal and vertical relationships in developing economies: implications for SMEs' access to global markets', *Academy of Management Journal*, **51**(2), 359–80.

Murray, J.Y. and Chao M.C.H. (2005), 'A cross-team framework of international knowledge acquisition on new product development capabilities and new product market performance', *Journal of International Marketing*, **13**(3), 54–78.

Nonaka, I. (1991), 'The knowledge-creating company', *Harvard Business Review*, **69**(6), 96–104.

Nonaka, I., R. Toyama and P. Byosière (2001), 'A theory of organizational knowledge creation: understanding the dynamic process of creating knowledge', in M. Dierkes, A. Antal-Berthoin, J. Child and I. Nonaka (eds), *Handbook of Organizational Learning and Knowledge Creation*, New York: Oxford University Press, pp. 491–517.

Phillips, L. (1981), 'Assessing measurement error in key informant reports: a methodological note on organizational analysis in marketing', *Journal of Marketing Research*, **81**(11), 395–415.

Polanyi, M. (1967), *The Tacit Dimension*, London: Routledge & Kegan Paul.

Rialp, A., J. Rialp and G.A. Knight (2005), 'The phenomenon of early internationalizing firms: what do we know after a decade (1993–2003) of scientific inquiry?', *International Business Review*, **14**(2), 147–66.

Ritter, T., I. Wilkinson and W.J. Johnston (2004), 'Managing in complex business networks', *Industrial Marketing Management*, **33**(3), 175–84.

Ruzzier, M., B. Antoncic and R.D. Hisrich (2007), 'The internationalization of SMEs: developing and testing a multi-dimensional measure on Slovenian firms', *Entrepreneurship & Regional Development*, **19**(2), 161–83.

Schroeder, R.G., K.A. Bates and M.A. Junttila (2002), 'A resource-based view of manufacturing strategy and the relationship to manufacturing performance', *Strategic Management Journal*, **23**(2), 105–18.

Spence, M. and D. Crick (2006), 'A comparative investigation into the internationalisation of Canadian and UK high-tech SMEs', *International Marketing Review*, **23**(5), 524–48.

Sullivan Mort, G. and J. Weerawardena (2006), 'Networking capability and international entrepreneurship: how networks function in Australian born global firms', *International Marketing Review*, **23**(5), 549–72.

Teece D.J., G. Pisano and A. Shuen (1997), 'Dynamic capabilities and strategic management', *Strategic Management Journal*, **18**(7), 509–33.

Thompson, J.D. (1967), *Organizations in Action*, New York: McGraw-Hill.
Thorpe, R., R. Holt, A. Macpherson and L. Pittaway (2005), 'Using knowledge within small and medium-sized firms: a systematic review of evidence', *International Journal of Management Reviews*, **7**(4), 257–81.
Venkataraman, S., I.C. McMillan and R.C. McGrath (1992), 'Progress in research on corporate venturing', in D.L. Sexton, J.D. Kasarda and E. Hippel von (eds), *The State of the Art of Entrepreneurship*, Oxford: Oxford University Press, pp. 487–519.
Wiklund, J. and D. Shepherd (2003), 'Knowledge-based resources, entrepreneurial orientation, and the performance of small and medium-sized businesses', *Strategic Management Journal*, **24**(13), 1307–14.
Yin, R.K. (1994), *Case Study Research: Design and Methods*, Thousands Oaks, CA: Sage Publications.
Yli-Renko, H., E. Autio and H.J. Sapienza (2001), 'Social capital, knowledge acquisitions, and knowledge exploitation in young technology-based firms', *Strategic Management Journal*, **22**(6/7), 587–613.
Zahra, S. and I. Filatotchev (2004), 'Governance of the entrepreneurial threshold firm: a knowledge-based perspective', *Journal of Management Studies*, **41**(5), 885–97.
Zhou, L. (2007), 'The effects of entrepreneurial proclivity and foreign market knowledge on early internationalization', *Journal of World Business*, **42**(3), 281–93.

10. Building competitive advantages in the process of business growth: the case of Bulgarian technology-based SMEs

Kiril Todorov and Iliya Kereziev

INTRODUCTION

Issues concerning competitiveness and development of technology-based SMEs (TBSMEs) are the subject of great interest for more and more researchers and practitioners. Nowadays the economic prosperity of countries increasingly depends on technological progress and the capacity for innovation of their economies and enterprises, including through creation and development of TBSMEs. On the other hand, creation and development of high-tech enterprises is an entrepreneurial dream for many entrepreneurs pursuing high business results and recognition, but also assuming high risk and uncertainty.

At the same time, a set of reports revealed that in comparison with their main American and Asian competitors, this comparatively small – but important for Europe – group of SMEs is lagging behind with respect to business and innovation performance. Moreover, there seem to be indications that only very few technology-based enterprises in Europe experience rapid growth (European Communities, 2002). The same conclusions are valid for Bulgarian TBSMEs as well, which, in respect of their number and quality, are at an unsatisfactory level of development (Applied Research and Communications Fund, 2006). This is confirmed by statistical data. For example it is clear that low added-value industries are the main Bulgarian exporters, and just 25 per cent of total export is represented by products with a high level of processing. Furthermore, the share of exported high-tech products is very low, or even insignificant. As a result, it is not surprising that Bulgarian and foreign entrepreneurs and managers continue to assume that Bulgaria is a favourable place only for inexpensive and low-technology production, subcontracting and outsourcing.

However, this ambiguity makes it even more important that our attention is focused on the performance of TBSMEs that have considerable potential for growth and internationalization. The weakness of Bulgarian TBSMEs requires powerful support especially regarding fostering their business growth, and to help their management development, which often lacks best practice. Success of these enterprises should be based on the creation of strong competitive advantages and their permanent improvement in the process of business growth.

The aim of this chapter is to reveal and highlight the relationship between creating and developing competitive advantages and growth management of SMEs, and on this basis to identify and analyse the main competitive advantages of Bulgarian TBSMEs and their prospects for development. In order to achieve this aim, the conceptual framework of Wickham (2004) is followed as a theoretical base for analysing competitive advantages and their relationship with business growth.

THE MULTI-FACETED NATURE OF FIRM GROWTH

Firm growth means more than an increase in the firm size. On the part of entrepreneurs and managers growth is a consequence of effective management. The firm grows when they are able to discover suitable business opportunities and the business competes effectively in the marketplace. Maintaining growth has proven to be difficult in the long run, therefore sustainable growth is considered a prominent indicator of business success.

Also, firm growth should benefit all stakeholders involved through the increase in available capital: customers receive better service, employees get more pay rises, as well as career advancement opportunities, the business has more money for expansion of products and markets, and shareholders can receive higher dividends. Because of its complex nature, firm growth can be viewed from a number of different perspectives. Wickham (2004) outlines four important aspects of firm growth that are important: financial, strategic, structural and organizational. The strategic aspect of growth must play a central role in firm growth management.

STRATEGIC ASPECT OF FIRM GROWTH MANAGEMENT

From a strategic perspective, the key to business success is to develop a unique competitive advantage, one that creates value for customers and is difficult for competitors to duplicate. A company that gains a competitive advantage becomes a leader in its market and can achieve above-average profits. However, business rivalry is a very dynamic process, and the competitive advantages are not static. For that reason, once created, competitive advantages require permanent enhancement.

In this respect, competitive advantages are very sensitive to business growth. Expansion of the business can be used to develop a sustainable competitive advantage. This is possible only if the entrepreneur and managers try to manage competitive advantages actively as the firm grows. And conversely, development and enhancement of strong competitive advantages can be seen as a powerful engine of firm growth. Gaining such a synergy requires taking into account the different characteristics of growth on the basis of the different types of competitive advantages. According to Wickham (2004), the competitive advantages are achieved through firm-specific sources of advantages. The most important are cost advantages, knowledge advantages, relationship advantages and structural advantages.

Growth Through Cost Advantages

There are a few sources of cost advantages: preferential access to important resources, economies of scale, experience curve effect and technological changes. The most useful is the relation between the growth and experience curve effect. The skills of a firm are developed and sustained only through experience, and in this way the experience of a firm is related to its potential for better performance. Gaining more experience in delivering output leads to a reduction in cost. This can lead to an uninterrupted 'circle'. Reduction of cost allows a business to offer a lower price, which leads to an increase in demand for the firm's products. However, cost leadership is a strategy which requires quite high output volumes and specific conditions to be met.

Cost leadership and growth complement each other because the experience curve effect is the most meaningful one in the growth phase of a product life cycle, and in the firm growth phase. Such a strategy, however, is not suitable for most firms, particularly for those with a smaller size, including TBSMEs. In spite of this, in technology-intensive industries, new and smaller firms can gain an advantage over established rivals through their potential for faster learning of new routines and better responsiveness to new clients' requirements (Grant, 1991).

Growth Through Knowledge Advantages

Knowledge advantages relate to a firm's know-how that its competitors do not possess. This could be knowledge about the customers, the market or the product, which enables the business to offer more value to the customers. The development of a knowledge-based advantage is dependent on two factors: the significance of the knowledge advantage and its rate of depreciation. If the business aims to grow through knowledge advantages, then it must conduct market research regularly and be active in offering new products and services to the customers. This is a particularly suitable strategy for 'high-tech' markets where customers are likely to respond well to new offerings and innovations.

In TBSMEs, where often a considerable proportion of personnel are highly-qualified, a very important role is played by those employees who are the generators and source of such knowledge and who know how to use it. These are the so-called key personnel on whom the firm's output depends to a great extent, and they are difficult to find, recruit and develop. Their departure may cause a serious crisis in the business because they are the source of experience and knowledge that are key for the development of other firms' employees and for the effectiveness of business processes. This is a common situation in knowledge-based firms, where knowledge management is an important unit for business success. The experience and skills of key personnel constitute intangible knowledge which is difficult to manage by capturing it in a formal system and structure. The knowledge of key personnel cannot be easily copied or transferred to other employees. Their importance increases because they are often members of informal networks of highly qualified and experienced experts. Participation in such social networks is a source of external intangible resources in the form of new ideas, information, contacts and know-how, which allow them to solve difficult business development problems. In general, key employees are a unique source of competitive advantage, and TBSMEs must pay special attention to their recruitment, development and selective motivation (Institute for Entrepreneurship Development, 2008).

Growth Through Relationship Advantages

Embedding the business in networks of positive relationships is the entrepreneur's key role. The challenge becomes, how the entrepreneur and the managers can maintain relationship advantages as the firm grows and further how they can use such advantages to drive growth in the business. As the firm grows and develops, so the web of relations becomes much greater and more complex.

The idea of building relationship advantages means entering the business in the web of relationships with other firms, which secures its access to external valuable resources. Besides relationships with other firms, the business can develop effective relationships with customers, suppliers, investors, employees and other stakeholders, which can lead to building advantages.

Growth Through Structural Advantages

Structural advantages give more flexibility and responsiveness to the firm in comparison with its rivals. This is often a key source of competitive advantage for smaller firms because cost advantages are unusual in the early stages of business development, relationship advantages need time for their establishment, and knowledge accumulation needs considerable investment.

The development of these advantages requires consideration not only of the formal organizational structure, but also of the informal side of the business, such as informal communications and relationships, and an organizational culture that supports or impedes growth. A central challenge of the growing SMEs is maintaining flexibility and innovativeness while at the same time introducing systematic processes. Overcoming this challenge is one of the factors that characterizes successful firms.

The main task of the firm's management is to keep its responsiveness and drive for innovation, to decentralize firm management and the decision-making process, and to successfully transform entrepreneurial into organizational culture as the business grows and increases in size. The key to this is the designing and development of the business structure and organization in a way which will allow structural advantages of the firm to be sustained in the future. For this purpose the role of the firm's leader (entrepreneur or firm's manager) is very important as they must keep the business on the right direction and identify and exploit new business opportunities (Todorov, 2001).

COMPETITIVE ADVANTAGES OF BULGARIAN GROWING TBSMES

Competitive advantages of TBSMEs can be established and developed on the basis of the sources mentioned above and a combination of them. In order to be long-term, the firm's growth must be based on sustained competitive advantages that are attractive to customers.

In this section the main competitive advantages of TBSMEs are identified and analysed, and their sources and relation to the firms' growth are discussed. Moreover, some data and results from the survey of growing TBSMEs are used. They are gathered in the framework of the research project 'Management of growth and competitiveness of Bulgarian

TBSMEs' (IED, 2008). Generally, in our case, a TBMSE is defined as an enterprise based on and highly dependent on the use of technological resources. Manufacturing products and delivering services in TBSMEs are based on the intensive use of scientific and technological knowledge.

Bearing in mind the specificity and complexity of the subject of research, we implemented a detailed and broad questionnaire to gather information about different aspects of the growth process and its management in the companies studied. Next we used personal interviews with some key entrepreneurs and managers to go 'deeper' into the problems we tried to analyse and understand. The interview and case study method allowed us to get inside the companies and to compare quantitative with qualitative information and impressions. The questionnaire embraced growing TBSMEs and covered issues related to their characteristics, behaviour, strategies, strategic orientation, and so on. Business growth was measured as increase in turnover and/or personnel in the last three years.

In accordance with the research methodology, the interviews were mainly carried out with entrepreneurs and executive directors of small and medium-sized enterprises, and just a few key employees, such as general accountants, project coordinators, and so on.

Thirty-one firms were interviewed. The industrial sector distribution of the interviewed firms was varied and was as follows: seven firms were related to high-technology industries (IT, electronics and engineering), 10 were related to medium-high technology industries (machine and instrument building, metallurgy, metal processing, chemical industry) and the remaining 14 were technology-based firms from traditional industrial sectors such as food processing industries, woodworking, furniture industries and light industry.

Firms' Performance and Competitiveness

All studied firms were experiencing growth during the period of 2004–2007. The entrepreneurs' expectations for future progress were positive and this was evidence that the studied firms were strategically oriented towards growth and development. The relatively long period of growth allows us to define them as successful businesses. This suggests that these firms have important achievements concerning their growth management. The presented data showed a tendency towards increase in firms' turnover for the studied period (Figure 10.1).

The main market of Bulgarian TBSMEs is the domestic market, where 83.9 per cent of the firms make a significant share of their sales revenue. Approximately half of them sell 50 per cent of their output on the Bulgarian market, and 19.4 per cent of firms sell 100 per cent of their

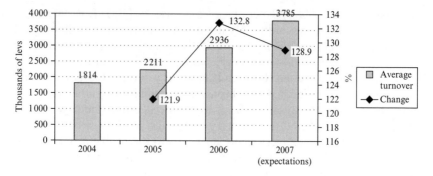

Figure 10.1   Firms' turnover and rate of increase

products and services on the Bulgarian market. Around a quarter of firms sell their products on the markets of Central and East European countries, and a third sell on the markets of West European countries. High competitiveness in an international context is demonstrated by 16.1 per cent of firms, who sell 90 per cent of their products on foreign markets. In comparison with the other subgroup of the SME sector, TBSMEs are more competitive on foreign markets. There are sectoral differences – the firms from high-tech industries are those which sell mainly on EU markets, and innovative technology-based firms from traditional industries are those which sell mainly on the markets of neighbouring and CEE countries, where the characteristics of the economic and marketing environment are similar to those in Bulgaria.

Competitive Advantages

Most of the interviewed firms pointed out that they relied on a combination of competitive advantages with a central role played by product/ service quality (Figure 10.2). This is reasonable because of their technological orientation, but it is not compatible with the high rate of answers revealing use of advantages based on low price. Usually SMEs find it difficult to follow a strategy based on delivering high quality at a low price. On the other hand, increasing competition in high-tech industries on world markets is influencing the price/quality ratio, which obviously has a negative effect on Bulgarian firms.

Under such pressure Bulgarian TBSMEs strive to offer high quality at an affordable price in comparison to their foreign manufacturers and well-known rivals' trademarks, and later become recognized for this. In addition, they often offer a high-speed service, which is particularly important for Bulgarian subcontracting and outsourcing companies.

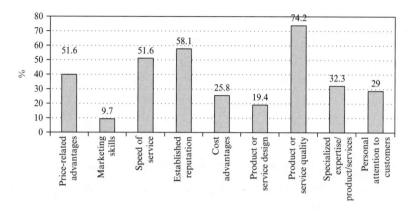

Figure 10.2   The main competitive advantages of TBSMEs (multiple entries possible)

But our observations lead us to the conclusion that attracting customers with a lower price negatively affects the long-term prospects for firm development.

The firms' main source of cost advantage is lower labour costs in comparison with their foreign rivals, including costs for highly qualified employees. Because of the lower price of their products and services, they are not able to amass enough resources needed for the development and pursuit of a long-term strategy. Therefore, relying on the combination of cost-related sources of advantages and price-related advantages puts high-technology businesses in an unfavourable position in respect of their prospects for long-term success and growth.

To extend the analysis we can provide answers to a variety of additional questions concerning the nature and quality of firms' technological base and firms' capacity for generation and transfer of new knowledge. As already highlighted, the main knowledge-related competitive advantages are those that are hard for other firms to imitate. In the case of TBSMEs, such advantages acquire a variety of intangible assets such as patents, licences and specific know-how. And although the nature of the business activity of TBSMEs supposes that their main competitive advantages are embodied in the intangible assets of the firm, the collected data shows a different picture. Over a third of the interviewed companies have not acquired intangible assets in the last five years. This means that these firms do not buy new knowledge and do not improve their own technological base. From the different types of intangible assets, the firms have most often acquired trademarks, technical documentation and licences. Few firms have acquired samples and designs, copyrights and patents

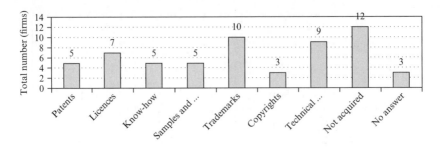

Figure 10.3   Intangible acquired assets in the last five years

(Figure 10.3). The situation concerning firms' self-created intellectual products is similar.

In addition, we can conclude that the majority of Bulgarian TBSMEs are not oriented towards the creation of new and advanced technologies, and most often adopt and use such technologies purchased or transferred from foreign sources. A small number of them rely on their own R&D as a prime source of competitive advantage.

In this situation, some Bulgarian TBSMEs are highly dependent on their key employees who have knowledge of markets and products. This knowledge is connected with the firms' ability to create and develop advantages on the basis of marketing skills, product design and personal attention to customers. But despite the presence of some success in this respect, there are important weaknesses. The management are not sensitive to the firms' needs for the development of such key employees and to the application of new and innovative practices for their motivation. The study shows that firms do not distribute ownership as an instrument for motivation, for example they do not offer shares to their employees, including key employees. Such practices are very suitable for growing TBSMEs, because their successful development and increasing turnover lead to an increase in the value of the company which leads to an increase in the value of employees' shares. Small high-tech companies can see a hundred- or a thousand-fold increase in the value of their shares between when their early employees start and when they retire.

The most powerful sources of competitive advantages for TBSMEs are related to the firms' involvement in innovation collaboration and participation in innovative networks. In this respect, Bulgarian TBSMEs most often create partnerships with suppliers – see Figure 10.4. The majority of firms have one or more innovation relationships with customers, competitors, same sector enterprises, enterprises from other sectors or large multinational companies. These partnerships are not based only on pure commercial relations, and we can define them as 'network' relations.

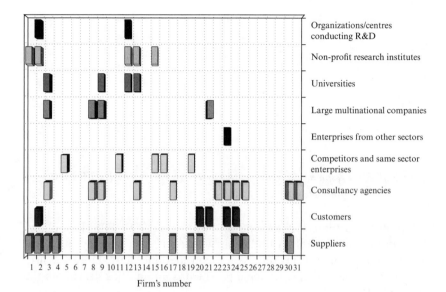

Figure 10.4   Innovation collaboration

Through their supplier–customer relations TBSMEs transfer new technologies (most often purchasing technological equipment) and through their 'network' relations (most often subcontracting and out-sourcing relations) they aim to acquire not just new technologies, but also managerial practices and sometimes funding. They rarely collaborate with consultants, other firms and research organizations in order to conduct innovation projects.

As the presented data show, the strongest and most intensive are relations with suppliers and other companies, which in the majority of cases are contractors. This suggests that Bulgarian TBSMEs do not manage to establish important competitive advantages on the basis of innovation partnerships and networks.

Competitive Strategy

The use of organizational structuring as a source of competitive advantages can be indirectly explored and assessed through competitive strategies of the firms and the way they formulate and develop them. Almost half the firms follow a strategy of product adaptation and an equal number adopt the competitive strategy of focusing on a market niche (Figure 10.5).

Nearly a third of the firms' answers reveal that they offer systemic

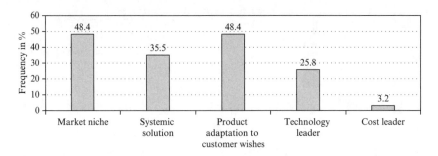

*Figure 10.5   Frequency of competitive strategies followed by TBSMEs
(multiple entries possible)*

solutions to customers' needs and problems. Bulgarian TBSMEs following a strategy of technology leadership which characterizes very ambitious
and growth-oriented firms represent a considerable share. Only one firm
follows a strategy of cost leadership, which is an unusual strategy in the
case of SMEs.

The above results show a strong marketing orientation and very flexible behaviour on the part of the firms studied, but this is not enough for
their long-term success. A more detailed exploration of the gathered data
revealed that according to the answers given by the firms, they rely on two
or three competitive advantages and then follow more than one competitive strategy.

The absence of a focus on development of competitive advantage and
the lack of a clear competitive strategy suggest problems with long-term
business success and also weaknesses in the strategic management of
Bulgarian TBSMEs. Furthermore, usually the interviewed firms very
rarely have and follow a written business plan or any kind of strategy.

Our observation and additional interviews revealed that the majority of firms do not follow a clear model for their future structural and
organizational development, and as a result their business development
is often poorly prepared and chaotic. Finally, instead of a conclusion our
opinion is that entrepreneurs and managers in Bulgarian TBSMEs are
not sensitive to the development of structural advantages, which is one
of the main sources of competitive advantage most suitable for smaller
firms. They focus their attention only on the use of price-based advantages and this negatively affects their prospects for long-term success and
growth.

CASE STUDY: SATURN ENGINEERING LTD ON THE PATH TO HIGH TECHNOLOGIES AND GROWTH

In spite of the prevailing unfavourable characteristics and assessments of the quality and maintenance of the competitive advantages in Bulgarian TBSMEs, amongst them we can also find positive examples. Saturn Engineering Ltd is a fast-growing and successfully managed Bulgarian technology-based small firm. The company business development is a good example of how, in an economy with low technological characteristics, a high-technology business can be started and developed successfully.

In the case study we analyse the firm's competitive advantages and how they are acquired, problems and factors that negatively affect the firm's competitive advantages, and the actions management take in trying to upgrade the present competitive advantages and establish new ones. Some managerial decisions are obvious and others are very creative. The firm's management is a good illustration of how Bulgarian TBSMEs can improve their competitiveness as they grow.

The Bulgarian engineer Mario Metodiev, who works and lives in the USA, founded the company. He was one of the first Bulgarians to leave the country after the beginning of the political and economical reforms in 1989. After some years of employment for American companies he decided that he had gained enough experience to start his own business, and he established Ultraflex International Inc.

Later, during one of his visits to Bulgaria, the entrepreneur saw that on the Bulgarian market there was a lack of consumer electronics. So in 1998 he founded Saturn Engineering Ltd, and started to import consumer electronics from the USA to Bulgaria.

Company Business Development

Company development is a good example of how its management succeeds in capturing new business opportunities, establishes strong competitive advantages and tries to actively maintain its competitive advantages to sustain them as the firm grows.

The entrepreneur's first business idea of trading consumer electronics rapidly ran out of market potential but he found new business opportunities. In 2000 the company started to diversify its activities and offer a variety of services such as web design, and internet and software-related services. At this time the IT service sector was in the early years of development and it offered good prospects for business growth. However, as in the case of the first business, the IT service market very quickly reached maturity, and many small and flexible firms came into the market to offer diverse and competitive services. The competition on the market grew, and the profit margin decreased.

At the same time, the entrepreneur and the management team found out that the demand for designing and manufacturing electronics and electronic components was growing on the global market. Ultraflex International Inc. started to contract out to Saturn Engineering Ltd some activities related to its projects. The initiative was successful and Ultraflex International outsources to the Bulgarian company the design and manufacture of electronic components. From just a micro-firm selling consumer electronics, the company became a specialized producer in the field of IT, and later provider of innovative engineering design, product development and contract manufacturing in a broad range of fields, including industrial, medical, dental and consumer electronics.

So Saturn Engineering Ltd has shown remarkable development and business growth in the last 10 years. The company started with five employees, but now it numbers 56, including 19 engineers engaged in R&D activities. For each of the last two years the company doubled its turnover. Saturn was awarded the Bulgarian Annual Innovative Enterprise Award for 2006 and 2007. In this way, the company developed its competitiveness and even showed a business capacity higher than the ordinary original equipment manufacturer.

In the early stages of development, the firm growth was supported by the orders from the American partner. This was meant to be an assured market. Another important success factor was the strong American dollar, because the firm's revenue was in American dollars.

Competitive Advantages and their Sources

From the start the company has relied on and developed its main competitive advantages that are traditional for Bulgarian outsourcing companies in the IT and electronics sectors, namely lower prices but high quality. Besides providing services from concept, feasibility and design, through prototyping and pilot production, the company offers full-scale assembly, final production and fulfilment.

We can try to identify and classify the variety of sources of the firm's advantages. Presented by type they are as follows:

1. Sources of cost advantages:
   - The lower labour cost that represents the main part of the firm's operating cost.
   - Saturn has developed a unique internal structure that is excep-

tionally cost-efficient yet flexible and powerful. To ensure the highest level of integration between the engineering groups, Saturn has developed a proprietary process that utilizes a powerful Online Project Management and Team Collaboration System for flawless execution. The process has proven so successful that it has been able to reduce development costs by as much as 50 per cent for clients.

2. Knowledge sources of competitive advantages:
    - At first these are firm-specific competences created in the process of firm development – applying advanced, field-proven engineering design and lean manufacturing principles; experience in management of research projects from concept, feasibility and design, through prototyping, production and post-production support; collaboration with companies that are world-leaders in electronics.
    - The firms possess a quantity of patents and innovations that span many fields. Often the company uses its customers' patents. This constantly increases and enhances the technological capacity of its R&D department.
    - The firm provides ongoing training for the engineers to learn new technologies. Certain training is implemented together with the American partner in its engineering base.
    - According to the company's CEO, the creativity of Bulgarian engineers is very important – a non-imitable resource. As a matter of fact, Saturn is recognized worldwide as a leader for its broad engineering talents.

3. Network sources of competitive advantages:
    - Through the partnership with Ultraflex International Inc., the company has access to cheaper funding, new and advanced productive technologies and equipment, employee training, and so on.
    - Close relations to producers of electronic components and firm's assemblers. Some of these are Bulgarian firms that offer favourable prices.

4. Organizational sources of competitive advantages:
    - The firm's organizational structure was designed right at the beginning of its development. From the start of the business organizational processes were foreseen that became necessary later. The company's management considered the firm's development and growth in advance – what department would be created, what their functions would be and what their interrelations would be with other departments.

- The organizational structure is flat, and the managers of different departments are empowered with considerable authority to make managerial decisions. The company encourages the flexibility and innovative behaviour of employees.
- Saturn offers design services and manufacturing in a modern ISO 9001:2000 certified facility. The firm uses an Enterprise Resource Planning (ERP) system.
- Special attention is paid to employees' development. The low employee turnover is an indicator of the high quality work conditions. The employees have the opportunity to learn and develop their skills, the work is creative and routine procedures are unusual.
- Every six months there are inter-firm assessments for all employees, departments and for the firm as a whole. For the engineers there is an incentive system based on their performance and achieved outcomes. Also one part of the company's profit is distributed among the employees according to their assessment.

In spite of the abundant range of sources of advantages, over the long term, competitive advantages and the returns associated with them are eroded, both through the depreciation of firms' resources and capabilities, and through imitation by rivals. After the Bulgarian accession to the EU, more and more foreign firms moved their production facilities to Bulgaria or to other CEE countries. These are well-known and developed companies that strive to profit from the sources of advantages offered by the growing Bulgarian economy. Moreover, at the moment in Bulgaria there is a shortage of IT and electronics experts. The number of experienced hardware engineers is limited; the most-skilled employees leave and start to work for big American and European companies, and in addition the universities do not train enough high-quality workers. This is the reason why the cost of labour is steadily increasing and gradually neutralizing the cost-related source of competitive advantages of Bulgarian firms. Saturn cannot always take advantage of the collaborations with comparatively inexpensive local suppliers and subcontractors, because it often encounters a number of problems in the quality and delivery time of contracts.

Another unexpected problem has appeared in the last two years. The decrease in the rate of exchange of the American dollar has led to the decrease in the company's turnover measured in Bulgarian Levs (and in euros) because the company's main customers are American firms, and the contracts are long-term and fixed in American dollars. Saturn is not able to move quickly on other markets because it does not own its trademark and is not known on the marketplace of final products. This is the

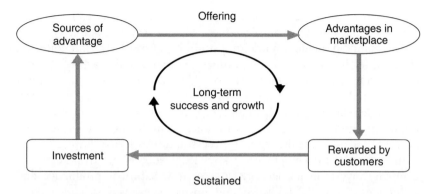

Source: Wickham (2004, p. 438).

Figure 10.6 Creating and sustaining competitive advantage

main reason for the company's management to start planning substantial investment in business development.

Prospects for Development

The case of Saturn Ltd is a good example of how strong competitive advantages can give a stable position and success. However, competitive advantages are not static, but are exposed to erosion from the competitors' actions and from environmental changes. However, building a competitive advantage is not enough. For long-term success a sustainable competitive advantage is necessary. This requires investing in maintaining and enhancement of the company's competitive advantages, upgrading of the current sources of advantages and even finding new sources when necessary. Saturn follows the idea of the model shown in Figure 10.6 to build and develop its advantages considering its growth challenges and the changes in the competitive environment.

The entrepreneur and the firm's management are aware that further business growth requires preparation, development of vision and growth strategy. In relation to this, the company is undertaking a range of actions and initiatives that will allow it to sustain its competitive advantages and upgrade its sources of advantages.

The major point in the new strategy is development of a marketing department and on this basis the sale of products with its own trademark direct on the European market. In the creation of the new marketing function, the company will be supported by the marketing knowledge and know-how of the American partner, but because of the differences in the American and European markets, these will not be applied directly.

The company made a marketing study in several European countries concerning the acceptance of products with the trademark of 'Saturn Engineering' and concerning price level. It was found that the current partners and customers were very positive. A lot of potential customers have trade relations with them and have even bought Saturn's products, but under another trademark. As a whole, the marketing study results are positive, and all in the firm expect successful future development.

In spite of the development of knowledge sources of advantages, the company invests in its network sources too. Saturn is productive and technologically well-established and possesses its own sustained competitive advantages. In the context of the scale and technological level of the national economy, the company has accumulated a critical mass that allows it to play a role of firm-locomotive in an innovation network embracing a considerable number of Bulgarian technology-based suppliers and subcontractors (Autio and Garnsey, 1997). In this respect Saturn has initiated a project to build a high-tech park 'Sofia'.

This is a very ambitious aim because a support structure of this type has not been built before in Bulgaria. In realization of this initiative the company has gained the support and collaboration of the Technical University Sofia, the Ministry of Education and Science, the Bulgarian Academy of Science, the Bulgarian SMEs Agency and foreign funding organization.

Gathering all these technology-based SMEs and important national institutions under one roof could play an important role for the support of technological transfer, the generation of innovative ideas and findings, the sharing of experience and knowledge, and the establishment of new and advanced cooperation and partnerships. Closer collaboration will decrease the relationship's problems between partners because proximity is a precondition for improving the control and diffusion of organizational culture characterized by correct and open relations. Also, the high-tech park will support the technological and business development of the smaller TBSMEs that cannot grow alone. On the other hand, the low level of technological and early business stage of local firms or their inadequate development may significantly impede the business growth of Saturn.

CONCLUSION

Identification of the main competitive advantages of Bulgarian growing TBSMEs and the analysis of the relation between them and firm growth show interesting and ambiguous conclusions. In the first place, this subgroup of SMEs is significantly more competitive than the group of SMEs as a whole. Their main competitive advantages are lower prices but high quality and high speed of service. The lower prices, however, are not the result of sustainable sources of competitive advantage, and this means that the companies cannot rely on them to earn long-term success.

The Bulgarian TBSMEs underrate the importance of development of knowledge-based competitive advantages. Usually they use available and well-known knowledge and very rarely generate new knowledge to give them an advantage on an international level. This weakness is balanced through the building and development of network advantages that positively influence their business growth. However, in most cases these are subcontracting and outsourcing relations in which Bulgarian SMEs are in a more dependent and unfavourable position in comparison to their partners.

Concerning structural advantages, we can conclude that Bulgarian TBSMEs show very flexible and market-oriented behaviour, but it is not based on proper developed and resource-assured growth strategies. Finally, besides the fast business development of studied firms, their competitive behaviour is not based on sustained competitive advantages and the firms do not have a clear vision and plan to actively maintain and develop them.

REFERENCES

Applied Research and Communications Fund (2006), *Innovation. log: Measuring the Innovation Potential of the Bulgarian Economy*, Sofia: Applied Research and Communications Fund.
Autio, E. and E. Garnsey (1997), 'Early growth and external relations in new technology-based firms', paper presented at USASBE Annual National Conference 'Entrepreneurship: The Engine of Global Economic Development', San Francisco, 21–24 June.
European Communities (2002), 'High-tech SMEs in Europe', *Observatory of European SMEs, No. 6*, Luxembourg: European Communities.
Grant, R.M. (1991), 'The resource-based theory of competitive advantage: implications for strategy formation', *California Management Review*, Spring.
Institute for Entrepreneurship Development (IED) (2008), '*Management of growth and competitiveness in Bulgarian technology-based SMEs* research project of Entrepreneurship Development Institute at UNWE, financed by Bulgarian National Research Fund, 2005–2008.
Todorov, K. (2001), *Strategic Management of Small and Medium Sized Enterprises*, 1st and 2nd edn, Sofia: Siela Publishing.
Wickham, P. (2004), *Strategic Entrepreneurship*, Harlow, UK: FT Prentice Hall.

11. Business pre-incubator as a learning network: a case study in the University of Applied Sciences

Kaija Arhio and Marja-Liisa Kaakko

INTRODUCTION AND BACKGROUND

The vision of the Central Ostrobothnia University of Applied Sciences is to be the most well-known and recognized University of Applied Sciences in Finland in the area of entrepreneurship by the year 2010. In addition to higher education, the main focuses are research and development and different services for regional business life.

According to these aims we have developed a model to support entrepreneurship in the Central Ostrobothnia University of Applied Sciences. In the pre-incubator all the activities will train the students towards entrepreneurship, to start their own enterprise and to make their first steps in business. This includes educational and learning processes, research and development processes, learning environment and 'be awakened to entrepreneurship' activities. Students are able to stay in the pre-incubator during their studies. After graduation they will have opportunities to continue developing and planning their businesses supported by regional incubators.

The history of the business pre-incubator in the Central Ostrobothnia University of Applied Sciences Ylivieska Unit goes back to the late 1990s. In 1997 there was a project (INSY) concentrating on the entrepreneurship of engineers and supporting businesses among engineers. This project was the beginning of the Technology Village (YTEK) and RFM-polis. New learning methods were examined and tested as part of higher education in the INSY project. Since those days the pre-incubator has played an essential role in the learning process at the Ylivieska Campus.

The more systematic activities in the pre-incubator started in 2004 as part of the developing project of RFM-polis, and in 2005 these activities continued in cooperation with YTEK. During this project the network model of the business incubator and pre-incubator activities was created and tested. In 2005 and 2006 there were a total of 28 students in the pre-incubator, and eight of them started their own business either during their studies or after graduating.

Starting a new business is a network process involving several actors: students, teachers as tutors, other university personnel such as laboratory staff, educators, client companies, public administration and financiers. In this entrepreneurial process, learning means both individual learning and organizational/network learning. The role of the learning process is underlined when, as a result of the coaching process, a student does not start their business and this decision is also an acceptable result.

LEARNING ORGANIZATION: LEARNING NETWORK

In this chapter, learning refers to something more (or wider) than learning in the traditional educational context. Organizational learning with all the knowledge behind the practice leads to continuous improvement (Argyris and Schön, 1978). Collective organizational learning is the process of continuous development of actions. Through the creation of new knowledge (both tacit and explicit) in teamwork new innovations are created and developed, too (for example Susimetsä, 2006). This creation process of new organizational knowledge combines the individual viewpoint with social perspectives of learning.

The concept of organizational learning combines economical (managerial) and educational theories (Engeström, 1994; Watkins and Marsick, 1993; Lennon and Wollin, 2001). Learning within firms has been a feature of the theory of the firm since Cyert and March (1963), and in the 1990s the work of Peter Senge launched these items into public discussion. In practical business management, learning has been studied from many different viewpoints that are often connected with environmental changes such as global competition. Through learning, organizations are able to avoid possible threats and instead create new innovations to ensure future business success. In business literature the concept of organizational learning refers closely to innovation and change (for example Fiol and Lyles, 1985; Levitt and March, 1988). Prahalad and Hamel (1990) linked collective organizational learning to the concept of core competence. A business strategy that is based on core competences means reasonable allocation of resources and in addition continuous improvement and learning. More and more focus should be placed on organizational and network learning in inter-organizational cooperation. It has also been said that in the future one of the core competences needed will be network management (Weil, 2000).

There are many different ways to define organizational learning. Many of these definitions emphasize social interaction between members of organizations and interaction between organizations and their environment. Also the organization's ability to change strategies, structures and culture is one of the key features of organizational learning. So organizational learning has a close connection with change, creativity and innovation. Knowledge management discussion emphasizes the strategic totality of organizations and has connected organizational learning and strategic learning. Strategic learning in turn is related to sustainable competitive advance (for example Kirjavainen, 1997). According to Kirjavainen (1997, pp. 293–301) strategic learning is a cyclical process where every step is based on a previous stage and at the same time builds the foundation for the next step. This is close to the model of expansive learning launched by Engeström (1987).

Argyris and Schön (1978) state that organizational learning is a metaphor, because organizations do not learn, but learning takes place in individual members of organizations. As a synergy process the organization's learning is more than the sum of individual learning results. Intellectual capital developing in a learning organization creates a competitive advance that is difficult to imitate. On the other hand this organizational knowledge is more difficult to duplicate than other resources such as technology, which can just be purchased (Senge, 1990; Nonaka, 1991; Lennon and Wollin, 2001). One example of the metaphors dealing with the learning organization is the intelligent organization. According to Quinn (1992), an intelligent organization concentrates on its core competences and is able to create synergy between these core competences. An intelligent organization produces innovative solutions for customers when analysing the value chain of actions. An intelligent organization learns more effectively than its competitors and is able to attain world-class quality and actions. A learning organization understands that in every single business action there is a new opportunity to learn.

Senge's model of the learning organization is based on five principles: systems thinking, personal mastery, mental models, building shared vision and team learning (Senge, 1990). In systems thinking everything consists of small connected actions, and the most important is the change of understanding. A team with positive social interaction and a safe atmosphere is able to behave as a learning forum of the organization. Many research results indicate the great effectiveness of teamwork. The development of an effective learning team takes time and requires commitment of all members.

Traditionally, organizational learning has been studied in the context of big companies, but, especially since the 1990s, researchers, practioners and policy makers have focused more and more interest on the small and medium-sized enterprise sector. SMEs are nowadays seen as a crucial factor when increasing knowledge and retaining competitive advantage in a changing environment. The concept of the learning network has mainly been used in the context of web-based learning environments, regional development and transfer of knowledge and technology between universities and small enterprises (Morris et al., 2006; Hanssen-Bauer and Snow, 1996; Tell and Halila, 2001). It has also been discussed as an aid in developing strategic capability among SMEs (McGovern, 2006).

In both literature and policy documents small and medium-sized enterprises are advised to build up networks as a route for acquiring the knowledge needed to survive in changing and competitive markets. Learning in small companies often means transferring technology between organizations. Learning from partners is one of the key elements in a company's success. Knowledge transfer between international partners has been a critical element within Japanese industrial networks (Chaston and Mangles, 2000). According to Chaston and Mangles' (2000) research in the UK, small firms in networks tend to adopt a higher-order (or double-loop) learning style with common features: (1) feedback is given to all employees on how they are doing their jobs; (2) employees are encouraged to participate in training and organizational development programmes; (3) employees will actively share their knowledge with others; (4) the organization's goals and strategies are clearly communicated to all employees; (5) employees, customers and suppliers are motivated immediately to let the organization know about failures; (6) the company is able continually to evaluate current working practices and rapidly identify actions to enhance customer satisfaction; and (7) the company is able to identify new ideas from any source within and outside the organization. These features are similar to those introduced by Senge (Senge et al., 1994).

People in learning organizations have a sense of the importance of their work and every individual is able to increase his or her own competences. In addition to goals and strategies, the organizational values behind the actions and the organization's tacit knowledge are known. Trust and willingness to cooperate are clearly seen in workers' behaviour. Also knowledge will be delivered at every level of the organization. In this kind of learning organization, experiments regarding new ideas and risk-taking are approved of and failures are understood as opportunities to learn. Organizational learning affects organizational competences and might be a way to strengthen market position (Senge et al., 1994; Chaston and Mangles, 2000).

Network learning is an integration process involving the mental models of separate companies to achieve common goals, models of actions and principles. Another point of view includes social processes and interactions in the network that promote the formation of common principles and rules. This means a common network culture, too. This kind of strong network culture remains in a network even when companies change. New enterprises will assume this network culture. Networking is a challenge to both coordination of actions and learning. Through learning, the network is able to act with quality and speed. One key element behind network success is learning (Toiviainen, 2003).

PRE-INCUBATOR NETWORK AS A PART OF UNIVERSITY STUDIES

The aim of the pre-incubator is to offer students the opportunity to find out whether it is feasible for them to start their own business. The essential questions refer to the enthusiasm for, and willingness and courage to undertake entrepreneurship. According to the 2010 entrepreneurial strategy of the Central Ostrobothnia University of Applied Sciences, the entrepreneurial process is a lifelong learning process starting as early as in childhood. During university studies entrepreneurial subjects are included in basic studies and in the wide range of professional and specializing studies. The main goal is to develop a positive attitude to entrepreneurship and to create entrepreneurial skills. This entrepreneurial learning occurs in different projects, practical work and in the final thesis.

This process is closely connected with the needs of society and business life. One element is the entrepreneurial culture of the university. The pre-incubator is part of a student's learning process through their personal study programme. Within the personal study programme the entrepreneur candidate is able to carry out plans and development work for their own business, such as product development, prototype manufacturing, market research, testing and cost accounting. Every student has his or her own individual pre-incubating process which differs from those of other students. In every case the beginning of the entrepreneurial path will be planned and studied separately. The goal of this process is to offer enough knowledge for the student to make the decision whether or not to start their own business. The business plan is the basis of this decision.

Information and marketing of the pre-incubator's activities are included in the basic business studies that are compulsory for all students. The student will receive information about university services supporting entrepreneurship and the services available in regional business incubators. After that the students themselves are responsible for activities and for collecting further information concerning opportunities. In addition, the pre-incubator arranges seminars or events supporting entrepreneurship and is active in different situations promoting entrepreneurship as a career. For instance they may visit and work with local companies.

Through projects the students are able to participate in research and development. R&D activities at the Central Ostrobothnia University of Applied Sciences are run in close cooperation with SMEs.

Pre-incubator activities at Ylivieska Campus utilize networking, so that there are as few stable constructs as possible. Because every incubating process is unique, services that are needed vary in every case, and so that is why we prefer to utilize local services networks (for example, incubators in the area). Activities are based on the student's needs in their business plan and tutoring. The model of action and process concerning cooperative partners and schedules will be planned case by case to offer the most qualified support and tutoring for the entrepreneur candidate. The pre-incubator acts as a tutor in a student's own learning process in a flexible and responsible way. Networking as a mode of action also means a low organizational structure with low permanent costs. At a small unit the number of entrepreneur candidates each year is small. By networking, a small unit with a small number of entrepreneur candidates is able to guarantee quality of action.

Working as a network means that the coaching of students is also connected with the region's incubators and municipal management consultancy. Our students can also take part in all training in the RFM-polis Incubator Centrum in Ylivieska. When our students start their own business, the new entrepreneurs will be guided to the regional incubator centre in the area in which the company starts up.

CUBICO CASE STUDY

As an example of the entrepreneurial process we examine the case of Cubico. The student involved started at the university in 2003. During his first year of studies he planned and manufactured a prototype loudspeaker with quite an unusual and challenging design. The manufacturing was carried out in cooperation with the CENTRIA woodworking laboratory. After registering the company under the name of Cubico he was able to continue manufacturing utilizing the CENTRIA laboratory resources. In 2006 the company signed an official contract with the regional business incubator. While running his own business the student is continuing to study. His specialist studies will be finalized as part of the Cubico business. These studies include product development, manufacturing, marketing and management accounting, and this means basically working as a entrepreneur in his own company.

Individual learning in this case has led to the establishment of a new company. Organizational and network learning become evident in this

---

BOX 11.1   ENTREPRENEURIAL PATH OF CUBICO

Start of studies at COU	Autumn 2003
Registration of company	Spring 2005
Contract with regional business incubator	Spring 2006
Working in wood-laboratory CENTRIA	To be continued
Studies	To be continued

---

process. There are many cases in which we can ask if this development process of a new company could have happened without the network of students, university, pre-incubator and regional business life.

RESULTS OF LEARNING IN THE PRE-INCUBATOR NETWORK

When we think about the Central Ostrobothnia University of Applied Sciences Ylivieska unit's pre-incubator services, we notice that the basic ideas and goals have remained the same during the ten years we have been active in this sector. Naturally the operational environment and the operational preconditions for new companies have changed. Because of these changes the pre-incubator's actions have developed to correspond with the current operational preconditions. In a continuously changing environment the activities of pre-incubators change; however, the basic principles remain the same.

In a pre-incubating process the activity is personal and trusting with mutual interaction. Each individual process differs from the other cases and every case is an opportunity for learning for the tutor. Hence the tutors are able to adapt this new learning in future processes. As stated in the organizational literature, the social interaction between an organization's members, between an organization and its environment in changing circumstances, and the development of an organization's activities through learning are emphasized in this continuous learning process.

The pre-incubating process always starts off the student's own bat and that is why the commitment and activity of the student constitute an important base in this process. As there are no permanent structures, the activities will be tailored to the student's need. The goal is for the student to grow to make a decision on whether or not to run their own business

– that happens through the composition of a business plan. During the process the student also gains practical skills needed in entrepreneurship, such as knowledge of marketing or accounting. The most important learning result in this pre-incubating process is the student's own ability to make the decision. When the pre-incubator acts as a network, so the student can utilize the whole network during the process. Every cooperational partner will support and supervise the student and so the entrepreneur candidate is part of a future business environment that is already at the planning stage.

SUMMARY

The focus in the pre-incubator process is on personal growth and learning. After establishing a company, the student moves on to develop and build up the company with the support of the regional business incubator and guidance systems. Cooperation between these and the university is very close. Since the beginning one of the basic principles of action has been that the university pre-incubator is a part of the regional support network of entrepreneurship. The pre-incubator process is one element of a whole, laying the foundation for the entrepreneurial path. This model of action offers opportunities for the development of tutors' knowledge and skills and for the continuous development of the pre-incubator activities as a learning network.

This chapter has introduced a practical example of how to support entrepreneurship as a part of university studies. From this single case the universities are able to learn when adapting this way of action. When supporting entrepreneurship this case is a way of benchmarking and learning from best practices. As an indication for future research we propose a wider investigation of similar cases from different universities in Europe.

REFERENCES

Argyris, C. and D.A. Schön (1978), *Organizational Learning: A Theory of Action Perspective*, Reading, MA: Addison-Wesley Publishing Company Inc.
Chaston, I. and T. Mangles, (2000), 'Business networks: assisting knowledge management and competence acquisition within UK manufacturing firms', *Journal of Small Business and Enterprise Development*, **7** (2), 160–70.
Cyert, R. and J. March (1963), *A Behavioural Theory of the Firm*, Englewood Cliffs, NJ: Prentice-Hall.
Engeström, Y. (1987), *Learning by Expanding: An Activity-Theoretical Approach to Development Research*, Helsinki: Orienta-Konsultit.
Engeström, Y. (1994), *Training for Change: New Approach to Instruction and Learning in Working Life*, Geneva: International Labour Office.

Fiol, C. and M. Lyles (1985), 'Organizational learning', *Academy of Management Review*, **10** (4), 803–13.

Hanssen-Bauer, J. and C.C. Snow (1996), 'Responding to hypercompetition: the structure and processes of a regional learning network organization', *Organization Science*, **7** (4), 413–27.

Kirjavainen, P. (1997), 'Strateginen oppiminen tietointensiivisessä organisaatiossa. Teoriaa luova case-tutkimus oppimisesta kahden tietoyrityksen strategisessa kehityksessä' ('Strategic learning in a knowledge-intensive organization'), Dissertation, Publications of Turku School of Economics and Business Administration, Series A-Z:1997.

Lennon, A. and A. Wollin (2001), 'Learning organizations: empirically investigating metaphors', *Journal of Intellectual Capital*, **2** (4), 410–22.

Levitt, B. and J. March (1988), 'Organizational learning', *Annual Review of Sociology*, **14**, 319–40.

McGovern, P. (2006), 'Learning networks as an aid to developing strategic capability among small and medium-sized enterprises: a case study from the Irish polymer industry', *Journal of Small Business Management*, **44** (2), 302–305.

Morris, M., J. Bessant and J. Barnes (2006), 'Using learning networks to enable industrial development: case studies from South Africa', *International Journal of Operations & Production Management*, **26** (5), 532–57.

Nevis, E.C., A.J. DiBella and J.M. Gould (1995), 'Understanding organizations as learning systems', *Sloan Management Review*, Winter, pp. 73–85.

Nonaka, I. (1991), 'The knowledge creating company', *Harvard Business Review*, November–December, pp. 96–104.

Prahalad, C.K. and G. Hamel (1990), 'The core competence of the corporation', *Harvard Business Review*, May–June, pp. 79–91.

Quinn, J. (1992), *Intelligent Enterprise*, New York: The Free Press.

Senge, P. (1990), *The Fifth Discipline: The Art and Practice of the Learning Organizations*, New York: Doubleday.

Senge, P., A. Kleiner, C. Roberts, R.B. Ross and B.J. Smith (1994), *The Fifth Discipline Fieldbook. Strategies and Tools for Building a Learning Organization*, London: Nicholas Brealey Publishing Ltd.

Susimetsä, M. (2006), 'Motivated and self-regulated learning of adult learners in a collective online environment', Dissertation, Acta Universitatis Tamperensis 1160. Juvenes Print.

Tell, J. and F. Halila (2001), 'A learning network as a development method – an example of small enterprises and a university working together', *Journal of Workplace Learning*, **13** (1), 14–23.

Toiviainen, H. (2003), 'Learning across levels. Challenges of collaboration in a small-firm network', Dissertation, Department of Education, University of Helsinki, November, also available at: http://ethesis.helsinki.fi/julkaisut/kas/kasva/vk/toivainen/learning.pdf.

Watkins, K.E. and V.J. Marsick (1993), *Sculpting the Learning Organization*, San Francisco: Jossey-Bass Publishers.

Weil, T. (2000), 'Innovation as a creative recombination and integration of existing components of knowledge', paper presented at the Conference on Knowledge and Innovation, 25–26 May, 2000, Helsinki School of Economics and Business Administration, Center for Knowledge and Innovation Research, pp. 5–11.

12. European entrepreneurship: future steps

Alain Fayolle and Kiril Todorov

The problems analysed in this chapter relate to growing challenges to Europe as a region and particularly to European enterprise as an engine of economic development. The intensifying processes of global competition, the development of the economy and projections of multicultural modern businesses are the main reasons for these growing challenges. To these may be added the effects of today's financial and economic crisis, whose demands distort the logical long-term decisions that were taken in periods of stability and growth.

Given the role and content of the enterprise, entrepreneurship can be seen as a means to reduce the negative effects of the crisis so that a way out can be found, and as an engine for development beyond. European entrepreneurship plays and will play the role of such a mega-instrument in the new 2020 Europe development strategy. A subtle point here is to consider the goal-setting gaps as well as the mechanisms for implementation of the Lisbon Strategy. This mostly refers to the generation of sufficient and adequate competitive innovation and their successful commercialization.

At the present time, in terms of competitiveness (especially regarding the level of innovation), production management and labour conditions, Europe is a region that is lagging behind the USA and Asia.[1] Therefore, besides the objectives, resources and mechanisms for implementation of the new European development strategy for 2020, it is necessary to define particular strands of development regarding European entrepreneurship which, as a phenomenon, has many different forms, ranging from start-ups to high-tech spin-offs of larger structures.

These requirements and problems can be synthesized based on summaries of research on existing practices and findings, which can also be found in the contributions to this volume.

It is vital that we have a clear theoretical, conceptual, systematic and comprehensive review of entrepreneurial activity as the basis for its explanation and support in a particular plan. Despite the great variance, in this plan can be found perceptions and concepts and perhaps the forgotten 'new Schumpeterianism', the role of innovation and its commercialization, as shown in the chapter by H. Pichler (Chapter 2).

On this theoretical and methodological basis, a range of appropriate tests should be formed, whose validity and efficiency can be used by different stakeholders and especially policy makers. These results, particularly in the methodological and implementation plan, could be fully integrated in the preparation of new and existing entrepreneurs and managers, who face growing requirements for the possession of specific knowledge and skills, not only in Europe but also beyond it, in a comparative plan.

All these directions and the implementation of the strategies to support entrepreneurial activity in the first place must concern leading sectors such as IT, communications and biotechnology, as shown by the chapters of D. Watkins (Chapter 5), M. Merlino and S. Testa (Chapter 8) and D. Tolstoy (Chapter 9). The greatest attention must be paid to cross-border entrepreneurship in the effort to align the levels of European regions (see the chapters by R. Saner and L. Yiu, Chapter 3, and J. Ateljevic, Chapter 6).

One of the most important aims is the strengthening of the relationship between science–practice, and in which the European universities play a leading role. Here the problem is not simply the creation of sustainable and competitive business sectors based on knowledge, but also the creation of a new generation of entrepreneurs–leaders (see the chapters by O. Pesämaa et al., Chapter 7, and K. Todorov and I. Kereziev Chapter 10).

The main objective of this chapter is to analyse and summarize the existing challenges and opportunities that face entrepreneurship development in European countries with a view to the globalization processes, current economic crises and the networking activities influencing the innovation-led growth of SMEs, and to provide directions for producing knowledge and reinforcing entrepreneurship in Europe.

Therefore, we may synthesize and outline the major directions in which to promote European entrepreneurship and the mechanisms for its implementation. The current economic environment for the development of entrepreneurship in Europe is changing faster today than ever in the past. The globalization processes, rapid change in information and communication technologies and the knowledge-based profile of high-growth firms across Europe are among the main contributors to these changes. The processes described above are connected to the re-emergence of entrepreneurship in the fourth quarter of the twentieth century as a key agenda item for European policy makers.

HOW GLOBALIZATION CHALLENGES AND THE KNOWLEDGE-BASED ECONOMY HAVE AFFECTED EUROPEAN ENTREPRENEURSHIP IN A PERIOD OF GLOBAL CRISIS

Internationally oriented entrepreneurs and emerging businesses face new challenges in an integrated global environment. International economic growth and innovation increasingly result from small or entrepreneurial companies.[2] Attention to the role of firms in the knowledge-based economy has resulted in policy makers counting on entrepreneurship to provide the engine of economic growth.[3] These are among the main reasons why entrepreneurship (and small business internationalization in particular) as a field of research is of increasing interest to policy makers.

The main challenges highlighted in most of the reports, studies and policy documents on entrepreneurship are the need to reinforce entrepreneurship, boost knowledge and further entrepreneurial innovation. In summary, the globalization challenges for Europe are of two main types:

- The first challenge relates to how to replace jobs lost in traditional industries, and the relocation of certain activities outside Europe, with new, quality jobs. In the future, this challenge will become critical as exports from emerging economies will increase rapidly, not just in the segment of traditional, labour-intensive products, but also in product segments with higher added-value.[4]
- The second globalization challenge relates to how to stop Europe from lagging behind the USA and Japan in innovation in high-technology sectors and how to increase its long-term international competitiveness. With a marked increase in investment in R&D and education by China, India and other emerging economies, it is realistic to expect that these countries are well on their way towards becoming strong international competitors for Europe in various areas of innovation.

To the above we add the demand for (mostly short-term) answers related to the financial and economic crisis in respect of the above two trends. We emphasize that short-term answers must not prevent the search for long-term, strategic solutions.

However, in defining these challenges, the ambition of the European Union to assert its leadership in the world is shown – an ambition that is all the more difficult in the context of EU enlargement, given the problems of transition economies, labour migration, energy and resource security and the negative demographic processes.

These challenges are related to some important features of SMEs that make them cope differently from large enterprises in an economic downturn:[5]

- Fewer SMEs are export-oriented, and contractions in global demand thus affect SMEs to a lesser extent than they affect larger enterprises.
- As SMEs typically have lower wages than is the norm in larger enterprises, there is also less need to reduce employment.
- Many SMEs are family-based and thus do not want to cut down on employment. The entrepreneur and the family members who are active in the company are more open to accepting a salary cut. Thus wage structure is more elastic to demand.

But despite the above comparative advantages to larger enterprises, SMEs are generally characterized by low labour productivity, which subjects them to chronic difficulties in covering their investment needs and in making more significant progress towards growth.

The impact of the global crisis on entrepreneurship is presented by an OECD report[6] incorporating the findings of a survey conducted among a number of countries, the European Commission, European Investment Fund, and the outcome of the discussion at the Turin Round Table. According to the survey results, 'at the present time, SMEs have been especially hard hit by the global crisis. These firms are more vulnerable now for many reasons: not only has the traditional challenge of accessing finance continued to apply, but new, particularly supply-side, difficulties are currently apparent'. Among these reasons are also the following:

- SMEs in most countries are confronted with a clear downturn in demand for goods and services;
- it is more difficult for SMEs to downsize as they are already small (and the number of company failures is increasing);
- SMEs are individually less diversified in their economic activities;
- SMEs have a weaker financial structure (lower capitalization) and a lower or non-existent credit rating;
- in a situation of increased payment delays and decrease in liquidity, SMEs are still heavily dependent on credit and have limited financing options.

In the pre-crisis period the majority of enterprises in Central and East European countries were cooperating with international firms from developed countries investing in their economies, that is they usually pursued a reactive strategy towards internationalization. This is illustrated by the case of inward-investing automotive firms in the Czech Republic and

Slovakia. Although there are potential learning benefits for local SME suppliers associated with such a strategy, there are also risks that need to be managed, associated with these firms ending up at the lower end of the supply chain[7] and becoming dependent on foreign contractors.

Currently in many countries anti-crisis packages and accompanying measures are addressing the financing problems of SMEs. As a response to the financial and economic crisis, policy measures to enhance SMEs' access to liquidity, especially to bank lending, through the creation and extension of loan and guarantee schemes for SMEs have been adopted by most member states (Austria, Belgium, the Czech Republic, Denmark, Estonia, Finland, France, Germany, Greece, Hungary, Italy, Lithuania, Luxembourg, the Netherlands, Spain and the United Kingdom).[8]

Notwithstanding the global economic and financial crisis, the current economic environment brings certain *opportunities* for fostering entrepreneurship on an international scale. In the current economy traditional barriers to internationalization have been reduced, resources have become more mobile and more easily transferable between countries, and information flows between countries have been enhanced. Thus it has become feasible for resource-constrained firms to seek to overcome these constraints through internationalization.[9]

As mentioned above, the biggest problem today in support of the European enterprise is how to combine anti-crisis (short-term) support with long-term and comprehensive support for European innovations and entrepreneurship. Only with such an approach with a theoretical and methodological plan, effective real policy and adequate research and training in the field of innovative entrepreneurship, will Europe be able to compete with the United States and East Asia.

ENTREPRENEURSHIP THEORY

In addition to the general recognition of entrepreneurship as an engine of economic development in recent years, it is the subject of increasing interest to theorists and applied researchers. In the last few decades researchers in various fields of entrepreneurship have been trying to systematize theories explaining this phenomenon. To date, we can say that there are a sizeable number of classifications and representations of various theories and concepts.

During the twentieth century, various economists clarified the process of entrepreneurship. Each has emphasized some different aspects of entrepreneurship and has contributed a furthering of the understanding of entrepreneurship and entrepreneurs.

Development of the modern theories of entrepreneurship has centred on either opportunity recognition or the individual entrepreneur. At the same time many theoretical insights have come from economics, sociology, management and psychology.

We can see the individual entrepreneur in a wide variety of approaches and different theoretical economic perspectives. Despite the well-known neo-classical school and Austrian school of economics there is a set of new theories with significant results in their application in entrepreneurship research. They are industrial organizational economics, the resource-based perspective, the competence-based perspective, transaction cost economics, evolutionary economics, economic sociology and so on.

While explanations of entrepreneurship have adopted different theoretical assumptions, most of these concern three central features of entrepreneurial phenomena: the nature of entrepreneurial opportunities, the nature of entrepreneurs as individuals, and the nature of the decision-making context within which entrepreneurs operate.

The overall conclusion in their presentation is that these explanations do not contradict each other, but rather the various theories complement each other, trying to explore entrepreneurship from different perspectives. The heterogeneous nature of entrepreneurial activity and entrepreneurs in different geographical, economic and socio-cultural contexts is reason to have no one valid and acknowledged mega-theory.

Of course, there is an evolutionary development of theories, which reflects the impact of different historical eras and their corresponding manifestations of entrepreneurial activity.

Important questions that seek answers in various theories are:

1. What are the factors determining the various levels of entrepreneurial activity observed in different historical, geographical, political and socio-cultural contexts, and differences in the forms of this activity?
2. Are those factors persistent enough in their nature and relationship to serve as a base to outline a theoretical model explaining entrepreneurship?
3. What are those factors (or at least part of them) that can be influenced and/or used as instruments in promoting entrepreneurial activity?

Each of the theories is based on various studies showing the relevant facts supporting it. To the extent that these studies are based on meaningful empirics, and on other appropriate theoretical models, it is actually difficult to designate a single theory or even a group of theories close in their field of study, which can be accepted as complete in terms of the above questions. For the same reasons, it is difficult to identify which theories can be rejected or even ignored a priori. This, of course, does not diminish the questions relating to the theories, but requires the search for answers to associate and combine the contributions of individual theories. In other words, it is necessary to cross the assumed boundaries of each theoretical field. And this applies especially to the third question, because of its political and practical nature.

In order to achieve this combination it is necessary to work with relatively large datasets reflecting different aspects of entrepreneurial activity and with data obtained by methods allowing comparability in different contexts over a long period. To some extent, a good basis for proving the validity of individual theories might be research such as the 'Global Entrepreneurship Monitor', the 'Index of Economic Freedom' and the like, because of the diversity of criteria used for the measurement of entrepreneurial activity.

In trying to explain entrepreneurship, representatives of the various theories are often limited to the instruments of particular established scientific fields and their projection of the very definition of the term 'entrepreneurship'. However, not a few economists (macroeconomists) almost ignore the role of entrepreneurship in their theories, which is paradoxical. The problems of modern economies (mostly developed economies, as seen in most European countries), and especially the demand for solving them, require an upgrade to the existing theories of entrepreneurship as well as avoidance of attempts to place entrepreneurship within established scientific fields. The basic issues common to most developed economies are twofold: the problem of competitiveness of local firms and the national economy as a set of such firms, and secondly, the problem of employment of the workforce. These issues are comprehensively represented in the 'European Competitiveness Report', 2009[10] and *Report on Employment in Europe* in 2009.[11]

Solving the first problem, that is increasing competitiveness, is a direct consequence of the extent and quality of entrepreneurial activity, but along with that many factors are included, directly and indirectly, which are objects of scientific research in other areas – innovation, technology, organization of labour law and so on. This just illustrates the difficulties in isolating entrepreneurship as a separate phenomenon. But also, this issue focuses the attention of entrepreneurship researchers on the manifestations and outcomes of entrepreneurial activity, which are observable and measurable parameters of the subject and which, to a certain extent, facilitate attempts to construct an entrepreneurial theory.

Solving the second problem – the generation of employment – in turn refers the research to the person as a subject of entrepreneurial activity. And there are attempts to construct an entrepreneurial theory based on the science of humans, their thinking and behaviour, as well as science for society, especially societal relations. And, as we know, most of these achievements in the sciences are still disputed (but not depreciated) due to difficulties in capturing sufficient data to support the lack of practical ways to measure a large part of the processes determining human thought and behaviour.

Concerning the future of entrepreneurship theory and entrepreneurship research, Aldrich noted three different paths of development.[12] The first path is that of classical sciences whose development is based on accumulation of empirically tested hypotheses and well-grounded generalizations. The second path is that of application of different theoretical frameworks and research methodologies borrowed from relevant fields such as economics, sociology and psychology, as well as related functional areas such as finance and marketing. A third way is less theory-driven, and considers practically important topics and perceived usefulness.

In other words, if we were to provide a summary, the problems facing entrepreneurial theories are related to the 'limits' of these theories, methodology and corresponding apparatus, and the validity of the different contexts (conditions). But in terms of questions that should address these theories and practical problems of modern economies, whose solution is based on entrepreneurship, the existing theories, while still developing and not comprehensive in their scope, can serve as complementary and competing approaches in the search for answers.

If we go back to tracing the evolutionary advancement of these theories, we find that there is increasing orientation towards the subject of entrepreneurial activity – the man and his environment in all its diversity – rather than seeking points of support in well-studied processes and economic indicators. This orientation means, at least, an increasingly multi-disciplinary approach to the study of entrepreneurship and 'crossing borders' between the established scientific fields.

Finally, it is understandable that, based on European traditions in the socio-economic theoretical developments, theorists should orient us in a European perspective and the role of entrepreneurship in it. In other words, the theoretical and conceptual views should be both the basis and input for subsequent applied research and for supporting the needs of specific policy and practice – enterprises, entrepreneurs and managers.

ENTREPRENEURSHIP RESEARCH AND TRAINING

Both entrepreneurship theory and research are defined as relatively young areas – actually research intensifies in the 1980s. This newness poses a number of issues concerning the subject of research and methodological apparatus that is applied by the researchers. The main issues are, of course, related to the adequacy of research and their results to the requirements of today and their users.

A good starting point for tracing the evolution of entrepreneurial studies is the book by Hans Landström *Pioneers in Entrepreneurship and Small Business Research* (2005),[13] which reflects the achievements of the most significant researchers, namely D. Birch, D. Storey, Z. Acs, D. Audretsch, G. Becattini, A. Cooper, I. MacMillan and H. Aldrich. From there can be seen the search for limits of entrepreneurial studies, as well as the research approaches and methods utilized. In general, the directions in which the research community develops are twofold: coverage of entrepreneurship as a manifestation of the macro level and the corresponding factors at this level, and the various aspects of entrepreneurship at the micro level – both regarding the individual and the company.

As regards the methodology of entrepreneurial studies, it follows the variety of existing theories of entrepreneurship: economic, managerial, sociological, psychological and multidisciplinary, taking into account both the object and the subject of research.

The diversity of topics is considerable – from the figure of the entrepreneur, to the environmental factors affecting entrepreneurial activity, to studies of specific problems of this business – finance, marketing, human resources, and so on.

The scope of research also follows the differences in understanding of the nature of entrepreneurship. Many researchers prefer to narrow the scope of their research to entrepreneurial situations characterized by innovation, rapid and significant growth, and high technology. On one hand this is explained by the difficulties associated with the heterogeneity of entrepreneurial activities, but on the other, these authors rather seek to study cases that have greater importance to the economy and society.

More specific issues outstanding from the entrepreneurial studies are related to seeking solutions to issues such as entrepreneurial activity among women, young people, minorities, immigrants and religious communities.

There are a number of researchers who focus on individual factors underlying entrepreneurial activity, policy, regulation, education, systems development and protection of innovation.

The results from a study on entrepreneurship research done in the 1980s and 1990s show that five converging axes have been attracting entrepreneurship scholars over time: research on personal characteristics of the entrepreneur; on factors affecting new venture performance; on venture capitalists' practices and their impact on entrepreneurship; on the influence of social networks; and research drawn from a resource-based perspective.[14]

There are also different approaches shown by American and European researchers. Differences in research approaches relate to the two essential characteristics of research – the subject of study and methodology.[15] Europe, in comparison with the United States, is a region of exceptional diversity in the entrepreneurial tradition, not only between nations but also within a larger country. This is among the main reasons why researchers from different parts of the continent focus on very different aspects of entrepreneurial activity. For example, if for the Scandinavians the focus is primarily on innovation and technological aspects, for the researchers from Mediterranean countries the focus will be small family companies; in German-speaking countries the focus will be on the regulatory environment, and for researchers from Eastern Europe, it is on the revival of entrepreneurship and the processes of transition to a market economy. Certainly, without making these characteristics an absolute, it should be noted that in the United States, where entrepreneurship is an inherent feature of the whole society, topics of research are not predetermined to such a significant degree by regional and other differences between the states. In terms of the second characteristic of research, the methodology, Landström underlines the strong orientation of American researchers to quantitative research methods, unlike Europe, which to a significant extent uses qualitative research methods.

The historical review of entrepreneurial studies also shows a change in research interest, following some, for a time, typical thematic preferences. For example, in the 1980s a wave of interest in cultural and cross-cultural aspects of entrepreneurship could be observed, which abated in the 1990s, to be forced to the background by the interest in connection with new technological entrepreneurship opportunities and related knowledge management. In the early twenty-first century preferences are directed to the process of globalization and its effects on entrepreneurial activity.

The development of theories of entrepreneurship will pose new questions which researchers will seek to answer. And because one of the first and fundamental questions have not yet found definitive answers, they will be even longer in focus. These are issues related to assessment of entrepreneurial potential of the individual; to conditions necessary for 'feeding' of entrepreneurship, and to the success and growth of newly established enterprises. Issues of entrepreneurship policy shape a separate, somewhat independent, direction of research. In its framework the experience with the politics and consequences of past interventions will be analysed and evaluated. Today the particular object of research is the study (measurement) of the effects of entrepreneurship education, which, in the last decades, has been recognized as an important tool in creating an entrepreneurial culture.

A separate direction, presumably, will be formed by attempts to penetrate the psychological (including cognitive) processes explaining the choice of an entrepreneurial career and the choice concerning further behaviour.

Finally, you can expect the continued divergence of topics related to entrepreneurship, crossing the boundaries of the established areas such as economics, management, sociology, and so on, and thus forming a new knowledge, which enriches other abutment areas rather than being mere theory. Here we have in mind the recently neglected role of entrepreneurship in the early-formed theories about economic and social development.

An important aspect in the prediction of future research questions is connected to sources of interest in entrepreneurial studies. Undoubtedly, as before, the leading source of interest to researchers remains the scientists dedicated to entrepreneurship. But in addition to this, we should mention the growing interest of policy makers who, on one hand, seek the correct mechanisms to promote entrepreneurship as a proven tool for solving economic and social problems, and on the other, seek some feedback from the effects of their policy. Of those who are interested in further research in the field of entrepreneurship, last but not least, are the entrepreneurs themselves, mostly represented by their associations, who are trying to achieve the necessary interaction with the business regulatory institutions, and who need the relevant arguments in defence of their interests.

As a number of the researchers in the field of entrepreneurship are lecturers in entrepreneurship, research results are becoming an integral part of entrepreneurship subjects. An example of this is the experience of the Institute for Entrepreneurship Development (IED) at the University of National and World Economy in its partnership with the Chair of Entrepreneurship at the same university and the Bulgarian Association for Management Development and Entrepreneurship (BAMDE). The result of this partnership is presented below as a model of their interaction.

The model was recognized as a best practice in European education in the framework of the EFMD project 'Quality of entrepreneurship programmes in Europe'[16] (Figure 12.1).

This model establishes a connection between: entrepreneurship research and education; hosting entrepreneurship events open to the community; training of trainers and consultants; the consulting activities and the practice. It was presented at various conferences and forums, [17,18,19] and institutions from different countries, including in Central and Eastern Europe and in Central Asia, demonstrated their interest in implementing it.

An important part of the model is development of entrepreneurship

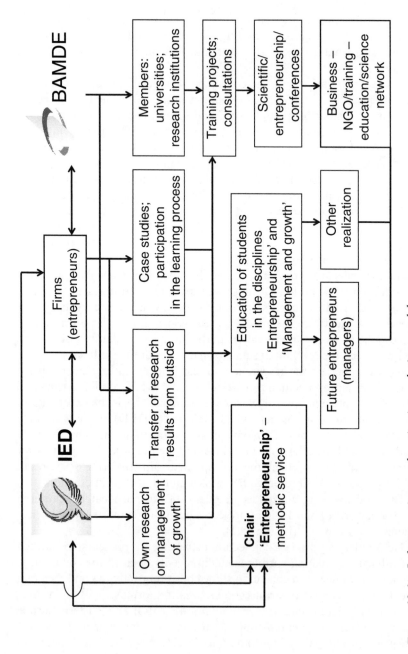

Figure 12.1 Industry–science–education interrelations model

education and training mainly through the efforts of IED and the entre-preneurship chair at UNWE. The historical development of the model shows that the need for survival in the phase of transition, the resource limitations and lack of support lead to the establishment of such a flexible mechanism, matching the specific conditions in the case of SEE and CEE countries.

So, we do expect to have a more intensive research effort on the broader introduction of research results into entrepreneurship teaching and the preparation of new, knowledge-based, competitive European entrepre-neurs. This subject could contribute by its synergetic effects to competitive development in the new, integrating Europe.

ENTREPRENEURSHIP POLICY

For historical reasons, it is difficult to highlight the development of poli-cies that relate to entrepreneurship in the European Union – many of them are extensions of the policies initiated in past decades and aim to resolve the occasional, isolated economic and social problems, and which in our times intertwine in the quest to achieve their goals. For illustration it may be pointed out that SMEs, as a typical representative of entrepreneurial activity, are still subject to individual policies, despite the fact that they constitute a significant part of the European economy, while issues such as competitiveness, innovation and the labour market are subject to other independent policies. This also applies to family businesses, which are not distinguished in terms of their size. Individual policies apply to busi-nesses related to the agriculture sector and there are other specific sectoral policies.

To some extent this 'dispersion' can be justified not only historically (concurrence of problem areas), but also by the heterogeneity and diver-sity of socio-business environments in which they operate, and the conse-quent need for specialized support, tapering fields of application of one or another policy.

The last decade has seen a trend of narrowing in the scope of policy entrepreneurship and its focus on the education of values, attitudes and development of knowledge in order to increase the proportion of people willing to take responsibility for their implementation through the crea-tion and development of their own business.[20] In line with that focus, a set of policies whose objectives are to promote a common environment is being imposed in parallel.

The creation of an environment for promoting entrepreneurship in the European Union is represented by policy measures in key areas such as:

- simplification of procedures for starting a business;
- facilitating the transfer of businesses;
- reduction of the regulatory and administrative burdens;
- training of employees in SMEs;
- building management capacity;
- starting a 'second career' (by staff at the contractor);
- access to public procurement;
- facilitating the recruitment of first employee;
- second chance after bankruptcy;
- tax relief;
- simplification of accounting procedures;
- common commencement dates (for the introduction of regulatory changes);
- encouraging social responsibility of entrepreneurs.

Each of these areas is well substantiated by a series of studies to justify the existence of matching problems. While European-level political consensus has been reached on the meaning and essence of the listed policies, only one small part of them has created mechanisms for implementation at national and local levels. This is true especially for the new member states of the European Union, which until the last decade had been trying to establish effective operational structures in support of entrepreneurship. A major problem with these structures is the motivation of employees in them, which is very often inadequate for the interests of entrepreneurs. Others, however, relatively easily solve problems arising from the intersection of the guidelines listed in the regulation objectives pursued in the social sphere (social and health insurance), occupational safety, maintaining different standards for goods and services (including safety standards), which by default are burdensome regulations on business or, in other words, render the business environment more complex.

As to the policy, focusing on entrepreneurship as mere attitudes, knowledge and individual behaviour, it also faces problems at national and local levels. For example, the part of the policy that affects entrepreneurship education is faced with the traditions (very conservative) and the consequent inertia of the education systems. The insufficient capacity to provide tools, covering the special needs of SMEs and their entrepreneurs and managers, has the largely negative impact here, rather than the practice of mechanical borrowing from the large firms. Even greater is the inertia in bringing new, entrepreneurial values, particularly in regions with a relatively weak entrepreneurial tradition.

Regional differences at a European level, and national differences are barriers that are difficult to overcome when attempting to create entre-preneurs through political measures. Such differences are the product of centuries of specific historical development, and are rooted in local cultures; an effective solution has not been found to overcome them, either suggested by the theories of entrepreneurship, or as a result of the practical interventions that have been made in some regions. It is enough to indicate as examples the differences between northern and southern Italy, and west and east Germany, although, with the enlargement of the European Union, other more notable examples could be highlighted. Not to mention the case of Bulgaria and Macedonia, where despite the historical, cultural and psychological similarities, the differences are very great.

If it is necessary to make a reference to some of the imposed theories about entrepreneurship as a source of ideas for intervention activities, it is undoubtedly at European level where more visible policies have been developed that are aimed directly at individuals and in particular target-ing their knowledge and competencies. In a sense, the emphasis of these policies – entrepreneurial values and behaviour – does not always suf-ficiently take into consideration the specificities of regional cultures. This is obvious by uniformity of the approaches when training entrepreneurial individuals – both as a system and in terms of content. One explanation is in the idea that the transfer of best practices from more developed European countries (in terms of entrepreneurship) and the countries with proven effectiveness of entrepreneurship policy (mostly Anglo-Saxon countries) is possible to be copied mechanically to societies where the envi-ronment determining the local culture is too different.

Observations in the development of various European regions, sup-ported by sufficient statistics did not prove in practice an early conver-gence of the regions, although there are a number of measures contained in the policy regarding regional cohesion, cross-border cooperation and unification of social policies.

Along with the acceleration and improvement of entrepreneurial activ-ity, the policy has set some specific objectives, which have become neces-sary as a result of increased global competition and pressure on European economies. Such specific policies are geared towards innovation and internationalization of SMEs.[21] And in implementing these policies no sig-nificant national and regional differences are observed, although here they are related not so much to cultural as to economic factors – levels of gross domestic product, infrastructure security, clustering economies and regu-lations, to a significant degree. This reflects the presence and behaviour of large enterprises, including multinational and transnational organiza-tions, with their inherent supply chain and subcontractors.

The policy for promoting entrepreneurship in the European Union could take into account the experience in this field in the US, where the Small Business Administration started its activities in 1953, and where later policies were established regarding entrepreneurship in rapidly developing Asian economies – first in Japan and South Korea.

Without stopping to examine in detail the work of the US Small Business Administration, which is just one of the policy instruments designed to provide technical and limited financial support to small businesses, we should emphasize the importance of the overall regulatory environment, providing a degree of protection for small businesses for more than a century, starting from the Sherman Antitrust Act of 1890. It is true that US enterpreneurship is one of the characteristics of American society and in political terms policy makers have sought to establish a common environment to support it, rather than to adopt meaningful intervention measures. In more recent times, under the pressure of competition from outside the United States (a result of globalization), the US are looking for such policy measures, at the federal and even state level mainly to support entrepreneurial initiatives in innovative sectors, creating products and services with high added-value. Although there are many traditions of policy measures in the field of entrepreneurship, the overall policy has been criticized for a lack of coordination both at the federal level and between different political levels – federal, state and local. But the most significant idea from entrepreneurship policy in the United States that can be transferred to the European Union is the strong focus of contemporary policy measures on high-tech sectors.

With regard to policies to promote entrepreneurship in Japan and South Korea, but also in Taiwan and Singapore, today they are confronted with many questions; the slow economic development in these countries over the past decade is to some extent reflected in the gap between the political measures against the background of global change in the balance of economic forces. There were two features that characterized policy in these countries in the second half of the twentieth century: (1) strong focus on promoting export-oriented sectors; and (2) greater attention to policies for large companies because of their important role in exports. Undoubtedly, the SME sector is also subject to strong intervention measures, but especially in the development of specialized companies (subcontractors) in addition to large firms through the supply chain. When China becomes the dominant producer in the region it ousts names traditionally strong in many sectors: Japan and the other countries mentioned above are in need of a new policy to revitalize entrepreneurial potential. This is, however, at a time when there is a relatively weak entrepreneurial culture among the younger generation of Asians, who are being offered better career opportunities in the next couple of decades in the world of big companies. So far the answers to these challenges are still being sought, but unlike most countries in the European Union, Japan, South Korea, Taiwan and Singapore are well positioned in numerous high-tech sectors that are more closely integrated with the US economy. It is considerably more difficult to find an answer to the question 'what can Europe transfer from Asia?', mostly due to significant differences in their economies and culture, and in their institutional and economic structure. Of course, these countries also buy from Europe, and not only museum tickets!

At present, it can be concluded that at the European level there is adequate understanding, supported by relevant studies, political will and legislative initiatives, aimed at accelerating the development and quality of entrepreneurship. However, this is still just a starting point for establishing effective mechanisms to achieve sustainable results, particularly in certain regions of the European Union. The main question for Europe is: how do they get from realizing something needs to be done to actually implementing it.

CONCLUSION

The challenges and opportunities facing Europe are the challenges and opportunities faced by European entrepreneurship as an engine of economic development. Therefore, it is extremely important to have public support for European entrepreneurship in theory, policy and research plans. The vision of a united Europe catching up with the US and Japan, notably in terms of the number and the importance of innovation and its successful commercialization, requires new responses to the challenges. These new responses also require changed attitudes towards entrepreneurship in terms of:

- Better links between theory, policy, research, training and real practice.
- Adaptation of a foreign practice with reference to European achievements, values, traditions and psychology. Particularly interesting are some achievements of countries in transition which are now new EU members.
- Development of working and effective mechanisms for involving young people in Europe, and especially from Eastern Europe, in entrepreneurial activity as a priority in innovative sectors. Particularly important is the combination of innovative technology

with entrepreneurial training so investors know early on which technologies will be adopted by the market and which will not.

NOTES

1. As shown by a number of research and analysis. See, for example, the project entitled: 'Manufacturing Visions (ManVis). Integrating Diverse Perspectives into Pan-European Foresight', in which 22 European countries participated. The project examines the state of European competitiveness and aims to create visions of new production and management in Europe for decades to come. These visions help the development of the policies and strategies that focus on increasing the competitiveness of the European economy. Results show that in the opinion of over 3000 experts, Europe is really lagging behind the United States and Asia.
2. Etemad and Wright (2003), cited in *International Journal of Globalization and Small Business*, **1** (1), 2004.
3. Garnsey and Stam (2007).
4. European Commission (2009a).
5. Erixon (2009).
6. OECD (2009).
7. Smallbone and Xheneti (2008).
8. European Commission (2009c).
9. Hessels (2008).
10. Commission of the European Communities (2009).
11. European Commission (2009b).
12. Aldrich and Baker (1997).
13. Landström (2005).
14. Grégoire et al. (2001).
15. Landström (2005).
16. European Foundation for Management Development (EFMD) (2008a and b).
17. Todorov (2008).
18. Todorov (2009).
19. Todorov and Kereziev (2009).
20. A 'Small Business Act' for Europe.
21. Unfortunately even back in 1999 at an international conference in Leeds, in his paper 'Seven steps to heaven', D. Storey indicated the inefficiency of European policy in supporting entrepreneurship and SMEs. Since then little has changed in a positive sense.

REFERENCES

Aldrich, H.E. and E. Baker (1997), 'Blinded by the cites? Has there been progress in entrepreneurship research?', in D.L. Sexton and R.W. Smilor (eds), *Entrepreneurship 2000*, Chicago: Upstart Publishing Company, pp. 377–400.
Commission of the European Communities (2009), 'European Competitiveness Report 2009', Commission Staff Working Document, Brussels, 1.12.2009, SEC (2009) 1657 final, available at: http://www.eurosfaire.prd.fr/7pc/doc/1268660562_european_competitiveness_report_2009_2.pdf.
Erixon, F. (2009), 'Powerhouses of recovery: small and medium enterprises during and after the financial crisis', research paper, Centre for European Studies (CES), 13 October, pp. 24–5.

Etemad, H. and R. Wright (2003), *Globalization and Entrepreneurship: Policy and Strategy Perspectives*, Cheltenham, UK and Northampton, MA, USA: Edward Elgar.

European Commission (2009a), *A Knowledge-intensive Future for Europe: Expert Group Report*, Expert Group on the 3% Objective: Progress Made and Post-2010 Policy Scenario, October, Luxembourg: Publications Office of the European Union, available at: ftp://ftp.cordis.europa.eu/pub/era/docs/kife.pdf.

European Commission (2009b), *Employment in Europe 2009*, Directorate-General for Employment, Social Affairs and Equal Opportunities, Unit D.1, Luxembourg: Publications Office of the European Union, available at: http://ec.europa.eu/social/main.jsp?catId=119&langId=en.

European Commission (2009c), 'Report on the implementation of the Small Business Act', Commission Working Document, COM(2009) 680, European Commission, Brussels, available at: http://ec.europa.eu/enterprise/policies/sme/small-business-act/implementation/files/sba_imp_en.pdf.

European Foundation for Management Development (EFMD) (2008a), 'Best practices & pedagogical methods in entrepreneurship education in Europe', Project Quality of Entrepreneurship Programmes in Europe, WP1, p. 26, available at: http://www.efmd.org/images/stories/efmd/intl_affairs/wp1.pdf.

European Foundation for Management Development (EFMD) (2008b), 'How higher education institutions in Europe deal with the quality assurance of their entrepreneurship programmes: case studies', WP3, pp. 9–17, available at: http://www.efmd.org/images/stories/efmd/intl_affairs/wp3.pdf.

Garnsey, E. and E. Stam (2007), 'Entrepreneurship in the knowledge economy', CTM Working Paper 2007/04, University of Cambridge.

Grégoire, D., R. Déry and J.-P. Béchard (2001), 'Evolving conversations: a look at the convergence in entrepreneurship research', in W.D. Bygrave, E. Autio, C.G. Brush, P. Davidsson, P.G. Greene, P.D. Reynolds and H.J. Sapienza (eds), *Frontiers of Entrepreneurship Research 2001*, Babson Park, MA: Babson College, available at: http://www.babson.edu/entrep/fer/babson2001/XXIX/XXIXA/XXIXA.htm.

Hessels, J. (2008), 'Overcoming resource-constraints through internationalization? An empirical analysis of European SMEs', Netherlands Ministry of Economic Affairs, available at: http://www.entrepreneurship-sme.eu/sys/cftags/assetnow/design/widgets/site/ctm_getFile.cfm?file=H200806.pdf&perId=0.

Landström, H. (2005), *Pioneers in Entrepreneurship and Small Business Research*, New York: Springer Science + Business Media Inc.

Organisation for Economic Co-operation and Development (OECD) (2009), 'The impact of the global crisis on SME and entrepreneurship financing and policy responses', Centre for Entrepreneurship, SMEs and Local Development, OECD, available at: http://www.oecd.org/dataoecd/40/34/43183090.pdf.

Smallbone, D. and M. Xheneti (2008), 'Policy issues related to entrepreneurship development and cross border cooperation in case study regions', CBCED Project Deliverable, Sixth Framework Programme, pp. 9–10; available at: http://crossbordercoop.net/Publications/D16_policies_governance.pdf.

Storey, D. (1999), 'Seven steps to heaven', paper presented at 22nd ISBA National Conference, Leeds, November.

Todorov, K. (2008), 'The role and activities of BAMDE in supporting the growth of SMEs in Bulgaria', presentation to the 35th International Small Business Congress, 4–6 November, Belfast.

Todorov, K. (2009), 'BAMDE activities', presentation held at the International Capacity Building Alliance Seminar, FIA (Fundação Instituto de Administração), São Paulo, Brazil.
Todorov, K. and I. Kereziev (2009), 'A successful model of entrepreneurial education and training in transition countries: the example of Bulgaria', paper presented at EFMD Conference, 27 February, Barcelona.

Index

additive complementarities 159–60, 162, 165
administration, proper 134, 135, 137, 139
age
 board members 135, 136, 138, 139
 company 135, 136–7, 139
Aldrich, H.E. 210
algae 91
 algal blooms 91, 97
 algal toxins 96–7
Allemanisch dialect 34
alliances 146
Alpha case study 161–70
American dollar 188, 190
AMOS software 139
anti-crisis packages 207
antithesis 15
application
 knowledge application 145, 146, 147, 152, 153
 knowledge produced in the context of 75, 77–8
Aranyponty Rt. Rétimajor Fish Farm and Eco-tourism 80–81
Argyris, C. 196
Asbjørnsen, B. 93, 95
Asia 203, 207, 218–19
auditors 127–8, 137
 number of relationships 134, 135, 136, 138, 139–40

BAK International Benchmark Report 31–2
Balkans, the 4, 100–122
Beijerse, R.P. uit 147
biodiversity 4, 69–99
Bioindustry Park Canavese 148, 151
BioMan case study 148–53
 business model 149

knowledge application 152
knowledge creation 150–52
Biopaint 148–9, 151
biotechnology
 international product venturing 5–6, 156–75
 knowledge management 5, 143–55
bivalves, *see* mussels
Black, B.S. 128, 132
Blackburn, R. 72
boards of directors 5, 125–42
 board, administration and performance model 128–37
 functions of a board 127–8
 linear regression analysis of network characteristics and company performance 137–40
Böhm-Bawerk, E. von 12, 13, 25
bonding social capital 30
Bosnia and Herzegovina (BiH) 100–122
 Business Association 114, 115
 cultural heritage 105–6
 geopolitical context 103–4
 tourism opportunities 111
boundary-spanning roles 3, 38–40, 41
branding 95, 118
Bratunac 104, 118
bridging social capital 30
Brockhaus, R.H. 73
Bulgarian TBSMEs 6, 176–7, 180–93
Bulgarian Association for Management Development and Entrepreneurship (BAMDE) 213–15
business biodiversity facilities 73
Business Diplomat role 3, 38–40, 41
business incubators 6, 194–202
 pre-incubator 194–5, 198–201
 regional 194, 199, 201